Angelic Magic

How to Heal Past Lives & What They Didn't Tell You About Manifesting Your Dream Life

Angela Grace

© Copyright 2020 - All rights reserved

The content contained within this book may not be reproduced, duplicated or transmitted without direct written permission from the author or the publisher.

Under no circumstances will any blame or legal responsibility be held against the publisher, or author, for any damages, reparation, or monetary loss due to the information contained within this book, either directly or indirectly.

<u>Legal Notice:</u>

This book is copyright protected. It is only for personal use. You cannot amend, distribute, sell, use, quote or paraphrase any part, or the content within this book, without the consent of the author or publisher.

<u>Disclaimer Notice:</u>

Please note the information contained within this document is for educational and entertainment purposes only. All effort has been executed to present accurate, up to date, reliable, complete information. No warranties of any kind are declared or implied. Readers acknowledge that the author is not engaged in the rendering of legal, financial, medical or professional advice. The content within this book has been derived from various sources. Please consult a licensed professional before attempting any techniques outlined in this book.

By reading this document, the reader agrees that under no circumstances is the author responsible for any losses, direct or indirect, that are incurred as a result of the use of the information contained within this document, including, but not limited to, errors, omissions, or inaccuracies.

Table of Contents

BONUS FREE 10 Minute Guided Meditation Mp3 12

Book 1: Archangelology: Zadkiel 14

Introduction 1

Chapter 1: Introduction to Archangel Zadkiel & the Violet Flame. 4

Chapter 2: How to Call on the Violet Flame to Focus Your Energy for Manifestation   7

Chapter 3: Exercises, Mantras & Affirmations to Transform Your Negative Energy   11

    Light of Spiritual Protection 11

    Violet Fire Decree 13

    Visualization 13

    Your Daily Exercise 13

    Other Mantras or Affirmations 14

Chapter 4: Karma Clearing and How Previous Lives Can Affect Us 15

    Ways Previous Lives Affect You 16

    Karma Cleansing 16

Chapter 5: Your Spiritual Body 19

    Signs You've Stopped Growing Spiritually 19

    Are You Spiritually Blocked? 20

    Release Your Blocks 22

Chapter 6: Violet Flame Meditations 24

    Preparing for Your Meditation 24

    Meditation to Experience the Violet Flame 25

    Meditation for Clearing and Healing 26

    Meditation for Energy Shift 27

Chapter 7: Transmuting 29

    Roots of Disease 29

Chapter 8: Violet Flame Reiki 33

    Common Violet Flame Reiki Session 34

    Reiki Meditation Script for the Violet Flame 35

Chapter 9: How to Spend Time With Archangels to Create a Heavenly Life   37

    Knowing Who to Call 37

    Call on Archangels to Create a Peaceful Life 39

Conclusion 42

References 44

Book 2: Archangelology: Michael 46

Introduction 48

Chapter 1: Michael The Protector 50
   Michael The Person 50
   Archangels and Their Elemental Energies 51

Chapter 2: How to Easily Call Upon Archangel Michael 54
   Steps for Calling Archangel Michael 55

Chapter 3: Exercises, Mantras, and Affirmations 57
   Opening the Mind and Body 57
   Meditation 58

Chapter 4: Protect Your Loved Ones and Pets 60

Chapter 5: Protect Your Aura and Home 62

Chapter 6: Archangel Michael Meditations 65

Chapter 7: Archangel Michael Manifestation, Chakras, Dreams, and Karma   67
   Chakras 67
   Karma 67
   Dreams 68
   Manifestation 68

Chapter 8: How to Tell When Archangel Michael Is Around 70

Chapter 9: Writing a Letter to Michael 73

Chapter 10: Michael Protector Reiki 74

Chapter 11: Daily Life with Archangel Michael 76

Conclusion 78

References 79

Book 3: Archangelology: Raphael 81

Introduction 82

Part 1: Angela's Story 84

Part 2: Including Archangel Raphael in Your Life 87

Chapter 1: Introduction to Archangel Raphael 88
   Raphael Throughout History 88
   Raphael's Healing Powers 90

Chapter 2: How to Easily Call Upon Archangel Raphael 91
   How to Communicate With Raphael 91
   Reaching out for Beginners 92

Chapter 3: Exercises, Mantras, and Affirmations 96
   Transforming Negativity 96
   Manifesting Abundance and Healing 98

Chapter 4: Healing Animals and Loved Ones With Raphael 101

Visualizing Healing and Protection 102

Chapter 5: Align Your Money Frequency With Archangel Raphael 104
Attracting Abundance 105

Chapter 6: Archangel Raphael Meditations 106
Abundance Attraction With Archangel Raphael 106
Meditation for Healing With Archangel Raphael 107
Meditation for Loving Your Body 108
Meditation for Life Direction 109

Chapter 7: Archangel Raphael Manifestation, Chakras, Dreams, Crystals, and Karma 110
Manifesting Abundance 111
Manifesting Courage 111
Manifesting Wealth 112
Manifesting Positive Change 112

Chapter 8: How to Tell When Archangel Raphael Is Around 114
The Signs 114

Chapter 9: Writing a Letter to Raphael 117
Your Close Friend 117
Read Your Letter 118

Chapter 10: Archangel Raphael Reiki 119
Archangel Raphael Reiki Meditation 119

Chapter 11: How to Spend Time With Archangel Raphael 121
Daily Life While Carrying the Emerald Flame Everywhere 121

Conclusion 123

References 124

Illustrations References 125

Book 4: Archangelology: Metatron 127

Introduction 128

Chapter 1: Introduction to Archangel Metatron 130
Metatron's History 131
Signs of Metatron's Healing Power and Influence 132

Chapter 2: How to Easily Call Upon Archangel Metatron 133
Meditation 133
Activating Your Pillar of Light 134

Chapter 3: Exercises, Mantras, and Affirmations for Transformation 136
Affirmations and Mantras 136
Prayer 138
Cord-Cutting and Energetic Shielding 138

Chapter 4: Metatron and How to Use the Power of Sleep and Astral Time   140

Chapter 5: Aligning Prosperity, Abundance, Love, and Well-Being with Archangel Metatron's Frequency 142

    Candle Magic 142

    Archangels Metatron and Haniel 144

Chapter 6: Archangel Metatron Meditations 145

    Metatron Meditation for Clarity and Focus 146

    Light Body Meditation with Metatronic Energy 146

    Divine Protection and Abundance Meditation............................147

Chapter 7: Chakras, Karma, and Crystals with Archangel Metatron   149

    Chakras 149

    Karma 151

    Crystals 152

    Sacred Geometry and Metatron's Codes 152

Chapter 8: How to Sense and Feel Metatron's Presence 154

Chapter 9: Write a Letter to Metatron 156

Chapter 10: Metatron and Reiki..158

Chapter 11: Spending Time with Metatron................................160

Conclusion 162

References..163

Book 5: Archangelology: Jophiel..164

Introduction 165

Chapter 1: Jophiel the Beautiful..167

    Jophiel and Wisdom 167

    Jophiel's Creativity 168

Chapter 2: A Flash of Color 170

    Colors and Smells 170

    Confidence 171

    Quiet Strength 171

Chapter 3: Serene Grace 173

    Calming 173

    Honesty 174

Chapter 4: Blessings and Healing 176

    Making Space for Love..176

    Healing 177

Chapter 5: Beautification..179

    Little Things to Try 179

  The Things We Say 181

Chapter 6: Magenta Meditation Moments 183
  Rubellite Reiki 183
  Chakra 185
  Meditation How-To 186

Chapter 7: Dreams and Vibrations 188
  Lucid Dreaming 188
  Daydreamer 189

Chapter 8: Communication and Patience 191
  Writing a Letter 191
  Conversation 192
  Patience 192

Chapter 9: Outer Beauty 194
  Churches 194
  Making a Place of Beauty 195

Chapter 10: Time With 197
  Understanding the Messages 197
  Paying It Forward 198
  Time For Prayer 198

Conclusion 200
  How Can Archangels Bring Us Closer to the Divine? 201

References 202

Book 6: Archangelology: Uriel: 203

Introduction 204

Chapter 1: Uriel the Wise 206
  Uriel in Scripture 207
  Symbolism and Associations 207

Chapter 2: How to Call Upon Uriel 209
  Beginning the Meditation 209
  Calling Out to Uriel 210
  Hearing Uriel's Voice 210

Chapter 3: Having the Strength to Ask 212
  Daily Exercises 212
  Mantras and Affirmations 213
  Cord-Cutting 213

Chapter 4: Calling Forth Uriel's Sword 215
  Protecting Yourself 215

    Protecting Your Pets 216

Chapter 5: Uriel the Role Model: Aligning Your Frequency 218
    What Is a Frequency? 218
    Completing the Alignment 219

Chapter 6: Meditations for Your Specific Needs.........................221
    Meditation for Body Positivity 221
    Meditation for Life Direction 222

Chapter 7: Utilizing Dreams, Crystals, and Candles 224
    Dreamwork 224
    Crystals 224
    Candles 225

Chapter 8: Seeing Uriel in the World Around You 227
    Animal Encounters 227
    Repeating Numbers 228
    Instincts and Ideas 228

Chapter 9: Writing a Letter to Uriel 230
    How to Write the Letter 230
    Example Letter 230
    Follow-Up 231

Chapter 10: Reiki With Uriel 233
    What Is Reiki? 233
    Incorporating Uriel's Help 233

Chapter 11: Spending Time With Uriel 236
    Beautiful Moments 236
    Venting 237

Conclusion 238

References 239

Book 7: Spiritual Discernment..242

Introduction 243

Chapter 1: Hearing God..247
    How Can I Tell? 250
    Now What? 253

Chapter 2: Purpose 257
    Why Does It Matter? 257
    Here's How You Know 259
    What You Should Do Before Listening 261

Chapter 3: Day to Day 263

    The Small Things Matter..263
    How to Listen 264

Chapter 4: Light of Darkness 267
    Nature of Spirits 267
    Here's How You Know 268
    Separate Bad Things from Evil...271
    People Under the Influence of Spirits..272

Chapter 5: Wisdom..274
    What It Is..274
    God's Wisdom in Action 274

Conclusion 276
    BONUS FREE 10 Minute Guided Meditation Mp3...................277

Want Your Next Book/Audiobook FOR FREE? 279

Download the 11 Hour + Long Audiobook 'Angelic Magic: How To Heal Past Lives & What They Didn't Tell You About Manifesting Your Dream Life (Archangelology 7 in 1 Collection)' For **FREE!**

If you love listening to audio books on-the-go, I have great news for you. You can download the audio book version of *'Angelic Magic: (Archangelology 7 in 1 Collection)'* for **FREE** just by signing up for a **FREE** 30-day audible trial! See below for more details!

Audible trial benefits

As an audible customer, you'll receive the below benefits with you 30-day free trial:

- Free audible copy of this book

- After the trial, you will get 1 credit each month to use on any audiobook

- Your credits automatically roll over to the next month if you don't use them

- Choose from over 400,000 titles

- Listen anywhere with the audible app across multiple devices
- Make easy, no hassle exchanges of any audiobook you don't love
- Keep your audiobooks forever, even if you cancel your membership
- And much more

Go to the links below to get started:

AUDIBLE US : *bit.ly/angelicmagic*

AUDIBLE UK : *bit.ly/angelicmagicuk*

BONUS FREE 10 Minute Guided Meditation Mp3

Wouldn't it be nice to have even more motivation, inspiration, and courage on your spiritual path? As a sincere "Thank you" from the bottom of my heart, i've given you access to a free audio Mp3 violet Flame guided meditation below.

If you're ready to drop all the negative energy that no longer serves you then get your Violet Flame meditation below.

• Easily use the violet flame to free blocked energy within you

• Cleanse your Karma to skyrocket your joy

• Start growing spiritually again & get back on your path to your destiny.

Go To: *bit.ly/zadkielmeditation* To Get Your FREE Violet Flame Guided Meditation Mp3!

Please Leave a Review on Amazon

From the bottom of my heart, thank you for reading my book. I truly hope that it helps you on your spiritual journey and to live a more empowered and happy life. If it does help you, then I'd like to ask you for a favor. Would you be kind enough to leave an honest review for this book on Amazon? It'd be greatly appreciated and will likely impact the lives of other spiritual seekers across the globe, giving them hope and power.

Thank you and good luck!

Angela Grace

Why not join our Facebook community and discuss your spiritual path with like-minded seekers?

We would love to hear from you!

Go here to join the 'Ascending Vibrations' community:

bit.ly/ascendingvibrations

Book 1: Archangelology: Zadkiel

The Violet Flame, & Angelic Karma Clearing Secrets (Archangelology Book Series 1)

Angela Grace

Introduction

"I AM the Violet Flame
In action in me now
I AM the Violet Flame
To Light alone I bow
I AM the Violet Flame
In mighty Cosmic Power
I AM the Light of God
Shining every hour
I AM the Violet Flame
Blazing like a sun
I AM God's sacred power
Freeing every one"
(Summit Lighthouse, 2014)

How do you feel after repeating this decree? Do you notice a difference from when you picked up this book? Maybe you feel more powerful. You might feel more motivated. Maybe you don't directly know how to explain the way you felt, but you know that you feel different. It's like there is a light that became a tiny bit brighter inside of you. Even if it faded quickly, you felt it and that's what matters.

This light is what people refer to as the violet flame. It's a part of you that creates more forgiveness, justice, mercy, transmutation, and freedom. Imagine the flame as not just glowing violet fire or a ray of light but as spiritual energy. It's the seventh ray of the Holy Spirit and helps you change your negative energy to positive. The violet ray gives you a platform for healing.

You probably know the Holy Spirit as the third person in the Trinity or see it as a relationship to God. While this is correct, there is more to the Holy Spirit than one high power. In fact, there are several and they are known as the archangels. They are the highest angels who work closely to God and your guardian angels. They each have their designated responsibilities. For example, Archangel Michael is the protector and highest archangel; he protects you in battle. Archangel Ariel works closely with the animals and nature, and Archangel Raphael works closely with people who are a part of the healing profession, such as doctors, nurses, and therapists.

The archangels and the violet flame are closely correlated, which means the benefits you receive come from several higher powers. Think of them as working together to create a powerful energy that helps you heal through the violet rays.

One of the benefits is the inner peace that grows inside of you. You'll start to feel it as a light, gentle feeling. The more you practice by stating decrees, remaining positive, focusing on forgiveness, and following the path that your higher powers lay out before you, the stronger the peace becomes.

Along with peace comes the ability to remain calm. Many people tend to feel that this benefit surprises them. For example, they'll find themselves in a situation that used to make them anxious or worried. They'll remember being afraid when it happened in the past but now feel calmer. They're able to think clearly and can come up with a solution to a problem without their previous struggles. It's at this moment that you take a step back and realize how much you've changed because of the violet energy surrounding your soul.

Another benefit is that your thoughts change. You no longer focus on the negative thoughts, even when they creep into your mind. You learn how to use the flame's powers to bring your positive thoughts into focus. It gives you the strength to accept your darker thoughts or emotions and then realize that it's in your power to change them. It's up to you to choose your thoughts.

The violet flame and archangels help you feel more balanced. They help create a union within your soul that brings stability to your chakras. You start to feel your heart soften as you find new compassion, understanding, sensitivity, joy, and freedom in your life. You then want to help other people open their mind and heart up to this new love that you feel. It's important to realize that what you're feeling is the warmth and love from the violet flame and higher powers. It's their energy that is filling you.

I wrote this book because I want you to feel this love. I want you to reach your highest self through the path of the violet flame. Archangelology isn't a topic that has academic experts. It's not backed by science. It's supported by your intuition and what you believe. To see the violet flame you need to open up your heart and mind. You need to tune into your gut feeling and understand that it's okay to believe in something that makes you feel beautiful inside and out. What feels best for you, what you believe in your heart is exactly the path that you need to follow.

You're not alone as you're walking because the energies from the archangels, guardian angels, and universe are always surrounding you. Join me in this journey of learning about Archangel Zadkiel, the violet flame, and how to spend time with your archangels so you can achieve the heavenly life you deserve.

Chapter 1: Introduction to Archangel Zadkiel & the Violet Flame

Archangel Zadkiel is known as the angel of mercy whose name means "the righteousness of God." He works alongside his brother and twin flame, Holy Amethyst, to serve mankind through the seventh flame. When called upon, whether through meditation or spoken word, they will come with other angels of the violet flame and help fulfill your request. For example, you might receive signs that they are near or they may give you a "gut feeling" of what you should do.

Zadkiel will help you become more compassionate toward yourself. He will help you find lost objects, with memory enhancement, and in healing physically, emotionally, and mentally. Zadkiel also supports you in learning how to forgive yourself and others, remember important information, and with studying. If you want to learn how to let go of your judgment, you should call on the violet flame angels through Zadkiel.

One of the archangel's main jobs is to help you see the light within yourself. You will stop focusing on your mistakes as negative pieces of your life and start seeing them as a way to learn and grow. You'll also see your personality flaws as a blessing in your life because you understand that it's not possible to be perfect. You begin looking at ways to focus on your character so you can reach your highest self, who is the best person you can imagine.

Some people believe that their best self is someone who never makes mistakes, doesn't have problems, is constantly positive, everyone loves, and is flawless. If this is the person you want to visualize for yourself, go ahead and write it down. But, it's important to realize that you don't need to imagine a perfect self—you imagine a realistic person that you wish to become. You might look at your long-term goals, such as graduating from college and obtaining your dream job. You want to get married, have children, and be as patient as possible with them. You want to become more compassionate and improve your self-esteem. Your best self understands that no one is perfect and you don't need to strive for perfection, but you *do* need to learn from your mistakes and control your inner critical voice.

Once you have an idea of who you want to become, write it down or create a visualization board with your main personality traits. Look at this creative piece every day so you're reminded of why you're working so hard. Keep in mind that you might change your ideal self over time, especially when you reach a goal. You're constantly developing as a human being and this can change your perception of what's important, which changes pieces of your highest self.

Archangel Zadkiel and his team help you turn your unhealthy habits and thoughts into healthy ones. God wants you to enjoy the beauty of the world and see yourself as a talented, amazing, and loved person. This attitude becomes hard for many people throughout their lives because of their environment, thought patterns, habits, and emotions. For instance, when you're stressed you're more likely to think negatively about yourself and people around you. When you have this thought process and emotion every day it develops into a negative mindset.

You can know Zadkiel is around through various signs. You might only see one of these signs or you could pick up on a few.

You remember something. If you're been struggling to remember anything important, his team is on your side. The thought will just pop into your mind or you might hear it whispered in your ear.

Seeing a purple or blue light. Even though it's a purple ray that you'll see in your mind's eye, shades of blue can also show that the team is near you. If you see either shade, it's time to note anything you feel, hear, or think because they're trying to communicate with you.

You feel him. You might instinctively know or feel that Zadkiel or someone on his team is near you. Don't doubt yourself, open your mind's eye and become comfortable with your intuition.

The Ascended Master, an evolved being who has walked earth, of the violet flame is Saint Germain who taught the seventh flame and is known as a legendary spiritual master of ancient wisdom. He focused on strategies to help people learn about the ray to improve themselves and their lives. He requested God to send the flame to earth so he could help humanity and the practice could continue for the rest of time.

The violet flame is a combination of two colors, blue and pink. The blue flame comes from God's will and power, which is also known as the Divine Father. The pink flame is known as Divine Mother and means divine love. When you focus on calling Archangel Zadkiel, exercises, karma cleansing, or prayer these two colors come together to create violet.

The flame is a tool of self-transformation and many people believe that now is a perfect time to start focusing on it. The world is going through so much and is tumultuous and constantly changing. There are a lot of negatives in the world, which continue to affect your mindset. The violet flame can help you overcome the struggles, tragedies, and negativity so you can transform into a positive, compassionate, and lovable person.

To activate it you need to call upon Zadkiel through affirmations or decree. It will start working right away by healing your soul and your body. You might feel that you're at a higher frequency after praying to the archangel or you could start to feel like you're vibrating. Your instincts will let you know that powers are working to help you heal and to let it continue as is. If you're meditating, you'll remain in this state until you feel that it's time to bring yourself back into reality. If you're trying to focus on a project, you need to follow your body, mind, and emotions to understand if you should take a break and bask in the energies sent to you or continue working on your project. The key is to allow the healing. Notice what is happening to you and accept it.

Sometimes you won't feel anything right away. The energies will start working, but it's not noticeable to you for several reasons. It might be because you haven't opened your third eye, which is your spiritual eye, that sits in the middle of your forehead. You might be unbalanced emotionally and mentally. Another reason is that you're not focusing on the vibrations that are being sent to you. Don't worry if you don't feel anything immediately. Understand that developing your spirituality is a gradual process but the more you practice and learn, the stronger it becomes. No matter where you are mentally and physically, if you invoked the violet flame, it's working.

Chapter 2: How to Call on the Violet Flame to Focus Your Energy for Manifestation

Archangel Zadkiel is a great power to call upon when you're frustrated, angry, sad or feeling negatively. His team can help you find the positives in the situation and feel better emotionally. However, there are a few important points that you need to understand before you call upon the violet flame.

The first factor you need to comprehend is that you must call on an archangel to help you with a certain situation in your life. Even though they can feel and sense what you need help with, it's still necessary to be clear with your intention. Tell them directly what you want and don't hesitate or feel that you're asking them too much. They're here to help you and they want to do whatever they can to ensure you live a happy life and fulfill your mission. However, keep in mind that you don't always have to call on your angels. They can help you in any situation, whether you ask for their help or not. In fact, you always have angels around you, called guardian angels, that are constantly supporting you in all parts of your life.

When you're setting your intention, you need to think carefully. You don't want to have any negative thoughts in your mind or emotions that can lead to the harm of others. Think about the outcome that you want from this connection and how you want to achieve it. You should use your energy to bring out the highest good within yourself, which is part of your best self. Always remember, when you're communicating with your angels and the violet flame you're aiming to become closer to your highest self.

Another factor to consider is how you're thinking at that moment. Your thought energy is one of the most important pieces of your life that you have the ability to control. If you're struggling to focus on the positive, you should use strategies like meditation to help change your thought pattern. You can also change your negative thoughts into positive ones during the process. For example, if you're feeling the warmth of Archangel Zadkiel's light coming toward you during meditation as you're asking for support and energy to make an adjustment in your life and you catch yourself thinking, "I can't do it" switch your thought to "I can do it and will do it with the energy from the angels surrounding me."

Before you start preparing yourself to call on them, you need to remember the word patience. If you're starting to open your third eye or this is the first time you've reached out to the violet flame, your connection might be a little staticky and this is okay. Instead of worrying, creating anxiety, or fixating on negative thoughts, think about ways you can open the door to the spiritual world. Ask yourself if you really believe in what you're doing, keep trying, and look at balancing your chakras.

You need to prepare yourself and there are many steps to this process. However, you want to follow the procedure that works for you. For example, you might find that starting with a prayer and then going into a meditative state helps your mind remain calm so you can feel the energies of the higher powers around you. Other people might feel that a prayer isn't necessary and they turn to breathing exercises or affirmations before they begin. Never believe that you're doing something wrong in the process because there is no clear-cut way to communicate with the angels. As long as you're not blocked, you're open to hearing and feeling the higher powers, and following your authentic method, you'll feel a strong connection.

Find a quiet and comfortable location. By now your intention should be clear, so it's time to find a place to communicate. I understand this can be hard if you have young children, but it's crucial. You might find that it's easier to connect with Archangel Zadkiel when everyone is asleep or they've all gone to school or work. Remember, your higher powers don't have office hours so you can connect with them at any time. You can also look at setting up a specific area by having a diffuser going, lighting candles, or playing relaxing music on low in the background. The key is to not let any noise distract you.

Ground yourself. Once you're ready to open the connection, you need to ground yourself. You can do this by visualizing roots coming out of your feet into the ground or vice versa. The key is to ensure that these roots reach the earth's core and that you feel it. It might come to you in a sense of oneness, calmness, or you simply might think that you're connected to the earth and can now reach out to your angels. You may also say mantras or prayers during this process or in place of imagining the roots.

If you want to focus on visualization, you need to put yourself in a peaceful and relaxed state, similar to mediation, and close your eyes. You will start by taking a few deep breaths and letting your muscles relax. You'll imagine roots, similar to roots of a tree, coming out of the soles of your feet. They're full of bright colors from your soul and aura. You might see them as yellow, orange, purple, blue, green, or a variety of colors. These roots continue to grow from you, out your window, down the exterior walls of your home, and into the grass. They gradually work their way into the soil, creating a sense of warmth and building the connection to the universe. You see the soil spinning as the roots dig further into the earth. The light becomes brighter as the connection grows deeper. It goes past the clay and water as it works its way to the center. When you take a breath in, the energy from the earth goes through the roots and into your body and soul. Let your lungs expand with each breath to bring in as much energy as you can. When you breathe out, the energy moves around your body, letting the energy soak into your bloodstream, bones, and cells. Once you're ready, you can open your eyes and continue with your connection process.

Affirmation. If you choose to go the affirmation route, or even a combination of the two grounding methods, you still want to put yourself into a relaxed state, but not a complete meditative state. You will start by closing your eyes and taking three deep breaths. Let your lungs expand as far as they can while breathing in slowly. Hold your breath for a couple of seconds before you gradually let the air out. Once you reach a state of relaxation, repeat a phrase that you feel will help ground you. For example, "Mother Earth and my roots are connected. We are now one," or "My roots are flowing deep into the ground and to the center of the earth. Mother Earth and I are connected." When you feel like you're ready to move on to the next step, you can open your eyes.

Recite a prayer of protection to Archangel Michael. When you begin opening the door to the spirit world, even if it's to connect with the higher powers, you allow any entities to enter your doorway. You can become comfortable and connect with the best intentions in your mind but find that your heart isn't following the same path. Instead, you notice there are bits of anger or frustration in you, which invites negative entities. Therefore, you always want to take time to say a prayer of protection to Archangel Michael before you start communicating with Archangel Zadkiel or any other angel. All you need to do is say, "Archangel Michael, my protector, I call upon your energy and love to help shield me from negativity during my communication with the angels. I thank you for your assistance." If you're in the middle of a connection and ever feel that there is a negative presence near you or knocking on your spiritual door, you can call Michael to assist you in any way, even by saying, "Archangel Michael, help me!"

Visualize the violet flame. Once you've found your way to connect to Mother Earth and requested protection from Archangel Michael. When you find yourself relaxed and ready to officially connect with Archangel Zadkiel, you need to find a transition to help you focus on the violet flame. For instance, you could simply imagine the flame burning in your mind's eye. You might start by seeing an angel light a violet candle and watch as the flame turns from blue to violet. You could also picture an image you find of it on Google. No matter what you do, make sure that it speaks to you as this is how you form a strong bond.

Chapter 3: Exercises, Mantras & Affirmations to Transform Your Negative Energy

There are many exercises you can do to invoke the violet flame. You can also use mantras and affirmations. As a beginner, you'll find your system and you'll stick with it for a while. However, it's important that you open yourself up to other ways to transform your negative energy once you become more comfortable with calling on Archangel Zadkiel.

The way you say these mantras or affirmations has a lot to do with how strongly you will come to believe in the flame and its powers. The spoken word has a lot of strength, so it's best to say your mantras and affirmations out loud. Another reason it's important to speak the words is because then they connect to your throat chakra.

If you want the violet fire to become more powerful, you should repeat the words for several minutes. The average is about 5 to 7 minutes but other people are known to go as long as 15 minutes.

Another way to bring more significance to what you're stating is to increase your volume. Start talking in your inside voice, you remember the one your librarian always told you to use, and then end by yelling it as loud as you can.

Light of Spiritual Protection

One of the first methods I tell many beginners to use is a simple two-step process of protection.

The first step is to *envision a white light surrounding you*. This is your bubble of protection from Archangel Michael and your guardian angels. It will protect you from negativity that's hovering around your environment, your thoughts, or any type of energies of malice that are trying to reach you. Some people refer to it as "armor of the Lord" while other people explain that it's the energy from Archangel Michael's sword.

The protective light will also help your energy. When you have so much going on around you, whether it's people or spiritual energies, you can start to feel drained. Think about the last time you went to the mall to go shopping or to watch your child play in a sporting event. You probably felt tired or emotionally drained afterwards because you didn't protect yourself from people that can unknowingly take your energy.

Another reason you want to visualize this light is because it can help your aura stay centered. You'll feel at peace and have patience for your learning and development.

The light won't fit you like a bodysuit as it surrounds your immediate environment as well. It's about nine feet in diameter and starts above your head and the encircles you all the way below your feet.

You can bring about this light by requesting Archangel Michael's assistance by asking him to protect you with his light and energy. You can then imagine the light coming from Heaven, growing bigger and bigger as it inches closer to you. Once it reaches above your head, it expands to create a large circle around you.

Another way is by saying a "I Am" decree. You want to create the presence of a bright tube of light and ask that you're calling forth the violet fire. For instance, you might repeat, "I am loved. I am in the presence of a bright light which starts above my head and circles me down beyond my feet. It's from the ascended master's flame. I call forth the higher powers of Archangel Michael and my guardian angels to help keep me protected. I am calling forth the violet flame that will blaze my desire. Together, as one, I am with the violet flame."

The second step is to *seal your aura and heart with the protective energy*. This will help keep the energy force field of the violet flame within you. It'll ensure you feel it's fire as you end the exercise and continue with your day. If you didn't call on Archangel Michael in the first step, you will do so now by simply requesting his assistance or saying a prayer. For example, you can repeat, "Archangel Michael, I call forth your blue sphere of protective energy. I ask that you surround my heart so the light can fill my chakras and aura. I am calling for your highest protection from the negativity that could steal my heart and bits of my soul. I ask for you to secure the original blueprint of my heart and soul."

You can also call on Michael through a decree. "Archangel Michael before me, Archangel Michael behind me. You are to my left, you are at my right. Archangel Michael you are above me and below me. Archangel Michael you are wherever I go! I bask in your protection. I am loved. I feel your loving protection surrounding me. Your protection is here! It is here!"

Violet Fire Decree

When you are calling out the violet flame, you want to believe you are the fire. You want to see yourself as this powerful force that can bring forth peace and harmony into your life. You want to believe that you can repair damage from your past, even your past lives. Therefore, you want to pump yourself up when starting the process. It's similar to all the football games you went to in high school and college where the cheerleaders would come out first and give a cheer. Then, the music would come on the speaker as the players ran out into the field one-by-one. They did this to get the audience and themselves excited for the game. You want to put yourself in a similar mindset.

One way to do this is to say a decree that makes you believe that you are the violet fire. You can create your own or state the following words, "I am a being of the violet flame. The fire flows through me. The brightness becomes one with my soul." You should repeat it several times and gradually increase the speed. You can also just repeat the first line, "I am a being of the violet flame" if you feel more comfortable keeping it short during your first few experiences.

Visualization

The violet flame works best when you see it in your mind's eye. If you're struggling to call on the fire, you will want to work on imagining it. If you need inspiration, start by looking at pictures of purple lights, flames, or even search what other people believe the flame looks like. Then, take a moment to find your quiet and comfortable location so you can focus on developing your own flame. You might imagine lighting a candle to help you get into a more peaceful mood. Perhaps you start by noticing a dim violet dot and then visualize it becoming larger. It's important to reach into your creativity and intuition. What do you think the violet flame looks like? Can you draw it? Even if you're not an artist, you can still sketch it out with a pencil and piece of paper. Even if it's a straight candlestick with a tiny oval flame, it's a step toward finding your creative outlet.

Your Daily Exercise

You should aim to call out the violet flame at least once a day. You can try to do it around the same time each day to give you a bit of a routine, but any time will work. You can even challenge yourself to help launch into a habit by stating you will practice one exercise for 30 days. This is helpful because it usually takes about 21 days to form a habit.

You don't need to spend a lot of time focusing on energy. For instance, one of the exercises is thinking or saying out loud, "I offer my gratitude and love to the violet flame. I give my love to Archangel Zadkiel as he sends me the violet flame." You can repeat this for a few seconds or as long as you feel the need to.

You can also set a time frame for your daily exercises. For example, you can repeat, "I am a being of the violet flame" for five minutes. You can also decide to say it a certain number of times a day. You might do this in specific settings or randomly speckled throughout, depending on what works for your schedule. For instance, if you're browning hamburger or stirring soup, you can repeat the mantra while stirring. You can also do it when you're washing your hands or every time you see a white vehicle while driving to work.

Other Mantras or Affirmations

Here are a few other mantras or affirmations that you can include in your daily practice or when you're trying to bring forth the violet flame.

- Let the violet light shine within my soul.
- I am that I am. Let the violet flame expand and blaze inside of me.
- Mother Earth is a plant of the violet flame. I am a being of the violet fire.
- I stand for peace. I stand for love. I stand for life and with the violet flame I end all strife.
- I breathe the violet fire into each cell. Every breath I take, the flame rises inside of me.
- Violet flame of freedom, you bring the beauty of spiritual truth.
- Let the violet flame pass through me. Let it bring light to every atom, cell, and all the electrons within my body.
- Today I bring God's freedom into my heart as I begin to love and forgive.
- Oh violet flame, bring your light to help set me free.

Chapter 4: Karma Clearing and How Previous Lives Can Affect Us

Karma refers to the spiritual principle of cause and effect. It means that the way you conducted yourself in the past can have an effect on what happens to you in the future. For example, you put money into the offering plate at a church and come home to find that you won a contest and will receive a handsome monetary prize. Karma can be good or bad. An example of negative karma is laughing when you see your ex-partner going through a bitter divorce battle and you find yourself in the same situation years later.

Many people believe in its energy, but on different levels. For instance, you might believe that karma focuses on your past lives along with our current life while your friend believes that karma only focuses on your present life. To you, karma can affect you because of an action you took 100 years ago that you don't even remember, while your friend doesn't believe in that possibility.

Another factor is that just because it comes your way doesn't mean it will leave. Some people believe they have bad luck because of their behavior in a previous life and it won't leave them until they cleanse their soul. Other people feel that they need to heal from past wounds in order to release the karmic energy surrounding them, meaning that karma can help your soul transform into a higher being.

Karma doesn't have an end date. It can travel from life to life with you without forgetting any important information. You can imagine it as a suitcase that your soul carries wherever it goes. It never gets lost and the only way you can heal yourself from it and release its chains is by opening it. But, this doesn't mean that you understand what's happening. In fact, you can be dealing with this energy without even realizing it.

No matter what you've done in your past, you can use karma clearing to release restrictive ideas, wounds, pain, problems, and negative emotions so you can walk along your path feeling free. It doesn't matter if it's something from a previous lifetime or an event from last week, you can clear your mind, body, and soul.

Ways Previous Lives Affect You

To understand this path, you need to believe in reincarnation. You need to feel that you've been born before on this earth and that you've been working toward your soul's purpose for centuries. Some people have dreams about their past lives while other people have a sense that they've lived in a certain area. There are also people who believe they know who they were 200 or more years ago. Others start to piece together a part of their past lives through their karma.

One of the ways you might be affected by karmic energy is the *feeling that you meet every person in your life for a reason.* You knew them in previous lives, but everyone played a different role. For instance, your brother might have been your uncle or friend. Your mother could've been your sister. You can start to understand why you know your friends, family, coworkers, and anyone else by asking yourself a few questions.

- Why are they a part of your life?
- What have they come to teach you?
- What do you need to teach them?
- What is the karma you need to experience with this person?

Karma can reverse roles so you start to understand a different side of the physical world. This happens because it helps your soul grow. For example, your soul decides to switch genders, live in a different country, or you and one of your parents from a previous life switch position. You become the parent and they're the child. Certain factors switch because you need to heal or learn from a previous situation.

Karma does repeat but for a reason—to help you reach your full potential. The phrase, "what goes around, comes around" is true. If you treated someone terribly in a past life you could be treated in a similar manner in this life. If you spent your time trying to help people, others will come to assist you. You can understand what your karmic energy is by looking at the themes in your life. Ask yourself questions, such as "What similar people continue to come into my life and why?" or "Is there something I can do differently to stop certain situations from happening?"

Karma Cleansing

You can call on the violet flame to help you heal and cleanse your soul to release your karma. The key is to understand what is following you and how to call the fire to correct your situation. Below are some of the most common areas that follow people from life to life.

If you find yourself struggling with illness, whether emotional, mental, or physical, you want to take the step to cleanse the karma that's following you. You can do this by calling Archangel Zadkiel and asking him to help heal your old wounds. Another way is through the use of crystals or through reiki. Disease affects you when your body isn't healthy, which means your soul isn't healthy. You're not spiritually balanced and struggling to communicate with your higher self. You want to find crystals that associate with your chakras that need assistance or with ones that can help you become more compassionate, patient, or healthy. For example, if you struggle with anxiety you can carry a moonstone in your pocket or as a piece of jewelry. Lepidolite is a crystal that focuses on balancing mood and depression. It's best worn as a necklace as it's part of the third eye and heart chakra.

Another reason karma can follow you throughout your lives is because you haven't forgiven people who hurt you. Even if it's been hundreds or thousands of years, your soul remembers and you continue to hold grudges. They might show up in stereotypes that you have against particular people or the way you treat others. You might also feel it through certain mental illnesses, insomnia, or through fears. One way to let go of your pain is through a prayer for forgiveness.

Start by saying out loud, "With these words, I send forgiveness into the universe so I can let go of the wrong I did to others and the wrong other people did to me."

Next, it's time to close your eyes and connect yourself to the higher powers by stating the following or a similar prayer:

"I am acting in forgiveness. I am setting myself free by casting out all doubt and fear. I am calling the full cosmic power to help raise my vibrations so I can overcome the pain my soul feels. I am calling for forgiveness every hour, to every place and all life. With this energy, I flood my life with forgiving grace."

You can also use the violet flame to help cleanse you when anger or frustration boils inside of you. It's often these feelings that bring you to holding onto your emotional and psychological wounds and scars so you're trapped in their chains. The key is to immediately release any negative emotions as quickly as they come to you. You can do this through various techniques.

- Say one or a few of your favorite violet flame decrees, such as "I am a being of the violet flame. I am pure and happy."
- Stop what you're doing and don't fall victim to the negativity. Instead, take a few deep breaths and ask the flame to help you by stating, "I call upon Archangel Zadkiel and the violet flame to transmute the reasons for my negative emotions immediately."
- After saying a decree, you can increase the power through visualization. Imagine the violet fire lighting up, becoming brighter and brighter as the negativity begins to disappear.
- You always want to end this process by taking another deep breath, but one more powerful than before. As you exhale, imagine the anger or frustration leaving your body and floating into the air for the universe to transform into positivity.

When you take immediate action to stop your negative emotions, you're able to end the karma that you've sent to someone else right in its tracks because you didn't let the negativity control you.

Chapter 5: Your Spiritual Body

You know all about your physical body through anatomy, but have you ever thought about your spiritual body? This is the part of you that travels from life to life and is referred to as your soul. How your soul develops is based on your beliefs, whether religious or otherwise. For instance, some people believe that God created your soul while others feel that it's a collection of energy from your lifetimes. Your soul can change over time through the lessons that you learn during your time on earth.

Your soul is a description of who you are; it's the whole of your personality. Of course, you have earthly features such as your childhood upbringing, your environment, and even society that helps shape your character, but the foundation is from your spiritual being.

People believe that the main goal in each life is to help your soul heal from past traumas and grow. Your soul has a mission and you continue to move from life to life until your mission is complete, at which time you'll transform into your highest self. The problem is, you have several detours and challenges that create issues during your growth. If you don't learn to overcome these obstacles, you can stunt your development.

Signs You've Stopped Growing Spiritually

You want to develop your spiritual being in every life, so you need to understand the warning signs that this part of you has come to a halt.

You're stressed and distracted. Of course, life is stressful and there are a lot of distractions that can keep you from staying focused on your life's mission. The problem is when you're too stressed, you carry negative emotions with you that stop you from entering into spiritual growth. You need to find ways to relax and release your tension, whether it's through mantras, meditation, aromatherapy, counseling, or affirmations.

You don't feel like you're developing. You might feel that you don't need to grow on a spiritual level or you're not focused on it. The main way to get through this situation is to understand, and remind yourself, that your whole life is centered on learning so you can reach your highest self.

You're too materialistic. Material items, such as cars, clothing, shoes, books, and all your purchases are a pleasure to have in your life. These things often give people a certain look in society, which makes you want more. You want to be on the top and you want people to see that you're financially doing well. However, this thought pattern can also disconnect you from your higher plain. Let go of the need to have these items around you so your soul can continue to thrive.

You feel disconnected. Your instincts can tell you that something is wrong with your spiritual connection. You might have a thought that you're not heading in the right direction and you need to strengthen your spiritual ties. You can do this by learning about your soul, meditation, and how to connect with your higher powers. You can also ask the violet flame to help increase your communication.

Are You Spiritually Blocked?

You can be born into this life with a spiritual blockage. You can also become blocked during your childhood or adult years and not even realize it. You might feel that you've reached spiritual enlightenment and then notice that something changed; it's almost like it vanished. You can experience happiness and peace for several years and then feel that it was taken from you.

Your soul carries your emotions and the burdens that you feel now. It can become weak if you don't take care of yourself, which is one reason why self-care is so important. To keep your soul healthy and happy, you need to release any blockages. But how do you know this is happening to you? Don't worry, there are simple and clear-cut symptoms. The key is to relate them to yourself spiritually instead of physically. For example, you might not be tired and lack energy because you didn't sleep well. It could be due to a spiritual wall that's keeping you from reaching your highest self.

Traumatic experience. One of the most powerful reasons for a block is a traumatic experience. If it's from a previous life, you might not know what happened but still fear certain life events. For example, you might have a fear of fire because you died in a house fire or are afraid of water due to a previous drowning. If you've had this type of experience recently, it's important to take the steps to overcome the situation. You might contact a therapist or face your fears head-on.

Here are a few symptoms that can indicate unprocessed trauma in your current life:
- Trouble sleeping

- Feeling stuck or like you are unable to break down an emotional or psychological wall
- Feeling like you are walking in a dark room with no direction or understanding of where to go
- Gaps in memory
- Intense feelings of anxiety, fear, anger, shame, and guilt—as they become increasingly unmanageable
- Trouble focusing on work and personal life duties, including relaxing or watching movies
- Recurring nightmares or night terrors of the traumatic situation (even if it's from a previous life)
- A feeling of "knowing" in your gut that something bad happened and having an idea of what it was, such as car accident or murder

Unable to relax. You're a dedicated employee at your company and work hard in your personal life, but you struggle when it comes to relaxation. You're aware of your constant need to feel busy, work tirelessly, and your inability to binge Netflix like everyone else. When you do try to relax, your thoughts make you anxious and you start to get fidgety.

Emotionally unattached. You feel that it's better to ignore your feelings and will go as far as ignoring other people's emotions to do so. Even when your partner or children try to talk to you about how they feel or try to help you, you close up. You might change the subject or try to convince them that you're feeling great and there is no need to worry. If they're struggling, you'll often find yourself saying, "Life happens," or "Don't worry about it because it's not that bad." You might also brush them off.

You're struggling on your life path. You know what your interests are and you have hobbies you enjoy. You even like your job but you still feel that something isn't right. You still believe there is a piece of you that's missing or you don't feel that you're on the right path. You have trouble choosing your direction and often seek the advice of other people, which can make you feel more emotionally and psychologically lost.

You lack energy. It seems like no matter how much sleep you get, you still don't feel rested. You might wake up feeling like you're ready to take on the world and grateful for a good night's sleep, but once you start moving and focusing on tasks, you become restless and feel the need to sleep some more. You crave naps and could take one every day, even though you don't understand why because you don't have children keeping you up at night or insomnia. It feels like you never have enough fuel to energize your life.

You feel happy but don't hold the happiness. You have so much to be thankful for from your job to your family, but you still find yourself lost in your emotions. You're drained and feel that you struggle with depression, but you can't understand why. You think about how you were happy yesterday, but now it's like you couldn't hold on to that emotion, even though nothing happened to drag you down.

Release Your Blocks

Once you've determined that you have a block, you need to take steps to overcome it so you can find a greater alignment and reach your full potential. You'll start attracting healthier relationships, increase your self-esteem, and discover more opportunities. One of the best ways to explain your life after release is you'll feel lighter. You'll become more radiant and you'll find more love in your heart. You'll also feel that people love you more.

First, you need to learn why you have a block and what it's trying to teach you. For instance, if you find yourself struggling with power dynamics, you need to learn how to find your own power. You need to become comfortable with the passion burning inside of you and let it out. But, you also need to keep yourself grounded and fill your power with love and compassion. If you're struggling to understand why, you may want to take time to reflect and ask the violet flame and your guardian angels to guide you to an answer. You can also write down your fears, why they happen, and brainstorm what you can learn from them. It's also critical to focus on your intuition, as you might have a feeling for the reason. If you do, write it down and reflect on this because your intuition will never steer you wrong.

You can also discover more about your blocks by making a list of your life patterns. Try to observe your behavior and thought process instead of judging yourself for certain situations. Another method that can help you discover more about yourself is to meditate. You can also ask yourself questions, like "What patterns do I have with my relationships?" and "How do I conduct myself at work?"

Next, you will want to state your intention to change to the universe and your higher powers. You can do this through meditation, by speaking it out loud, or simply thinking what you're feeling. For example, you might say, "I surrender to the universe and my higher powers. Please guide me in my spiritual healing so I can create a stronger connection with my highest and truest self. I am open to your love, grace, and healing."

It's important to note that during your transition you might struggle mentally. You may sink into a depression or feel blue for a few days. You can also feel more exhausted than before, which is normal when you're changing on a spiritual level. If you have anxiety, it can become worse for a short period of time. If you feel like you're healing, take these negative signs as positive indicators because they mean you're about to reach your higher state of consciousness.

Now, it's time to use your moments wisely. Focus on becoming the person you imagine yourself to be or your highest self. This might mean you use techniques to become more patient, compassionate, or understanding. One of the best ways to help yourself heal is by using the time you're given to guide yourself down a healthier path.

Time is on your side during transition. You might not feel that you have enough hours in a day to work on your career projects, but you always have the time to focus on you. If you make a mistake, forgive yourself and learn from it. If someone harms you, forgive them and then yourself, if necessary. Take time to learn strategies to help increase your self-love. Focus on tasks that lead you to feel happy and see the beauty in your life.

Chapter 6: Violet Flame Meditations

There are several violet flame meditations that you can use to help transform your life. Each one has its own special purpose. For instance, you can use one meditation to bring powerful spiritual energy into your life and another will help you heal from your past lives. Others will focus on your relationships, career matters, health, and well-being.

Preparing for Your Meditation

Your preparations are similar to how you get ready for visualizing, praying, or saying an affirmation. However, there are also a few special, significant steps that you'll take to help yourself reach a meditative state so you can truly see and feel the flame. It's at this point you'll bring in the energy to help transform your life. You'll also learn about the critical steps that will help you release yourself back into reality.

Step one: Find a comfortable and quiet location where you can be alone and without interruptions. You might find yourself lying down in the grass, on a couch, or sitting on a chair. Before you start, you need to ensure that your surroundings are conducive for bringing peace into your heart and soul. You should avoid feeling uncomfortable or in a place where you are struggling with negative thoughts during meditation. The energy that you hold at this time is the energy that you'll bring in. For example, if you feel stressed, you'll bring in more stress and the meditation won't work.

Step two: Ground yourself with the center of the earth. As in other grounding exercises, imagine your roots coming from the bottom of your feet and reaching into the earth. The roots pass the grass, soil, clay, rocks, and water to finally make contact with the center. Once you see a connection, visualize the energies of the earth reaching you through the roots and into your entire body.

Step three: You need to clear the negativity out of your mind, body, and soul. You'll do this by bringing yourself into a semi-meditative state through your breathing. Start by taking a deep and slow breath in. Let your lungs fill with air. Once they are full, slowly release this breath into your environment. Take another deep, slow breath in the same manner but this time start visualizing your negative emotions and thoughts leaving your body. They flow out of your body with the air and you begin to feel more relaxed and calm. Repeat this process until you start to sense your body sinking into the foundation you're lying or sitting on. Your limbs will start to rest and become heavy.

It's important to never move onto a full meditative state until you are confident that all your negativity has left your body, mind, and soul. If you're struggling, take your time. Be patient with your first few meditations because it takes you a while to get into your positive mindset, especially if you're dealing with depression, anxiety, are overworked, angry, or frustrated.

Meditation to Experience the Violet Flame

Close your eyes and take a deep, slow breath. Shift your awareness from the outside of your body into the inside. Imagine your guardian angels and other higher powers surrounding you as they start to move back to let the higher powers associated with the violet flame move forward. You see Archangel Zadkiel, his brother, and their team gliding closer to you, bringing forth a bright divine light.

Now switch your awareness to the message that further connects you with your guides and higher powers. You are indeed in their presence. You are in the presence of light, love, and peace. Let yourself relax as you find the rhythm of your breath. Once you are in a calm state, you will tune into the higher vibrational light that the Archangels bring to you.

You are aware of the light they bring, the violet flame. See this light. Visualize and sense the violet flame as it grows brighter and brighter. Imagine the light appearing right in the center of your mind's eyes. It surrounds your body, over your head and below your feet. The warmth of the light covers your body.

Breathe and let your awareness focus on your heart, the area of your soul. Visualize the light of the flame opening and expanding in your heart chakra then moving up to your throat, opening and expanding. Imagine the violet light moving into your crown, opening and expanding. Allow your awareness to connect to the oneness of the violet flame.

Focus your awareness within you as the flame brightly shines around you, connecting you to reach your highest consciousness. Stretch to reach the higher vibrations. Take a deep breath in through your mouth to let in all of the high vibrations. Hold in these vibrations and then release your breath. Feel the lower vibrations flow out of your body. Each time you breathe in, the violet light brings in more awareness to a higher consciousness and higher realms. Every time you release your breath, your stress, worries, and negativities leave your body.

Relax your breath and let the violet flame start transmuting negativity into positivity. Transforming judgment, ego, pain, bad experiences, loneliness, depression, anxiety, and feelings of worthlessness. Let it transmute fear and release the lower levels of density and manipulation in your light. Allow these lower energies to dissolve into the light.

Breathe in and let the energies of the violet flame enter your body. Let it enter your soul. Bring in the positive feelings from the universe. Feel happiness and joy. Allow the energies to cleanse your energy.

Focus your attention back to the violet flame as it continues to shine brightly. Breathe in and wiggle your toes and fingers. Feel the foundation beneath you as you start to shift your attention from inside to outside. Open your eyes and focus on becoming one with your environment before you continue on with your day.

(Go to: bit.ly/violetflameguided to Get Your *BONUS* Violet Flame Guided Meditation Mp3.)

Meditation for Clearing and Healing

Slowly breathe in, hold your breath, and breathe out. Close your eyes and observe your breath. Notice how the air feels as it comes into your mouth, down your throat, and into your lungs. Feel the coolness of the air in your body as you slowly exhale. Let the air flow back out of your lungs, into your throat, and out of your nose.

Breathe normally. Find the rhythm of your relaxed breath. Breathe in, breathe out, in and out. Your body is calm and your mind is at peace.

Bring your mind to the violet flame. You see a dim violet light in your mind's eye. As it comes closer, it becomes brighter. The flame starts to move. The flame is full of divine light. The violet color in the center of the flame is light. Your eyes move to the edge of the flame, where it's darker in color.

Watch the flame as it dances in front of you. It holds within its vibration the energy to help you cleanse your soul and heal your heart. As you continue to watch the flame, send out a message from your heart into Archangel Zadkiel and the universe. As you ask the angels and universe to heal you, the violet flame grows more vibrant.

The flame starts to circle around your body as you continue to send out your request. The violet flame becomes larger and larger as it surrounds your body from above your head to around your feet. You're entirely consumed in this beautiful orb of a violet flame.

You start to feel the vibrations of the flame as it connects to you. It reaches your mind and moves down your body, into your throat, heart, and then swirls into your bloodstream. The vibration reaches your cells, bones, and down through your legs and into your feet. The healing and clearing energy continues to circulate inside of you and begins to center at your heart, the location of your soul. The light becomes brighter as it connects to your soul. Let the warmth of the flame heal your soul.

As you bask in the warmth, thank the energy from the flame for its healing and cleansing powers. When the flame starts to go back toward the universe, slowly backing away from your mind's eyes, bring your attention again toward your breath. Focus on the sensations of your body by wiggling your toes. Wiggle your fingers and feel the foundation that you're lying on. Slowly open your eyes and let yourself adjust to the world around you.

Meditation for Energy Shift

Close your eyes and feel the warmth of the energy that is coming closer to you. They are your angels, bringing the energies of the universe. Right now, you see them as a ball of light, a bright light that is coming closer and closer. In the center of this light you start to see a bright violet ray.

Archangel Zadkiel is in the center, coming closer to you. You see him holding out his hands as the violet flame shines brightly from his palms.

The violet flame grows larger. Focusing your eye on the flame, you see it waving back and forth with the energy from the universe. As it closes in on you, the warmth from the flame reaches your heart. It spreads throughout your body and into your soul.

Allow the energies to flow through your body, circling around your heart. The violet rays from the energy become brighter as it connects to your soul. Visualize your body lighting up in the same color, from head to toe. You're radiating the warmth, love, and peace of the energy.

Let yourself bask in the energy for as long as you need. The light will continue to grow brighter until you feel the connection throughout every cell of your body. It's in your mind, shifting your thought patterns. Your emotions are more balanced, creating a peaceful energy that covers you like a warm, violet blanket.

Turn your attention back to your breath, allow the light to soak up inside of you. Wiggle your fingers and toes to feel the sensation of your body as you slowly open your eyes. Glance around your environment as you start to become one with your new energy shift.

Chapter 7: Transmuting

When you're transmuting, you're changing the state of your current being. You're altering a part of your memories, your personality, or anything you choose to focus on. You can change the appearance or nature to a higher standard or belief. The goal of the violet flame is to help you reach your highest spiritual self. It helps you discover the realm that you can't always physically see with your eyes. It allows you to open up your mind's eye, learn about the universe, angels, archangels, and all the powers that surround you.

Transmutation can help you understand the cause of disease. You'll learn how to purify atoms and electrons, strengthen your forgiveness process, transform your negative emotions, and even change your heredity. You can alter painful memories, However, you can't dive into any of these changes without the violet flame.

Today, many people believe that violet flame transmutation is a modern technique for people who are interested in reaching a higher spiritual being, but it's been around for centuries. People used to visualize and pray to Archangel Zadkiel and St. Germain to help them with life's struggles and woes. They prayed that Germain would return to earth to help improve the world. While the popularity of the flame died down for many centuries, it was brought back to life in the late 1980s during a Harmonic Convergence. People felt that they needed the power of the fire to help improve the conditions of Earth and help others find a better way towards enlightenment.

Roots of Disease

When exploring the root of disease, you need to look at the larger picture of disease. You usually refer to it as a physical illness whether it's a common cold, Type 2 Diabetes, eczema, or cancer. But, the roots of it goes further than anything physical. In fact, it starts at the emotional and mental level. This allows you to use the violet flame to transform your emotions or thoughts in a positive direction that will help you fight off any illness that you have. Think about it this way, you've heard survivors of cancer talk about their mental health and how they focused on the positive, even telling themselves they would beat it again and again. They believe they wouldn't have won the battle if they didn't have this strong mindset. Many experts agree with them, as physicians will always keep the conversation as upbeat as possible and explain that the way you face your disease builds your foundation for recovery.

It's important to note that the positive mindset doesn't mean you won't have negative thoughts or feel like you're having a bad day. It doesn't mean that you'll never question yourself again or wonder if you could've handled a situation better. Rather, it means that you learn how to stop these moments and turn them into a positive. In a sense, the violet flame helps you learn how to choose your thoughts and control your emotions so you can overcome any obstacles in your path.

One way that can help you transform your life is to say this common mantra to St. Germain. It's called the "Mantra of Affirmation," and focuses on your past, whether from your current or previous lifetimes. It helps you transform your method of thinking so you can start to let go of the negativity that holds you back. All you need to do is repeat, "I am a being of violet fire. I am the purity of God's desires" (Vaashiisht, 2019). When you say this mantra, it helps to set a timeframe. I suggest around 15 minutes, wherein you will speed up the mantra as the time ticks by. You will find that this two-sentence mantra helps improve your mindset immediately. In fact, take time now to try it. Set a timeframe and start repeating. Make your heart and soul believe the words that are coming from your mouth.

Another way to help you decrease negativity in your life is to improve the environment of your home. When you use the powers of the violet flame, you don't even need to take a step into your home to give it a lighter feel. What you need to do is concentrate on visualizing the flame wherever you are. Ask St. Germain and Archangel Zadkiel to help bring the light into your home. Imagine the flame coming down from the sky and flowing into your front door. Go room to room in your mind's eye as the fire helps lighten the mood by bringing peace, happiness, and strength. As unwanted thoughts and emotions are released, the fire grows brighter. Imagine that the colors of the flame are left in the individual rooms, hallway, and stairs. It leaves a trail of beautiful violet colors wherever it goes. The more the negativity caused by clutter, heavy emotions, frustrations, arguments, and illness is let go, the brighter your home becomes. As the flame leaves, imagine it soaring back up to the sky as you look at your home and see different violet rays illuminating your house.

When it comes to releasing parts of the foundations of disease, you always need to focus on forgiveness. You might tell yourself that there is no one you need to forgive, but it's likely that you don't realize how much you're holding in your soul that you're not consciously aware of. You've already learned a decree for asking the violet flame to help you let go. Now you should take it a couple of steps further and visualize the fire of anger disappearing.

Begin with the decree of forgiveness or calling forth the violet flame. Visualize it coming toward you and into your body. Feel the warmth of the sweet fire as it circles around your heart and then spreads throughout your bloodstream, cells, and bones. Focus on the fire filling your aura with its radiant light. As it continues to grow, imagine a dark flame of anger in your center. This is where you house your struggles to forgive and other negative emotions. They're trying to stay hidden from sight so they're not banished, but with the violet flame you have the power to see, feel, and release.

Visualize the flame circling your unwanted light. Now, imagine a deep pink flame coming down from the Heavens and into your soul. This is the fire of love and compassion. It meets the violet flame and together they envelope the darkness, transmuting your anger and negativity into positive emotions. The flames now work together to circle around your soul, giving you feelings of peace, forgiveness, love, and compassion.

The key to using the violet flame of forgiveness is to practice it often. Start by saying a decree or mantra and then finish with the visualization. You can decide to incorporate this process into your daily routine or use it every time you feel the need to forgive yourself or someone else.

Sometimes it's the people you see every day who bring forth your anger and challenges of forgiveness. While the best steps to take are to distance yourself from people who elicit negativity, you can't always do this. For example, when you have a coworker who is often angry and unforgiving, you still need to maintain a healthy work relationship. You must work with this person so you can maintain your job and do your best. Therefore, you need to find other ways to help you through this process so you don't lose sight of your transformation.

One way to lighten up the mood at your office is to ask Archangel Zadkiel to bring the violet flame into your employment building just as you did your home. You can be at your desk, on your couch, or even sitting in your car to follow this process. The key is to ensure that you make sure the flame travels through every nook and cranny of the building, from the basement to the top floor. If you don't know all of the space well, do what you can to get an idea, especially around your personal work environment. Walk around the building and remember as much as possible because your goal is to not only enlighten your office but also those around you. If you bring work home, visualize the flame going into your home and around the area where you work and the objects you use, such as your briefcase and supplies.

It's important that you don't forget about your physical health. You should focus on your overall health (emotional, mental, and physical) to assist in decreasing the roots of disease. If you feel that you're under the weather or a part of your body feels different, ask the violet flame to heal this part of you. You can also imagine the fire coming into your body and blazing away the old energy that's causing the pain. For example, you have a sore throat, so you visualize the flame moving around your throat and transmuting the unhealthy energy into new, healthy energy.

One of the factors that many people don't realize is that a physical ailment often means that something is wrong with our spiritual self. If you have a sore throat you might be keeping yourself from saying what you really feel. A stomach ache can symbolize that you're unsure about your path or a process in your current life. It can also signify that you feel something is wrong but you're not noticing the signs. You can also ask Archangel Zadkiel to use the flame to help heal your friends, family, coworkers, or anyone you see suffering. However, when you're asking the higher powers to help someone else, make sure you tell them to help only if their soul grants them permission.

Chapter 8: Violet Flame Reiki

Violet flame reiki is a powerful healing energy that provides stress reduction and relaxation. It's a part of the reiki energy that focuses on bringing more balance and harmony into your life. The problem that many healers find is that there are some areas in a person's life that create blocks. They also run into people who have stubborn patterns and feel like they are not allowed to be healed. They're usually filled with an abundance of negativity, specifically at the unconscious level, and it's hard for them to see the light.

Not every reiki healer practices the violet flame technique, but those who do state that it allows them to reach deeper into a person's soul, so they can truly heal. They see the fire as a powerful tool that can unblock the connection they can't reach. It works because unlike mindful meditation that tells you to release the negativity through your breath, the flame comes in and transmutes the darkness into light. It follows the pattern that good will always win over evil.

If you've used reiki before, it's important to note that the feeling you receive from the violet flame method is different. It's a softer and gentler feeling that washes over you. Some people describe it as a cool sensation, which is different from the normal methods used in this type of healing. The change in energy can make people feel that it's not working as well as other strategies, but this isn't true. This is the kind of vibration you want.

This type of reiki is meant to be used with your regular sessions. It's not meant to replace other types but to strengthen the energy you receive. The key is to accept your attunement naturally. Don't think of it as a separate form but visualize the power coming together to form one. For example, if you're channeling "Level 2 Reiki" and you include the flame, you want to continue on with this level. Don't see yourself as reaching a higher level.

One of the benefits of using the violet fire in this way is you can visualize the flame or feel the energy without needing to call on Archangel Zadkiel or ask the power to come your way. Instead, you just continue with your session and allow yourself to feel the vibrations as they will come to you naturally. However, this doesn't mean that you absolutely shouldn't call or ask. If you're used to calling on your higher powers for their help or you want to include added protection as you work with energy, call the archangels and St. Germain to help you. It's always a good idea to follow your instincts and regular process.

Common Violet Flame Reiki Session

If you go to different reiki masters, you'll find that they all have their unique way to conduct an attunement, but they also follow a similar pattern at the same time. One reason for this is because of their levels. Experienced masters will feel energy easily when beginners are still learning, so they might be slower or add a few steps in the process.

Before you start, take time to ask Archangel Michael to protect you. You can think or say a prayer out loud. You can keep it small by stating, "Archangel Michael, please protect me," or you can try "Dear Archangel Michael, please surround me with your golden light of protection as I prepare for this session. Thank you."

Then, you will want to call on Archangel Raphael to help you with the healing procedure. You can do this by stating, "Archangel Raphael, angel of healing, I ask that you guide me with your presence and power during the session. Please help me clear the blocks from my soul so I can reach the highest energy field. Thank you." From here, you can call upon Archangel Zadkiel and St. Germain by asking them to help guide you with the healing violet flame.

Next, you should prepare yourself to start healing by taking a few (at least three) deep and slow breaths. It's at this point you can visualize the higher powers coming toward you to help and invoke the violet flame through prayer, a decree, or affirmation. For instance, you could say, "Dear violet flame, please accept my blocks and darkness into your loving and gentle light. Take it into your power and transmute it into positivity." If you have not started imagining the fire coming toward you with its vibrate violet shades, you can try to visualize it burning right in front of you. Let your face feel the warmth of the fire.

Now, open up your fingers as far as you can. Let them stretch as they reach for your blocks of negativity that are keeping you from achieving your full potential. Visualize that you have grabbed the blocks and you can now remove the darkness from your body and soul. Look deep inside of yourself to see if there is any part of the blocks leftover and scoop it out with your fingers. Imagine holding the blocks above the candle's flame and watch them melt as they become hot by the energy of the flame. They are not mixing with love, compassion, forgiveness, and relaxation. They are transmuting through the violet energies.

Once you feel that you've completed this process, express your gratitude to all archangels and any other higher powers you called upon. Thank the violet flame for its energy and imagine that they all are gliding themselves back into Heaven. You can now continue on with your regular reiki session.

Reiki Meditation Script for the Violet Flame

Another option is to use meditation during your reiki session. This is something that your master might help you through or you can do in the comfort of your home, just like you would with your daily meditation. Before you begin this process, you should make sure that you prepare yourself by focusing on clearing as many thoughts as possible. There is no need to cleanse yourself of all negativity because you will do this during meditation. You also will want to ask Archangel Michael to protect you with his light and Archangel Raphael to help you with healing. Below is an example guided meditation for reiki.

Start guiding yourself into a meditative state by focusing on your breathing. Once you feel calm and relaxed, focus on your inner self and bring your thoughts to your crown chakra. Visualize the positive energy from the universe coming through the top of your head and down into your top chakra. Let the energy flow down your body, circling around your heart and then into your soul. Focus on the energy as your breathing forms a relaxed rhythm.

Now, call on Archangel Zadkiel and the violet flame. Ask St. Germain to help bring forth the vibrant fire and visualize the team coming together for you. In your mind's eye see the fire of a violet candle burning brightly in front of you. As it hovers, the fire begins to turn a light shade of purple. It then spreads around the blue and yellow, turning in a light shade in the center and a darker shade of violet at the ends.

Allow the flame to begin transmuting your blockages and negativity through its light. Imagine the candle floating toward your heart as it starts to illuminate around your body. The shades of violet flow over your head, down toward your legs, around your feet, and then connect at your heart.

Take a moment to state your intentions to the higher powers. Tell them that you are ready to release your old, negative energy and bring forth new, bright energy full of passion and forgiveness. You want to release your energy to make room for all the good energies from the universe.

Silently say, "I am at peace. I am loved. I give love." Repeat these words to yourself as many times as your heart desires. As you state these words or something similar, imagine the vibrant colors becoming brighter and stronger. They are clearing your energy and bringing in the positive energies of the violet flame.

Bring your attention to the flame. Say quietly, "I am the violet flame" repeatedly as you scan your body and visualize any leftover blocks leaving your body and aura.

Once your energy is transmuted by the flame, it will start to decrease in intensity. As you watch the flame gradually dissipate, thank the higher powers for their assistance. Take a few deep and slow breaths as you start to bring yourself back into focus with your outer self.

Stretch your body gently and begin wiggling your fingers and toes. Move your body little by little and then open your eyes. Connect yourself to your surroundings as you get yourself ready for the rest of your day.

Chapter 9: How to Spend Time With Archangels to Create a Heavenly Life

Even though you need to call on the archangels when you need their help, they're always nearby, regardless. They know what you want and need, but they can't officially help you unless you request their assistance. The main reason for this is because you have guardian angels and their job is to intervene when necessary, without you asking them. Once you call to them, they will come down from the Heavenly post and work with your guardians and other angels to help you.

Knowing Who to Call

There are several main archangels so it's useful to know who to call when you need help. Think about what you need help with and then look below to see which one concentrates on your needs.

Archangel Michael helps you in battle. If you're in war or you feel like you're in an emotional, mental, or physical fight with someone, call on Michael to assist you. He will also protect you in all matters, even when you're meditating. His color is usually blue.

Archangel Gabriel comes to you in copper shades. He is the angel of communication and can help you voice how you truly feel when you're afraid or not sure how to explain yourself.

Archangel Ariel is associated with animals. Her color is pink and she helps you connect with your pets and other animals. She also protects them, so if you're ever worried about animals, you can request Ariel to look out for them.

Archangel Raphael helps with healing and health. His color is an emerald green and you can call on him when you're not feeling well or are about to have a reiki session. He can also assist you with your thoughts and emotions if you feel chaotic or out of balance. He will push you to formulate healthy thoughts and emotions.

Archangel Raziel is referred to as the magician angel because he helps with so much. He is the colors of the rainbow and you can call on him while using the violet flame when you're focusing on past life traumas and healing.

Archangel Metatron is a purple color and another archangel who works closely with the violet flame. You can call on him along with Archangel Zadkiel when you're trying to clear blockages or negativity from your body.

Archangel Zadkiel is often seen with the violet flame but has a deep indigo blue color. His main focus is with forgiveness, which is a large part of the flame, too.

Archangel Jophiel encourages you to see the beauty of the world around you. When you're struggling or feeling like you're lacking the ability to sense the good in people or nature, call on her. She will come in a deep rose color.

Archangel Uriel is the archangel of inspiration, ideas, and divine insights. He is usually seen as yellow.

Archangel Chamuel is another angel that you can use with the violet flame as he is the angel of peace. His color is pale green and you call on him when you're having trouble with your negative thought patterns or you need an extra boost of calmness, relaxation, and peace in your life.

Archangel Sandalphon helps you receive messages around you. For instance, if you're struggling accepting compliments or you feel disconnected when people are communicating with you, call on him to help. He will come to you in a turquoise color.

Archangel Raguel is known as the harmony angel. He can be a part of the violet flame because he can help you create a sense of centeredness and peace. You will see a pale blue color when he is near and might hear music, such as a violin or harp.

Archangel Jeremiel is another angel that works closely with the violet flame. He is part of Archangel Zadkiel's team and will come to aid you in reviewing your life, including past lives, and to release energy that no longer serves you. When you look at the flame, he is the dark violet color.

Archangel Azrael assists anyone who is dealing with loss. He comes in a pale yellow color and will give you a sense of comfort.

Archangel Haniel is associated with clairvoyance and intuition. When you're first learning to connect with your angels and trust your gut, she is a good angel to work with. She comes in a bluish-white color.

Call on Archangels to Create a Peaceful Life

You might think that what you need support with is minor, but they don't. They want to assist you in every possible way. For example, you drop a pill from your medication box and can't find it. You worry about your pets coming across it and eating or playing with it. You might feel that this isn't a job for your angels, but Archangel Ariel wants to guide you to your medication to protect your fur baby—so let her. Call on her by stating out loud or mentally, "Archangel Ariel, help me find my medication" and she will be there.

You can also ask them to assist through meditation. It's important that you listen closely when using this method because you can hear them talking to you. At first, you might only understand what they're saying in your mind. Their words will come to you like thoughts. Once your connection is stronger to the spirit world, you'll begin to hear their soft voices through your ears. Don't question what they're telling you. When you first hear them, it's easy to question if it was your own mind or them. Follow your intuition and if you feel that it was right, believe it. Don't second guess yourself. If you sense that something is wrong, such as not hearing the message correctly, ask them to repeat their words.

Another option to connect is to write a letter. You can say the same words you would say out loud or mentally or write more than that. It's a great way to request their assistance if you need their help and if you're not comfortable talking out loud or can't concentrate mentally because of what's going on around you. For instance, if you're surrounded by friends and uncomfortable with a situation or you're afraid of someone who is near you, this is a perfect time to write. Maybe you write a letter because you express yourself better when writing and it's easier for you to ask them for help. Always start the letter with the archangel you're trying to connect with, such as "Dear Archangel Ariel or Heavenly Archangel Michael."

You can visualize that the archangel is around you and ready to assist. Start by imagining the Archangel that you want to call and say their name in a way that can strengthen your visualization. For example, you might say in your mind, "I am visualizing Archangel Gabriel coming to help me now." You can also use your mind's eye to see all the angels floating around you, ensuring that your prayers are answered.

You can call on the archangels through emotion. Each angel brings forth certain feelings to know that they are with you, such as compassion, love, and warmth. When you're struggling with anger, frustration, or other negative emotions, ask them to come and make you feel better. Tune into the way you're feeling so you can notice the change when they come. You will start to feel lighter and calmer. Your thoughts will become clearer, and you'll feel that they're near you.

One of the strongest ways to create a Heavenly life is to follow a special bedtime prayer that includes Archangels Uriel, Michael, Gabriel, and Raphael. God assigned these archangels to be the four cardinal points (north, south, east, and west) of the world. By calling on them, they can help balance your life in many ways during a time when you're closest to them and more open to their help, when you're asleep.

Uriel is focused on the north, Michael on the south, Gabriel is the west, and Raphael is the east. When you say your prayers, you should start by bringing these archangels to their correct direction in connection with you. For instance, if the south is to your right, you can say, "To my right, Michael, and to my left Gabriel, in front of me Uriel and behind me Raphael" (Hopler, 2018). The reason why you should do this before you fall asleep is because you complete most of your spiritual growth during this time.

Another way to spend time with the archangels is to talk to them like you would anyone else. You can do this when you're outside alone or lying in bed. You can even connect with them when you're in your car. You don't need to talk to them exclusively when you need them to assist with something. You can strengthen your connection with them by just telling them how your day went or about your plans to create a better life. Once they know what steps you want to take, they will start to work with you so you align with your goals. The archangels, angels, and your guardian angels are the biggest supporters you have in your physical and spiritual life. They always do what they can to ensure you succeed and have a happy, healthy, and well-balanced life.

Once you ask them for assistance, you need to look out for signs. Even when you meditate or talk to them, you might not hear them or receive messages of what they're saying through your thoughts. In fact, the main way they answer your questions or help guide you on your life's path is through signs. You might smell a certain fragrance, such as lavender, which can tell you that an angel is near. You might notice repetition of numbers for a period of time, such as "44" or "333." These are known as angel numbers and each number gives you a certain message. For example, the number eight means that you need to become comfortable with your personal power. You need to build your self-confidence, talents, skills, and realize that what you're feeling and doing is your truth. When you see the number "888," it means that you've been working on building your confidence and the angels know this. They're proud of the work you've completed and want you to know that your prayers will soon be answered through unexpected rewards or material abundance. Each number, one through ten, has a special meaning. Once you feel that the repetitive number is a sign from your angels, Google the meaning so you can follow the message to reach your full potential.

Conclusion

Repeat the "I am the violet flame" decree to yourself. You can go back to the introduction and read it or state your favorite one. You can also just repeat those words several times. Now, notice how you feel. Do you feel different from what you did when you started reading this book? You probably feel closer to the violet flame. You might visualize it immediately as you start repeating the decree. You might also feel that you're calmer and more centered.

The violet flame begins to work immediately once you start using it. While some of the benefits come on gradually, you can still feel it functioning to harmonize your life and give you a stronger sense of peace.

Do you notice your thoughts changing? Do you feel like you're starting to understand where your negativity is coming from and how you can change it? It's important to note your progress as you continue to connect with your higher powers and the vibrant fire. You can do this by writing down your emotions, thoughts, and anything else in a daily journal. Once a week, go back and read over the last few weeks to note your progress. If you see a gap in your healing, take time to focus on that area. Call the archangels to help guide you.

Continue to connect with the archangels and the violet flame, even when you feel that you're in a good place in life. When you're at your happiest, you should call on them to help you continue walking along your path. Always take notice of the signs they give you, whether it's through angels numbers, messages you hear and see, or your dreams. Write down the messages so you can bring the pieces together because they don't always answer you directly. Sometimes it can take you days or months to receive a message for a variety of reasons. They might feel that you need to work on yourself before you understand the full message, or you might have blocks that don't allow you to get the whole message right away. But, if you let go of the negativity holding you back, then you can understand what they're trying to tell you.

A key takeaway point to carry in your heart and soul is that you need to trust your intuition. The violet flame and the higher powers are not a science. It's not a topic that you can back-up through studies and research. It's a power within you that you feel. Your gut will tell you when something is wrong or right. You need to let go of your doubt and believe in yourself.

Also important to remember from this book throughout your journey is to take your time. You can't learn to connect with them clearly overnight. It can take months to let go of your blockages completely, it all depends on how deep they are and how much you allow the angels to help you. You will also never stop strengthening your relationship with the higher powers. It's something that you will work on the rest of your life, providing you take this step. Your heavenly life is waiting!

References

Abraham, L. (2015, August 30). *A guide to archangels and how they can help you.* Intuitive Medium Healer | Laura Ashley-Abraham | United States. https://www.lauraashley-abraham.com/single-post/2015/08/30/A-GUIDE-TO-ARCHANGELS-AND-HOW-THEY-CAN-HELP-YOU

Angels and Masters. (n.d.). *Archangel Zadkiel.* Www.Angelsandmasters.Net. Retrieved June 20, 2020, from http://www.angelsandmasters.net/A21.html

Beckler, M. (2015, May 7). *5 ways to ask for help from the angels.* Ask-Angels.Com. https://www.ask-angels.com/spiritual-guidance/help-from-angels/

Browne, S. (2019, May 22). *7 ways to work with the violet flame of transmutation.* Angel EFT. https://angeleft.com/violetflame/

Carol. (2017, June 5). *Healing with the violet flame of self-transformation.* Light Being Messages. https://lightbeingmessages.com/healing-with-the-violet-flame-of-self-transformation/

Dixit, S. (2018, July 10). *Spiritual growth: What are the signs that you are not growing spiritually.* Lifealth. https://www.lifealth.com/mind-body-and-soul/spirituality/signs-not-growing-spiritually-sd/82508/

Gracy. (2020, March 3). *Anxiety crystals | calming crystals for depression and anxiety - crystalis.* Crystalis - Crystals Shop. https://crystalis.com/crystals-stones-anxiety/

Harra, C., & Harra, A. (2015, June 12). *5 ways karma from your past lives affects you today.* Mindbodygreen. https://www.mindbodygreen.com/0-20223/5-ways-karma-from-your-past-lives-affects-you-today.html

Hopler, W. (2018, August 19). *How archangels can help you balance your life.* Learn Religions. https://www.learnreligions.com/archangels-of-four-directions-124410

Hopler, W. (2020, February 1). *How to know when archangel zadkiel is near.* Learn Religions. https://www.learnreligions.com/how-to-recognize-archangel-zadkiel-124287

Horvath, T. (2019, May 16). *Violet flame reiki*. The Sacred Wellness School of Healing Arts - Edmonton Reiki Training, Crystal Healing & Aromatherapy. https://www.sacredwellness.co/violet-flame-reiki/

Prophet, E. C. (1997). *The violet flame to heal body, mind, and soul*. Summit University Press. https://amethistpers.nl/wp-content/uploads/2016/06/Violet-Flame-Ebook-Free-Download.pdf

Summit Lighthouse. (2012a, April 17). *Use violet flame decrees to balance your karma and heal planet earth*. The Summit Lighthouse. https://www.summitlighthouse.org/violet-flame-decrees-benefits/

Summit Lighthouse. (2012b, July 2). *How to use the violet flame in 9 easy steps*. The Summit Lighthouse. https://www.summitlighthouse.org/violet-flame-9-steps-howto/

Summit Lighthouse. (2014, April 22). *Violet flame decree - personal transformation - I am the violet flame*. The Summit Lighthouse. https://www.summitlighthouse.org/i-am-the-violet-flame/

Suraj, H. (2014, May 15). *The power of the violet flame in reiki healing*. Reiki Rays. https://reikirays.com/10749/the-power-of-the-violet-flame-in-reiki-healing/

The Violet Flame. (2018, January 16). *2 steps to invoke protection*. The Violet Flame. https://www.violetflame.com/2-steps-to-invoke-protection/

Vaashiisht, S. (2019, July 18). *Using the holy fire violet flame to cleanse yourself*. Thriveglobal.Com. https://thriveglobal.com/stories/using-the-holy-fire-violet-flame-to-cleanse-yourself/

Valentine, R. (2017, November 14). *15 archangels to call on everyday*. Www.Healyourlife.Com. https://www.healyourlife.com/15-archangels-to-call-on-everyday

Book 2: Archangelology: Michael

Protection and Secret Angelic Codes (Archangelology Book Series 2)

Angela Grace

This book is for those who often feel vulnerable, unprotected, depressed, anxious, and alone. If you are one of such people, do not lose hope. Saint Michael is filled with light and love, and he wants to dispel these lower energies from your life.

You have not come upon this book or are currently reading this description by accident. This moment has been divinely orchestrated to make you enjoy a fulfilling and happy life on earth.

Those who are already believers in the archangel and divinity in general will find increased enlightenment and a deeper appreciation for the power and beauty of Michael. If you are not a believer, then you are truly fortunate to have found this guide. Michael's energy is ancient, sacred, reliable, and powerful. He can protect you in a crisis and give you courage to face any challenge.

It doesn't take much to invite such supreme and benevolent energy into your life. However, many have failed, repeatedly, to do this. You may even be reading this kind of book (the spiritual kind) for the first time. This guide will reveal to you the simple and effective way to form a lifelong relationship with the archangel.

Each page of this book has been blessed to bring you ever closer to complete healing. From the first chapter, you might feel Michael's warm presence. This, you will learn, is a sign that the archangel is with you. He is on your side.

If you desire the wisdom, protection, and guidance of Archangel Michael, proceed to the first page and be enveloped in light.

This book contains:

- Exercises on mantras and affirmations which you can use to transform the negativity that usually clings to us.
- Archangel Michael meditations and visualizations.
- How to heal your family, friends, and pets with the help of Archangel Michael.
- and much more...

Wishing love and light to all readers...

Introduction

My life, before I would become engrossed in what one might term esoteric spirituality, was quite lovely. There was nothing particularly striking or fulfilling about it. But with a house that provided a scenic view of the ocean, a relatively rewarding job that allowed for such luxuries, and a spouse who complemented me physically, financially, and mentally, you would agree that a lot of people would envy and aspire for that life. What more could I ask for, right?

To be fair, I *was* grateful for the things and people I had. However, neither material possessions nor a populated and active contact list of mostly superficial friends is enough to give anybody a true sense of fulfilment and success. This is most likely not the first time that you are presented with this school of thought, and you might roll your eyes at it. Yet it stands as one truth that many people would only discover after they have given up years of their life for a false vision of success. I felt divided between trying to be productive at work and being the fun, loveable, and put-together person that my friends and partner expected. This meant that I had very little time (if any at all) to attend to my personal concerns.

Suffice to say that I was constantly enveloped by anxiety, and it wasn't helped by the fact that no one in my life could relate with me. I would reach out to my partner, family members, and friends, but what was now my aching reality seemed abstract for them. As you might expect, this made me think that I must be damaged somehow. I needed some escape. Whenever people are dissatisfied with what they used to long for, they might act out. For me, this was by consuming scary volumes of alcohol and, by any means necessary, demanding a confrontation. Since not many people can exist in the toxic environment I had created around myself, I started to lose those I cared about. My partner called it quits and some of my friends stopped coming back after I pushed them away.

My mental health was in shambles and I was getting increasingly depressed. The combination of a spiraling mental and emotional well-being is never a good recipe for success at work. And, sure enough, my productivity saw an all-time low. The poor maintenance of my body meant that I was constantly ill, and I was quickly coming to the resolve that no longer existing was the only solution to my mess of a life. I no longer had a partner who would miss me. My parents had never thought much of me, and were vocal about how useless they thought I was. My friends, for all I knew, were not only shallow individuals, but they had no emotional connection with me. Taking my own life, at the time, seemed to me a more appealing thought than continued existence.

As you will discover in your journey with the beautiful archangel Michael, nothing in life happens by chance. I would find the light I desperately needed in the most unusual of places—on a shopping trip. I, quite literally, stumbled on crystals in a shopping center. As I moped out of the building while staring at the floor, I bumped into an old lady. This snapped me into reality, and I quickly apologized and bent to pick up her shopping bag. Then I stood up to behold, in a store window, the blue, starry and mesmerizing wonder that was a geode. In my book, *Crystals Made Easy*, I discuss how this moment in time turned me into a fervent crystal collector. Even though I could not explain what made them such spellbinding objects, their beauty and calming effects were irresistible.

Again, fate would direct my path towards further enlightenment and peace. This time, it was through my friend, Linda. All the books I've written, the people I've been able to help, and the joy and contentment that I now enjoy in my life may never have happened without the gentle guidance of the friend who was unlike the others I kept. She came to visit, and we launched into a long conversation about my personal healing, crystals, Reiki, self-acceptance, and more. With her prompting, I continued the research that would bring more concepts like chakras and archangelology into my field of view. I began to let go of the hurt and accepted a peace that was superior to all the mental and emotional trauma I had suffered.

The archangels are superior to every other angel and most supernatural beings. Michael is even more special, as the archangels are his subordinates. He is an especially pretty, yet terror inducing sight. The archangel Michael is often shown in paintings resembling a winged human and wearing colorful robes, exuding light from his face, wings and other parts of his body, and wielding a bright sword. He is God's warrior and the protector of everything pure and good. The first aspect of Michael that I experienced is his ability to heal. As I described earlier, I was broken and felt no reason to continue living. The crystals and Reiki started the healing that I needed, but it was Michael who gave me the determination to continue on that path. Michael has the power to heal the body, mind, and spirit. Through love, he can fill you with the courage you need to dive beyond the hurt and into the depths of your soul where your immeasurable strength and real beauty lies.

I can only imagine that, at this point, you are anxious to know more about this powerful and loving archangel. It is true that the greatest forces in life are those that we cannot see. No one can see depression, yet we feel its grip around our necks and its weight pushing down on our chests. To live without the protection and guidance of Michael is to become overpowered by your fears and hurt. The level of bravery and confidence that you need to stare down a terrifying diagnosis, the loss of a loved one, or extreme loneliness is inhuman. Without confidence and calmness in trying situations, one is most likely to make all the wrong decisions. You need Michael in your life to fight for you and help you stand tall. And Michael does not discriminate. He is willing to help defend even your pets from harm, if you need him to. The mission of this book is to help you see the beauty and necessity of Michael, and teach you the most effective ways to call upon him. I encourage you to open your heart to the friendship of this extraordinary archangel and all the goodness he is prepared to flood your life with.

Chapter 1: Michael The Protector

Even God must have been in awe of his creation when he named the leader of angels Michael. This name is translated in English as "who is like God?" and the sheer might and courage of this archangel exemplifies this name. In the Bible, we see the loyalty and bravery of Michael at play when he stands up against the rebellion started by Lucifer. With no direct help from the Almighty, Michael battles with the firstborn of the angels and defeats him. The Torah describes an angel who is assigned to be the protector of Yahweh's people, Israel. The Kabbalah, a faction of the Jewish faith, presented the archangel as the one who guides the souls of the righteous into heaven. Muslims also acknowledge the existence and power of Michael. The Quran explains that he blesses the righteous for their good deeds. Michael is able to share his strength of character with those who shun evil and bless them with protection in dangerous situations.

Although the belief in Michael extends to numerous religions, his responsibilities are often the same or similar. Lutherans believe that he is the guardian angel of those whose jobs are inherently dangerous. These include soldiers, police officers, and first responders. Jehovah's Witnesses insist that he and Jesus Christ are the same person. However, the consensus remains that Michael is the loving and magnificent protector of all things good. The Curanderas, who are traditional healers in Latin America, call on Michael to protect everyone from sailors, swordsmiths, the dead and dying, bakers, to bankers. In time of temptation, they ask him for the strength to put up a worthy resistance. The Curanderas create many protective *Amparos* or amulets. One of which is called the Saint Michael Amparo. This particular protective charm is considered one of the strongest, as it is dedicated to the warrior archangel. The Saint Michael Amparo can shield you from lower, malevolent energies.

It is surprising that, as devoted and awe inspiring as Michael is, he is mentioned less than five times in the Bible. Could this be by design? In those few instances where he appears in the Christian scriptures, people attempted to worship him. John in revelations fell to his knees in worship when he was faced with the archangel. This apostle, by all accounts, was fully dedicated to Yahweh and Jesus Christ, and never would have knelt to other gods. But he assumed, through Michael's appearance, that he was in the presence of God. Michael emitted a light so bright that it was impossible to look at him for too long, and his voice could stop the hearts of even the bravest men. As such, he might try to limit his visit to man to avoid being worshipped as God. However, we *can* pray to him, as you will soon learn in this book.

Michael The Person

Note that the word person does not always refer to human beings. In the context of this subtitle, it will be used to describe Michael as a conscious individual who displays emotions, a sense of reason, intelligence, and a complex psychology.

Michael is a fighter, and it is in this role that we often find him in many stories. In his legendary and heroic battle against the devil, Michael singlehandedly engages Lucifer in both his angelic and dragon form. Although, there is a lot to learn from this story, it would be remiss of us to ignore the conflict that the archangel Michael must contend with in his existence. You might possess prior knowledge and appreciation for the archangel before reading this book, but you were probably only looking at his status as an icon. If you would like to build a real, loving, and lasting relationship with Michael, then he must have a form outside art and folklore. He must become living, breathing, feeling, and palpable to you. Let's attempt to understand the person that is also Archangel Michael.

He is both a warrior and a healer. You might think that since Michael is the defender of good, it would be easy for him to also be the healer. With appreciation for the complexity of his divine personality, the warrior and the healer are still two distinct archetypes. This is made even more pronounced by the fact that he was created to excel in both abilities.

The warrior archetype puts Michael in a position where he is persistently beset by the need to conquer. Even though he might want to try more peaceful alternatives and appeal to his desire to heal, the archangel cannot afford to be seen as vulnerable. His courage and willingness to keep fighting not only keeps the enemy—Satan, in this case—hesitant, but emboldens the angels in his charge. If all aspects of the warrior archetype stays true for the archangel, then he very likely wrestles his craving for praise and adulation too. Since he is also Michael, the loyal and devoted archangel of God, this can be very challenging when men seem all too eager to bow at his feet.

However, the stories we have heard of Michael and the experiences of those who have accepted him into their lives would suggest that the archangel manages these conflicting archetypes well. He, in fact, seems to favor the healer in him more than the warrior. And when he must defend, we see his loyalty and courage, as opposed to any kind of hubris. as human beings, whether you're a man or woman, we also have the potential to be warriors and healers. And many of us struggle with these choices every day. Since television and popular media would have us think that warriors are violent and that healers often get the short end of the stick, we might respond with aggressiveness when a much calmer frame of mind is a better solution. When you pray and ask for Michael's protection and guidance, it is not wrath or vengefulness that you would feel. Rather, Michael's presence is as energetic as it is peaceful and comforting. We have a lot to learn from the leader of angels, and he is all too eager to teach.

Archangels and Their Elemental Energies

Fire

If you have ever seen a painting of Michael, you may recall that he was enrobed in blue cloth or wearing blue armor. At the very least, there is often something blue on his person. This color is symbolic of the might, Godly devotion, and courage that Michael personifies. Other times, the archangel is seen wearing red, which could be a result of his connection to the element of fire. In many religions, fire symbolizes awakening, truth, and purity. Michael can help you pursue not just the truth about your environment, but yourself too. He can hold your hand as you resolve to live a more righteous and disciplined life.

Air

Raphael (which means "God heals") is an archangel who is associated with air. While Michael is both warrior and healer, Raphael's primary role is healer. He can mend every aspect of what constitutes a human being, and help people live more fulfilling lives. He is most commonly depicted in art wearing the color green, which is an energy associated with prosperity and healing. This color also illustrates his connection to the earth. He is quite skilled in making medicines, and can utilize everything from fish to leaves in order to treat injuries and various ailments. Raphael can also help you deal with mental, emotional, and spiritual turmoil. You can call on him for strength, solutions, and guidance if you struggle with depression and addictions. This archangel not only brings new knowledge about general health, but also has a charming sense of humor. If you visit the bookstore and find a healing book on the floor and in your path, this might be Raphael making himself known to you.

Earth

According to science, the earth is about 4.5 billion years old, and life has existed on it for three billion of those years (Redd, 2019). This means that the earth is reliable, and this is a virtue associated with the archangel called Uriel. Another reliable phenomenon is wisdom. Uriel devotes most of his existence to learning and gaining wisdom, and he occasionally shares this with mankind. If you also feel like some parts of your life are out of control, archangel Uriel can grant you stability. His name is translated in English as "God is my light," and he can help you deal with confusion and doubt. As such, students are often encouraged to reach out to Uriel when they are preparing for a test and need the extra support (Patel, 2018).

Water

If you were suddenly asked to name an archangel, Gabriel might be the first that comes to your mind. His name is translated to mean "God is my strength," and you might think that, like Michael, he is frequently in battle. But this is not the case, as God often relies on Gabriel to reveal important information to people. Water is synonymous to clarity and reflection, and Gabriel's revelations often achieve these two. Typically, his messages are never confusing. Like water, Gabriel helps people to pursue purity of the soul, body, and mind. However, he does not stop at delivering messages. Some of the information that Gabriel conveys can be quite heavy, painful, or even scary to the receiver. This means that the individual would require superhuman strength and courage to take the news and act on it. Gabriel can and does empower people with the boldness to do the will of God and make the best decisions for themselves.

Chapter 2: How to Easily Call Upon Archangel Michael

As humans, we feel the need to connect, to feel loved, protected, and safe. It's why we marry, have friends, and socialize! But beyond human socialization, there is a part of ourselves that craves a connection to a higher power. One that has driven us to different forms of religions to find answers to our many different questions. In finding answers, we go through different means. But one, which has worked well for me, is calling on Archangel Michael. We've all led pretty long and interesting lives one way or another, but we have also had our down moments as well. Moments when we are at a crossroads, or aren't feeling very good about our current path in life. This point is when you reach out to the archangel, who never fails to show up.

"Why not go to God instead?" you might wonder. The answer is simple: angels are around us every day of our lives, and serve as messengers and servants of the divine. Nevertheless, they aren't gods, and are limited in their abilities and services. The coming of Michael is swift, and you will feel his presence, like a warm light enveloping you with a sense of protection.

Calling upon Michael is as easy as can be. All you need to do is say it or think it. Matter of factly, the mere intention to have him with you invokes his presence. In doing this, you are invoking the divine part of yourself, which is your divine strength, willpower, higher consciousness, and ability to keep yourself space. And as I said earlier, Michael is a part of the divine. Meaning, you are connecting to the same source from which he comes to draw him to yourself. What draws him to you is your willingness and openness to experience his presence.

So, a simple, heartfelt prayer like "I need your help," can invoke the archangel. Think of it as calling a friend. When you pick up your phone and dial a friend for a helping hand, the response he or she would give depends on how urgent help is needed. If there is no urgency, that friend might not show up as quickly as when it's an emergency. But Michael beats any human friend because he shows up regardless of the situation. You need not have an emergency to call Michael. A happy prayer expressing your desire to feel his presence is enough to invoke him.

Intention and willpower are a key part of calling on Archangel Michael, because he functions on the ray of divine will. It is that divine consciousness to which you connect to, when you open your heart and mind to call on him. However, when invoking the archangel, refrain from giving yourself away. It's best to not commit yourself to anything not part of you, angel or not. For example, beckoning on him every other time you feel scared isn't advisable, because at those points, you tend to give off the wrong kind of energy. We were all designed as self-sufficient and capable of looking after ourselves. So, surrendering your every fear to the archangel distorts that notion. Also, it means you keep inviting something outside of you to come in and rescue you all the time. If that's not possession, pray, tell, what is it?

Remember that Michael is merely an angel—a guardian of light given to servitude, who doesn't have the willpower to help you without your permission. However, in all your asking, understand that even though he's a part of the divine, you are also a part of that divine wholeness, and are the best protector of your person.

Steps for Calling Archangel Michael

1. **Prepare yourself**: There's a reason many appearances of divine beings take place in quiet environments. For one, distractions are less, allowing for divine instructions and interventions without intrusions of any sort. So, to begin your journey of contacting the archangel, find a quiet spot. To start, concentrate on your breathing and try to relax. Then, imagine yourself surrounded by a brilliant, golden light as you envision the presence of Michael. Allow the energy from within to lift you into the divine realm as you sense the presence of the archangel. With an open heart and a willing mind, reach into your divine self and experience Michael's presence around you. At this point, endeavor to be mindful of everything around you as you wallow in the living and blissful energy he resonates.

2. **Be intentional**: The need for intention cannot be overstated, so be prepared to be granted your needs. The words "I'm ready" is a powerful statement capable of engaging the archangel to fulfil your desires. This statement is especially helpful when you try making positive changes in your life. For instance, if you are grieved, and wish for comfort, you can call on the angel by saying, "Archangel Michael, I'm sad, comfort me. I'm ready to be at peace. Guide me in the divine path towards the peace that I seek. Thank you." Ensure that your needs are positive and not overboard. Remember that the archangel is still limited in what he can do for you. Also, don't spend your time wondering how he will do what you ask. That's not your job. You do the asking, and let the archangel bother with how he's going to supply your needs. Feel free to repeat your needs or intentions again, but avoid nagging. Constantly invoking Michael for the same need shows a lack of faith, which is a bad energy. The divine realm operates with faith, and faithlessness doesn't help. After making your request, listen for guidance or pay attention to any opportunity or ideas that may come your way. It could be Michael offering you intuitive guidance to help achieve your request(s).

   As humans, we often require help from others to reach our goals, especially when these goals are related to our life purpose or business. Archangel Michael is a valuable asset to have in such endeavors. Isn't he here to offer divine support and guidance after all? Sometimes, directly asking for help can help with faster replies. Remember, you're an intent away from calling on Michael and asking him for help. So, don't think about it and just do it. Are you stuck in a situation where you have to think on your feet but have no idea? Say the words. Make a direct request. Michael is at your beck and call, and he will answer in a snap. Do you need the right resources and people to push things forward? He can lead you to them. He's all about guidance after all, isn't he? He will whisper your name to those people that matter, and they will contact you.

3. **Visualize help coming**: Picture Archangel Michael attending to your needs and rounding up other angels to help you. Envision a golden light bathing you from heaven as you receive that idea, opportunity, or contact you asked for. Don't worry. Don't fret. Don't doubt. Just open your mind to the possibility of your request being answered. Feel your energy grow as you absorb the divine intervention of Michael. Believe that the situation is in control, and that the archangel is doing as asked to get things running. If you feel your request is taking too long to be processed, or help doesn't come as quickly as you like, don't be discouraged! It could be a test of faith to validate your trust in the divine power. Losing your faith would mean that you never truly believed in the ability of the archangel to bring your wishes to life. Hold fast to your faith and wait for the answers, which will come in their due time.

Chapter 3: Exercises, Mantras, and Affirmations

The Indians believe in chakras, the Chinese chi; but one thing remains common regardless of beliefs: we are all made of energy. The universe is a vast span of expanding energy in various degrees, and we are a part of this energy. In moments when we are down, sad, or unexcited, we experience a period of low energy. In contrast, when we are at our highest and happy, we radiate positive, vibrant energy. These energies are what help us stay grounded and connected to the universe and those around us. Without them, we would be incapable of connecting with the divine. Think of the divine as a sacred energy channel, like a plug you connect to for the surge of the supernatural. When you connect your phone to an outlet using a charger, the battery receives a surge of energy that powers it. That is exactly how our connection to the divine works.

According to Buddha, living is suffering, and he couldn't have been more correct. We live life trying to survive and do better than we did the previous day. Put simply, we are on a merry-go-round of avoiding suffering. Meaning, we are constantly surrounded by negative energies that may disrupt the brilliance of our intrinsic energy. This explains why we need to engage the archangel, Michael, to help drive any form of negativity that might cling to us. But such a feat cannot be achieved by wishful thinking or speaking the word. For instance, to improve your battery percentage, you have to plug in your phone. So, to get rid of negative energy, you have to plug into the energy channel. Let's consider another instance: when tragedy strikes, we tend to send thoughts and prayers or love and light to those in distress. It doesn't seem like much, but in doing that, we tap into their energy, putting ourselves in their shoes. In turn, we give them some positive energy to help them through the dismal situation. There are no benefits to taking on the pain of others, and you must understand how these energies affect you.

The divine isn't a physical channel you can plug into; thus, begging the question: how do you connect to it? There are several exercises, mantras, and affirmations that can get you hooked, but they all boil down to the technique of opening your mind and body, and aligning your energy. An open mind is one that perceives, and an open body is one that receives! In opening your mind, you create a means of connection with the archangel, and an open body presents a route through which positive energy is received.

Opening the Mind and Body

Exercises to Open the Body

1. Find a quiet place to sit. Ensure that the place is comfortable, so you don't get distracted by discomfort over time.

2. Sit upright with your spine aligned, and your chest pushed forward slightly in a receiving position. This posture opens up the body to receive the energy. Aligning the spine allows the energy channels within you to connect throughout the body, from your crown to the base of your spine.

3. You can hold up your hand in a prayer-like posture, but this is optional.

4. Close your eyes to shut out distractions from the environment. Doing this will allow you to be more aware of what is going on within you.

5. Be in tune with your body, and block out your perception of the external environment.

6. Listen to your breathing, and focus on it until you feel yourself grow calm with each breath.

Exercises to Open the Mind

1. The first step is to be mentally prepared for the process. Be intentional about wanting to receive positive energy and dispel negative ones.

2. Clear your mind. Avoid thinking about anything at this point. It can be challenging, given how the mind can be easily distracted! But focus on nothing more than the goal, which is to connect to Michael.

3. As you picture the archangel, take in deep breaths through your nostrils. Visualize the breaths you draw as living, positive energy.

4. Hold your breath for about seven seconds before exhaling through your mouth. Picture the exhaled breath as negative energy leaving your body.

5. Repeat the breathing exercise for as many times as you feel necessary.

6. On your final exhalation, picture the positive energy you have taken in flooding your body with light. Picture it revitalizing you, charging your mind and body.

Meditation

The technique of opening your mind and body leads up to the final technique, which combines mantras and affirmations to rid you of those pesky negative energies. While meditating with the archangel, he will protect and shield you from negative energies, helping you rise to the strongest version of yourself!

As you imagine your body being recharged by the healing power of the positive energy you inhaled, you can use this mantra (or other affirmations) to call on Archangel Michael:

"Now, I call in all my guides to be present with me, including all those that are in the highest of love and light: Archangel Michael, guardians, spirit guides, ascended masters, and loved ones. I ask that you surround me with your healing light, and rid me of my attachments to negative energies like worry, stress, and any other lower energies. Help me to be free from any attachment to fear. Help me to let go of my ego, as I ascend into the higher place of my being that only sees and knows love.

I ask that you take away any old energy still within me, and retract any form of thought that takes semblance to fear and ego. Help me to reconnect with the fragments of my soul, experiencing the wholeness of my divine birthright. And as I let go of every form of stress and fear, may I feel the intrinsic divine power at work in me. That I may be filled with the courage and strength to know my identity and work in the divine light. As I breathe in and out, I refill and recalibrate my mind and body with the divine energy that bursts with love, joy, and peace. I ask, Archangel Michael, that you shield me, sealing these positive and whole vibrations into my physical and emotional bodies.

I ask that you stay with me, helping me to continue in the divine light of God. Amen."

Chapter 4: Protect Your Loved Ones and Pets

Loved ones are more than a set of people who share the same surname with you. They are the people who rejoice, mourn, and stay by your side throughout the rest of your life. They are the ones you call home, without whom there would be no memories to make or cherish or recall. They are family that back you and friends that cheer for you. The ones who are there when you hit a roadblock. The people you call when in need. They are everything that makes life meaningful. As such, they must be protected. You can call on Michael to protect your loved ones, and keep them safe. You can pray for their protection and happiness in the same way you pray for yours.

Like family, pets are the perfect balance of happiness and anger. We love when they snuggle close to us when we sleep, but are horrified when they take a leak on the car seat. So, basically, they are family. Due to how much time we spend with our pets, we tend to develop strong bonds with them. To the extent that they sometimes put themselves on the line to save their human friends. With this in mind, it makes sense why you should not leave your pets out of your prayers. These animals are a source of joy, love, compassion, and peace to us, especially when we are at our lowest moments.

Committing your pets into the protection of Archangel Michael makes them safe and sound even in your absence. While it might sound silly to invoke the archangel around your pet, it is no strange tradition. In Christendom, animals played a crucial role in the liberation of the Israelites. More so, they were one of God's earliest creations, and our relationship with them stretches as far back as Noah and Adam. Pets have a more limited lifespan than us humans, meaning we will most likely witness their passing at some point. This can be a low point in our lives, so we have to make the most of the time we have with them. To ensure that they live out their days, you have to commit them into the care of Archangel Michael.

Remember the story of the Passover? When the Israelites smeared the blood of an animal on doors of their houses and the Angel of death spared them? The Archangel is not beyond catering to our pets and loved ones if we ask him to protect them. He is a guardian and a servant of light, so he is obliged to help you. And since they are family, he is obliged to protect them as well. Call upon the Archangel as you would at any time by reaching into your inner connection with the divine. Bid him to come to you with his host of guardian angels, and ask him to surround your loved ones and pets. Ask him to protect them from the evil of the days and the pestilence of nighttime.

Here is a prayer you can use:

"Dear, Archangel Michael, I ask that you come to me with your host of angels." As you say this, visualize him descending to meet you with his band of angels in a brilliant blue light. "I ask that you surround my pets and loved ones (family and friends), and shield them even as you shield me." You can call the names of your loved ones and pets. "Protect them from negative energies and the results of their errors. Give them your guidance to walk in the divine light, that their paths may be illuminated by the brilliance of your divine light. Be by them all day, every day. Be their guide and defender. Amen."

Now, visualize Archangel Michael dispatching his angels to surround your loved ones and pets. They are safe now, thanks to you!

Chapter 5: Protect Your Aura and Home

In our day-to-day lives, we experience negative vibes around us, coming in the form of colleagues, family, friends, social media, and even the mass media (who especially thrive on reporting gloomy news). Even the people you find on the streets, at the marketplace, and any other public place tend to have a low energy about them. Public places aren't usually cleansed or protected, and with people going about with low energies, it's easy for you to pick it up. The longer you stay exposed to these low energies, the higher your chances of noticing the effect of those negative vibes. This explains the importance of cleansing both your body and environment, as they work hand in hand to define your energy levels and aura.

Asides experiencing low energies from the physical world around us, we also have to be wary of negative vibes that can be picked up from the spiritual realm. But don't beat yourself up about this detail, because you have a shield in Archangel Michael, who will be there to guard and warn you at all times. All you have to do is ask. However, bear in mind that you can unintentionally let in energies that won't act in your best interests. For instance, following a depressing situation due to curiosity can introduce negative energies into your aura. But with the right form of protection from Archangel Michael, and the intention and willingness to connect with your spirit guides, you will be able to avoid crossing paths with the wrong energies.

But how would you know you haven't picked up any negative vibes or low energy if you can't see them? It's easy to find out if you have low energy or negative vibes, because you will experience crankiness and exhaustion. So, even after a good night's rest, you would still wake up feeling drained. You may especially feel this exhaustion at noon as you constantly try to avoid dozing off. As this continues, your focus will be diverted, and it becomes a chore to go through your daily tasks. However, it could also be that you feel ill, because poor health can also be responsible for exhaustion and low energy. As such, do well to see a doctor first to confirm you are in good health. However, if after trying everything, and you can't find any underlying health concerns, then it's time to focus on the spiritual part, which is cleansing your energy to rid yourself of low or negative energy.

Alternatively, to ensure that you get it right and remove every form of low energy safely and entirely, you can try seeing a therapist, but not just any therapist will fly with this task! You need an expert at removing low or negative energies and cleaning auras. Ensure to take the time out to carefully select the right therapist for the job. He or she has to be able to carry out the procedure safely, so they don't damage your aura any further or let in more negative energy. If you can't find a therapist to help with this, you can do it yourself. All you need is the archangel Michael to get rid of those low energies within and around you. Steps on how to carry out the procedure yourself will be covered in a later part of this chapter.

How can you use Archangel Michael to protect and cleanse your energy and aura?

We have all been in the position when someone needed help. At that point, you have a choice to let the energy of others affect yours. For instance, someone may have asked you to attend to their needs and forego whatever you were doing at some point. You ended up saying yes, even though you really wanted to say no. Or, have you helped someone out only to return feeling drained for days, and can't understand why? Then you get a text from the person you helped telling you how good your help was to them, and how they feel great. This happens because you swapped your positive energy for their negative one. So, you take home their burden, and leave them with your wholeness. Here is a step by step guide to rid your aura and environment of negative energy:

1. Every morning, visit your quiet place. Start by grounding yourself with some breathing exercises to calm your mind and body and reduce distractions. Shut your eyes, and listen to your breathing until you block out every sound from your physical environment.

2. Next, invoke the archangel Michael using a mantra of your choice. You can use: "Archangel Michael, I invite you to this place right now. Let me feel your presence." Now, envision him coming to you, and ask for protection. "I ask you to protect me as I commune with you. Guide my heart and mind, and shield me from distractions." Practice your mantra regularly until you know it by heart. Knowing it will help you summon Michael faster.

3. As you meditate, prepare your mind and heart to draw the archangel to yourself. Take a deep breath, and feel the radiation of his angelic energy surrounding you. You may see the blue energy he radiates, or feel it around you.

4. Picture yourself as an airship surrounded by Michael's divine blue light. Imagine other airships taking shots at you with several weapons. These weapons are the negative energies being sent your way. Envision these attacks bouncing off Michael's light, as you stay safe within the shield of his presence. Practice this when you run into someone radiating negative energy, or listen to some negative happening on the news. Picture yourself shielded by Michael, so that the negative energy has no effect on you. Doing this means you are reinforcing your intention to be under Michael's protection. Then, mutter to yourself or think about Archangel Michael standing next to you with his host of angels. Imagine them fending off the negative energy, and preserving your positive energy. Doing this doesn't mean you are less interested in helping others. No, you can help others as much as you want. Just ensure to do it safely within the confines of Michael's protection to protect yourself from swapping energies. As a matter of fact, you are in a better position to help others when you take care to cater for your energy.

5. After fortifying yourself against negative energies, the next step is to extend that protection to your environment. From your car, to your work area, to your house, to every other place you spend time at. To fortify these places under Archangel Michael, all you have to do is envision his light spreading from you around your present environment at any one time. Picture that place bathed in that brilliant blue light that surrounds you.

6. Remember, the archangel Michael can be reached at any time. The construct of day and night doesn't apply to him, so he is ready to protect and shield you at any time. All you have to do is say the word, and he will be obliged to help you. Also, you can extend this protection to the places of your loved ones too.

Chapter 6: Archangel Michael Meditations

Meditation is a process that combines several techniques such as concentration and mindfulness to achieve a certain goal. When meditating, you focus on a specific activity, thought, or object and train your awareness and attention on it until a clear, stable, and calm emotional and mental state is reached. In this chapter, the objective of this meditation is to call upon Archangel Michael and bask in the comfort of his protection.

A step-by-step guide on how to call upon the protection of Archangel Michael is covered below:

1. Shut your eyes and relax your body. Soften yourself and let go of any tension.
2. Focus on your breathing: inhaling and exhaling. Breathe deeply and let go of anything that doesn't serve you in the here and now. Release them as you exhale.
3. Train your focus on the present moment, and take note of your breathing.
4. Prepare your mind with the intention to feel supported, protected, and safe.
5. As you take deep breaths, feel your consciousness sink deeper, traveling further into yourself as you anchor onto your soul space.
6. From this space, call on Archangel Michael to come to your aid. Invite him from the divine realm to be present with you now.
7. You might experience him in a human-like or angelic form, or as the blue energy he radiates.
8. As he presents himself to you, you will feel every anxiety, worry, and stress melt away.
9. In the presence of the archangel Michael, you can only feel protected, loved, and safe.
10. As we've talked about throughout this book, you are created with free will. So, the only way the archangel can step in to help you is if you ask. So, ask him. "Please, Archangel Michael, keep me safe. I ask that you keep this feeling of security and safety with me always. Please, protect me wherever I go."
11. Envision the archangel receiving your request and casting a ball of blue energy around you as a protective sphere to protect your energy from being depleted or disrupted by any external force, so that your energy might be protected from those that will drain you, or anyone that wants to take from you what you aren't willing to give up.
12. Take a deep breath in this space filled with love, protection, and safety. Enjoy the feeling of knowing that within the confines of this space, you can't be touched by anything that can affect you negatively.

13. Know that Archangel Michael is by your side all the time, willing and ready to come forward and help you find your way to this space whenever you feel like reconnecting. All you have to do is ask.

14. Thank the archangel for his presence and the divine blessings he has showered you with.

15. Commit to take this feeling of protection, love, and safety with you as you return your consciousness to your physical body.

16. Breathe in deeply as you ground and anchor yourself to this blissful feeling.

17. Slowly, make some gentle movements like stretching and opening your eyes when you feel ready to return back to your day. Remember to reconnect to your protective sphere whenever you feel negative energy or emotions.

The benefits of this meditation routine cannot be overstated. Not only does it allow you to take charge of your day, it also helps you start out and finish on a high note. This spells a great frame of mind for you, which would allow you to function at the top of your game throughout the day! Also, with that much positive energy, you will be able to help others and spread the good vibes.

Chapter 7: Archangel Michael Manifestation, Chakras, Dreams, and Karma

Chakras

Chakras are energy centers or inner lights within the body that are lit up when we meditate. In Eastern religions, they are usually depicted as spinning wheels. A smooth and fast spin shows a higher likelihood of connecting with the divine. The idea behind this notion is that angels can be summoned through meditation and their respective connections to the chakras in the body. When chakras spin, they produce unique divine vibrations that connect to the divine realm. Angels respond to their chakras and grant us our requests. Sometimes, chakras can also be a source of connection for angels who wish to communicate with us. This is especially so for chakras like the solar plexus, heart, and crown chakras, from which we received intuitive guidance.

Archangel Michael is responsible for the throat chakra. So, when you connect with him, you are tapping into and activating the throat chakra. This chakra is linked to the color blue, hence Michael's distinct aura. Blue gems like sapphires can help you connect with the throat chakra and Archangel Michael better. But sometimes, the chakras can get blocked, cutting off your connection with the divine. To prevent this, here is a prayer to help you cleanse your chakras system:

"Archangel Michael, please come to me. I ask that you purify and cleanse my entire chakric system. I ask for your pure, concentrated light to flow through me, cleansing, purifying, and strengthening my chakras. Let the energy within me grow under your guidance, fueling my chakras with your love and blessings. Let every bad energy within me, blocking my chakras be completely erased now and forever. Amen."

Karma

Karma is a relatively common term, which is feared by many. While karma should not be feared, it should absolutely be respected! Karma is usually drawn by your actions. As much as you have free will to do as you please, you also pass judgement on yourself for your deeds. Karma is believed to be accrued from previous lifetimes. According to the belief, you decide what is missing in your life and how to go about it. The next time you reincarnate in a different lifetime, the choice is yours to choose what you have to learn. It's at this point that karma steps in. For instance, if you hurt someone in a previous lifetime, you will pay for that hurt if you don't unlearn the toxic behavior.

Dreams

Archangel Michael works with us when we dream to help ease our fears, and guide us to new peaks of peace and happiness. He teaches us when we sleep, and provides answers to our questions. He helps to construct the foundations of our purpose in life as we lay lost in slumber. Even though you don't remember your dreams sometimes, the information they contain isn't lost to your subconscious and aids you in several ways. To access the counsel Michael offers during sleep, you can keep a dream journal to record your dreams. You can use any notebook. Ensure to keep said book close to you as you go to bed, so you can easily record your dreams. Over time, you will start to see patterns in symbolisms and themes that will guide you when you wake.

When you have recurring dreams, it's likely that Archangel Michael is emphasizing on a particular subject, so pay attention. Get a book on dreams or reach out to a dream expert if you are confused or need guidance. Also, ensure to get a good night's rest. Refrain from retiring to bed intoxicated because chemicals tend to disrupt dream sleep (REM sleep). Here is a prayer to call on Archangel Michael before bed:

"Archangel Michael, I thank you for putting me to bed and helping me to enjoy sound sleep. I ask that you come into my dreams to teach, heal, and guide me. I beg that you show me (mention any request about a situation) on a spiritual level. Guide me to your understanding. Amen."

Manifestation

The world we live in thrives of experiences and variety. Every one of us has the inherent ability to give life to what we desire the most.

Manifestation is a natural occurrence that happens regularly for as long as we live, and is independent of whether or not we are aware of it. You can begin living in dominion, feel empowered, and have your needs met when you own your ability to manifest whatever you choose. We are blessed with the ability to merge with the divine in conscious co-creation. This ability is one that can be harnessed through a variety of ways, particularly through Archangel Michael. In this chapter, we will explore some of the most powerful and consistent methods of reaching for and focusing on the power of manifestation deep within us. To tap into this ability, one key element is intention. Unconsciously, we spend our days setting intentions as we go, in conversations, our mind chatters, and even to-do lists. These three examples are some of the basic forms of intentions we set.

However, the magic doesn't come from setting intentions unconsciously, but when we become mindful of the process and align it with our energy and perspective. It's all about posing yourself and being deliberate about receiving and giving. One of the most potent ways to create intentions is with a specific ritual, like the meditation we covered in the previous chapter. That said, intentions need certain elements to function, some of which includes:

- being conscious and deliberate
- maintaining integrity and authenticity in your demands

- trusting your intentions
- keeping a flexible and clear mind
- staying emotionally prepared

How to call on Archangel Michael for manifestation, positive shifts, and imaginative power.

1. **Be clear about your goals:** To manifest your desires (wealth, power, dominion, etcetera), you must know what you want. Otherwise, you can't take any steps to make it work, and summoning the archangel would be in vain!

2. **Ask Archangel Michael:** Once you know what you want and align your intentions to it, the time is right to tap into your innermost self, connect with the divine, and invoke the archangel. Tell the archangel what you want to manifest for him to begin the process.

3. **Work towards achieving our results:** Remember, manifestation is the process of co-creating the divine. So, working towards reaching your desires improves the likelihood of getting what you want. For instance, if you wish to manifest wealth, don't stay idle. Get busy!

4. **Believe in the process:** As you commit to work towards your desires, you might tend to doubt the feasibility of manifestation. Frustration and discouragement is only natural. Don't sit in the struggle, pondering what went wrong, or if things could work out. Doing that means you don't trust Archangel Michael enough to come through. If you are too afraid to fly for fear of a crash, you will never know what it feels like to be above the clouds.

5. **Be open to receiving and acknowledging what you get:** Archangel Michael is present to give you help along the way as long as you ask. However, it's easy to miss his signs, especially when they don't come in the way you expect. The minute you begin acknowledging and receiving the signs given by Archangel Michael, you will succeed in whatever you do.

6. **Maintain high spirits:** Based on the universal law of attraction, you get what you give. A classic case of what goes around comes around. If you want to get more of what you want, commit to walking with Archangel Michael and adhering to his guidance.

7. **Check for resistance:** Sometimes, it's not that Archangel Michael hasn't granted your wishes, it's that you might be resisting it. Resistance comes in the form of frustration, fears, doubts, procrastination, among other negative emotions. Keep a clear head, and ask for his guidance in removing these resistances.

Chapter 8: How to Tell When Archangel Michael Is Around

Life is never one smooth and happy ride until our passing, unfortunately. At many different points, we will be faced with difficult choices, uncertainty, fear, grief, and other challenging situations. Sometimes, the shoulder of a loved one is enough to keep us from falling. But, more often than not, we need our spiritual guides. In many trying moments, nothing else will do except, quite literally, the help of an angel. Thankfully, angels know when we are in trouble and the precise help to offer. They are everywhere, and might be beside you as you read this book. They, however, refrain from tinkering with human choices and its outcomes without permission. They might get involved to stop evil occurrences in times when people may not have the chance to say a quick prayer and invite the help of angels—as in the case of car crashes and the likes. In most cases, they stand aside and try to make their presence known in several ways.

The archangel Michael, can be especially persistent when trying to communicate his presence. Those who are ignorant of the operations of spiritual entities may just chuck it up to gut feelings. However, those who have taken the time to gain knowledge on this subject are comforted by the signs that are outlined below.

1. **You feel at peace:** Although this sign is common to all the angels, Michael's peace is more comforting than most. He often appears in crisis situations, when human judgement is ordinarily impaired. It is, in fact, in such scenarios that we notice his unmistakable calm the most. You can also feel the peace of the archangel when you are anxious and angry. He envelops us in his wings and will stay for as long as we need him to.

2. **You see his aura:** In chapter 1, we saw that archangels are associated with certain colors. These colors are their auras, and every angel has one. It glows brilliantly, and might be observable by humans in some cases. Michael's aura is blue. If you suddenly see a shimmer or flash of blue, this could be the archangel making himself known.

3. **You come upon a feather:** As pointed out earlier, Michael is a very persistent angel. He understands that human beings are doubtful creatures and that we are not likely to be convinced by one sign. As such, he will leave multiple clues to help you recognize his presence. One of such clues is a feather. If you remain skeptical after seeing the light of Saint Michael's aura and feeling the angelic calm, you might begin to see physical evidence of the fact that he is close to you. This is a calling card that should awaken and reassure you of God's love. It should neither alarm, nor scare you in any way.

4. **You hear his voice:** Have you ever been upset or anxious about any matter, and then you hear, seemingly out of nowhere, someone speak? This might be in a whisper or a more audible tone. If the voice seems to come from no apparent source, this could be an angel trying to communicate with you. Michael might whisper to you or speak in his characteristic clear, deep voice. While hearing his voice might be a bit jolting, his words and messages are those of peace and love. Oftentimes, they are also laced with humor. He wouldn't be forceful or commanding. Remember that Saint Michael is also a healer, and he is gentle with humans.

5. **You see his name everywhere:** How often do you hear or see the name Michael in a day? Even if you have a friend, pet, and sibling named Michael, and you live on Michael street, chances are that you won't stumble on the name at every turn or hear it at work, in your car, and other places that aren't your street. So, if this happens, don't be quick to dismiss the sign. This is even more true when you find the name three times. You might receive help from someone named Michael (or Michelle) or hear the name on the radio. It is more rewarding for you to acknowledge the archangel's presence, accept his heavenly calm, and ask for his help where you need it.

6. **You know it's the truth:** "Am I just hearing what I want to hear?" you might ask yourself. However, Michael's signs and messages cannot easily be dismissed as an overactive imagination. Whether they are practical or easy, it will be clear that you are neither hearing a lie, nor seeing an illusion. While the ego is powerful and cunning, it is incapable of mimicking angelic signs and messages.

7. **You feel hot:** You might feel a warm sensation when Michael is close to you. Before adjusting the air conditioner or worrying that you might be coming down with something, consider the possibility that an archangel has honored you with his presence. This warm feeling is noticeable even in generally cold temperatures. Michael, as we saw in chapter, is associated with fire. This is not just an element that is imagined by artistes and storytellers. It is a truth. Michael is often regarded as a sun deity by some because of the sheer amount of heat that he conducts. Thankfully, Michael will not cause you any harm with this heat. It often feels no hotter than the rays of the sun on a warm afternoon.

8. **You see repeating numbers:** Again, how often do you see the number 777? Even accountants and mathematicians rarely stumble on a specific order of numbers multiple times in a day. Since we always expect randomness in many aspects of our daily experience, Michael could try and get your attention with some order and repetition. You may have heard a lot about 11:11 and now reflexively dismiss such phenomena. However, the fact that you are now reading this book means that you want to be more open-minded to the idea. You have everything to gain by doing so. When next you find repeating numbers throughout your day, know that Saint Michael is reaching out to you.

9. **You see symbols of protection:** This usually happens after someone prays to Saint Michael. Think of what makes you scared, anxious, or apprehensive. When you call to the archangels in such times, he immediately wants to help. To do so, he might direct your

attention to objects that symbolize his protection over you. He will also provide you with the clarity to understand the meaning of such symbols. You might see a cross while waiting to be called for an interview. If you feel anxious about going out in public, you might notice a sword—this could be as a mural or on a poster. Even umbrellas can be shown to you by Michael, since they provide a hiding place from the rain.

10. **You hear his guidance as your thoughts:** In the depths of a depression, it is nearly impossible to have uplifting or optimistic thoughts. If you have ever gotten to such a point in your life, then you fully understand the ever-sinking feeling that follows depression. Even worse is the fact that you might want to keep drowning in the negativity and darkness that cloaks your mind. If you ask Michael for help, your mental image of your situation will gradually become less bleak. First, you will feel calm and relaxed. You might have a funny thought and chuckle. Then you gain an astronaut's perspective of your life, and all your problems will become less overwhelming than they were. This is Archangel Michael speaking to you through your thoughts.

Chapter 9: Writing a Letter to Michael

When you love and trust someone, you would miss them when they are not around. In the case of your relationship with the archangel, that would be when you *feel* they are not around. You enjoy communicating with them as often as possible, and employ various means to do so. Thankfully, Michael is ever ready to listen, reply, and assist you. You can communicate with him meditatively through prayer, and by writing letters. Not everyone is experienced with being still and meditating. Also, you might have doubts about your prayers reaching Michael (you shouldn't), and want something physical to strengthen your belief.

Before writing the letter, it is important that you *know* that you are worthy of angelic attention! These powerful spiritual beings have loved you unconditionally from the moment your soul was created by God. They never want to lose sight of you, and are eager to help you. Uncertainty and self-doubt might affect your expectation, which could hinder you from hearing your angel. Cynicism and dishonesty may also hinder your communication with Michael. You must be sincere when writing to him!

While writing the letter, do not be surprised if you feel the presence of the angel you are trying to reach. For Michael, as you already know from the previous chapter, this is the warm sensation, comforting feeling, and glowing, blue aura. As you pour your heart out in your letter, the archangel's presence might become more palpable. This is him urging you to hold nothing back. Express the full range of your emotions—from hurt feelings to gratitude—and make all your requests known. You can ask Michael to grant you physical or emotional healing. If you need the help of a therapist, ask him to guide you to the right one. Ask for courage and his protection if you are about to engage in something that is both positive and dangerous. Archangel Michael can also ensure that you get justice when you deserve it. But your requests do not necessarily have to be serious. You can ask for Saint Michael's help to fix a faulty television set. At the end of this exercise, you might choose to burn the letter or save it, but be confident in your belief that you have been heard.

Arrange the letter like you would if you were addressing a close friend. Write the angel's name at the top of the page, and follow this with your name and the date. Now, write *Dear Archangel Michael*, and begin expressing your sincere thoughts. You can sign the letter by writing thank you, yours faithfully, I love you, or whichever way feels right to you. That's it. Your letter has been sent to and received by Michael.

The archangel might reply through your dreams. As such, it is important that you do not sleep late or wait until you are exhausted before going to bed that night. You want to be able to remember what instructions and revelations are shown to you. When you wake up, record what you saw while dreaming. This can be done by writing down what you remember or using a video or audio recorder.

Chapter 10: Michael Protector Reiki

The modern-day practice of Reiki is credited to the 20th century Japanese monk, Mikao Usui. He taught his students, as he believed, about the various energies that traveled through the human body, and how these could be guided to help people achieve a more relaxed and happy state of being. Mikao Usui would place his hands a few inches from his patients' skin, focusing on the life force energy in different parts of the individual's body—head, feet, stomach, and so on. While Usui was not a scientist, those who came for Reiki treatment did attest to its stress relieving and healing abilities. And so, the practice grew in popularity and gained practitioners across the world. In 2006 alone, 1.2 million adult Americans paid for a Reiki session to help them deal with health issues including depression, anxiety, and chronic pain (Barnes et al., 2007).

Although the energy healing properties of Reiki are immensely beneficial, it should not be used as a replacement for orthodox treatments. However, it complements and enhances the results of standard medicine.

Reiki practitioners are not faith healers, and would not profess to be the cause of the healing that takes place after a successful session. Think of them as conduits for positive energy. Through years of training, such people master the ability to channel that energy through themselves into their patients' bodies. This enhances the positive flow of energy in the recipient's body. Energy healing can help to improve sleep, reduce anxiety, and give the patient more control over their emotions.

If you have decided to attend an energy healing session, the question then becomes which Reiki master to go to. Since one of Archangel Michael's abilities is to heal, he can guide you to the practitioner that is best suited for you. Saint Michael has watched over and loved you from the day you came into existence, and, hard as it might be to believe, he knows you better than you could ever know yourself. In leading you to the Reiki practitioner that you need, he will consider things like your history, personality, finances, phobias, and values. He will also protect you by making sure you go to trustworthy and right-thinking individuals. If you are yet to write Michael a letter or are planning to write another, you can ask for his guidance as a part of your request.

Since Reiki is about channeling positive energy, unblocking your *ki*, and living a more rewarding life, it often involves a lot of meditation. No, you do not have to be an expert to effectively meditate. It is also not always necessary to remain in a single spot. All that is important is the right atmosphere and singularity of thought. For this reason, consider getting as much Reiki music as you can find. They are everywhere and often downloadable for free. It is as easy as opening your YouTube app and typing *"Reiki songs."* If you went for a session, your Reiki master will play such songs to make sure you are relaxed as good energy sweeps through you. In the midst of such calming and cleansing songs is the best time to receive from Saint Michael. The songs are typically devoid of words, and only contain the healing instrumentals. Let them play while you sit, lie down, or go about your daily house chores. However, you do have to desire the healing and cleansing energy that is activated by the Reiki. Do not resist or forget it. You should remain willing and accepting in both your mind and soul. Whether you are cleaning or writing a book, make sure to not speak. This is because, while Reiki songs are powerful, your attention to them will further guarantee their effectiveness. Also, drinking water after a Reiki session aids your energy healing. By doing all these, your connection with Michael is strengthened, and he will bless all your benevolent wishes.

Chapter 11: Daily Life with Archangel Michael

Although Saint Michael is unarguably superior to human beings, he does not behave like a boss, lecturer, dictator, or an uptight parent. The relationships formed with Michael or any other angel are usually the happiest and most fulfilling. We are, in fact, incapable of forming such a bond with any other human being or animal. Archangel Michael is kind and humble, and seeks to teach us how to live our lives in the same way. As you interact with other people in your life, ask Michael to teach you the best way to treat them. You might be a parent, manager, employee, or entrepreneur. Michael can teach you how to always arrive at win-win scenarios, and the right way to get people to do things without being manipulative.

Your romantic life should not be exempt from Michael's counsel. If you find yourself in constant disagreements with your partner, ask him for guidance. You need to know which battles to fight with your romantic partner and how exactly to fight them. No such relationship can last for years without some arguments, but Michael can teach you to approach them with love, kindness, and respect. Graciously, the archangel is also willing to teach you about forgiveness. Some relationships are worth sticking out. However, it might be impossible to do so if you cannot move past hurt feelings and certain betrayals. If you ask for his help, Saint Michael will bless you with the courage to forgive the missteps of your loved ones, and he will also heal the broken relationship.

You also need angelic wisdom to know when a romantic partnership is no longer healthy to continue. To remain in such toxicity is to invite the lower energies of anger, depression, fatigue, and anxiety into your life. But, human discernment in such issues is quite unreliable. Your decision could be marred by your lack of foresight, your growing sexual interest for another person, and other biases. To ensure that you make the right choices, you must depend on the judgement of Archangel Michael.

Were you cleaning the kitchen sink and it suddenly became clogged, and you are now at a loss for how to fix the problem? Before reaching for your phone to use Google, call on Michael first. Even though it seems like a silly thing, Archangel Michael wants to be involved and wants to be included in every area of your life. Let him instruct you on how to fix the clogged sink, or guide you to the right online information. You must understand that you will never be a bother for Saint Michael. If your car battery dies on your way to work and you are about to spiral into self-hate and anxiety, put on some Reiki music and say a quick prayer to the archangel. Accept his divine wisdom, peace, and humor into your soul. Soon, you will be relaxed, happy, and gain understanding on how to deal with that issue.

It is good that you respect and revere Archangel Michael. But he wants to be your friend—and friends share everything with each other, don't they? He wants to cradle you in his wings when you are sad, laugh with you in life's funny moments, and celebrate with your joy. He is an archangel that wants to be with you at your most human times. You have everything to gain by accepting him.

Conclusion

Every journey begins with a desire, but it will require determination and courage to complete it: two virtues that you have proven to have by getting to this part of the book. Please, do not stop here. Let your walk with the archangel continue to flourish long after reading. Be reassured by the fact that Michael's love, light, and strength will always be with you.

Hopefully, you have resolved to let the archangel into every aspect of your life. Whether you need help with training or treating your pet, fixing home appliances, applying for a job, or handling your spouse's emotions, Michael is by your side to help you. Write him a letter and focus your energy for the manifestation of your desires, as you have learned from this book. Also, be attuned to the various ways by which he might reply to you. Take water after a Reiki session and try to sleep early. Take care of yourself. You can come back to this book whenever you need to, and as often as you need to. Best wishes on your journey with Michael.

References

Barnes, P. M., Bloom, B., & Nahin, R. L. (2008). Complementary and alternative medicine use among adults and children: United States, 2007. *National health statistics reports*, (12), 1–23. https://pubmed.ncbi.nlm.nih.gov/19361005/

Bedosky, L. (2020, May 13). *All about Reiki: how this type of energy healing works, and its health benefits*. Everyday Health. https://www.everydayhealth.com/reiki/

Camp, L. (2018, March 29). From archangel Michael: karma. Lacey Camp. https://www.google.com/amp/s/www.laceycamp.com/single-post/2018/03/29/From-ArchAngel-Michael-Karma%3f_amp_

Gray, K. (2015, February 10). *How to connect with your guardian angel through writing*. Heal Your Life. https://www.healyourlife.com/how-to-connect-with-your-guardian-angel-through-writing

Hopler, W. (2019, January 15). *How to recognize archangel Raphael*. Learn Religions. https://www.learnreligions.com/how-to-recognize-archangel-raphael-124281

Hopler, W. (2019, March 18). *Meet archangel Michael, leader of all the angels*. Learn Religions. https://www.learnreligions.com/meet-archangel-michael-leader-of-angels-124715

Hopler, W. (2019, April 29). *How to recognize archangel Gabriel*. Learn Religions. https://www.learnreligions.com/how-to-recognize-archangel-gabriel-124274

House, A., & Pichereau. C. (n.d.). *How Reiki works with the chakra system*. Dummies. https://www.dummies.com/religion/spirituality/how-reiki-works-with-the-chakra-system/

How to tell when St. Michael is watching over you. (2017, April 25). Original Botanica. https://www.originalbotanica.com/blog/st-michael-watching-over-with-you/

Newman, T. (2017, September 6). *Everything you need to know about Reiki*. Medical News Today. https://www.medicalnewstoday.com/articles/308772

Originals, M. (2012, June 22). *Archangel Michael*. Medium. https://medium.com/mysticaltalk/archangel-michael-7897ad931ae3

Patel, K. (n.d.). *Reiki healing for beginners*. Goop. https://goop.com/wellness/spirituality/reiki-for-beginners

Patel, R. (2018, July 10). *Working with archangel Uriel*. Reiki Rays. https://reikirays.com/42828/working-with-archangel-uriel/

Redd, N., T. (2019, February 7). *How old is the earth?* Space. https://www.space.com/24854-how-old-is-earth.html

Saint Michael archangel. (2015, November 17). Curious Curandera. http://curiouscurandera.blogspot.com/2015/11/saint-michael-archangel.html?m=1

St. Michael amparo for protection. (n.d.). Creole Moon. https://www.creolemoon.com/store/p677/St._Michael_Amparo_for_Protection.html#

Virtue, D. (n.d.). *8 ways to recognize archangel Michael.* Belief Net. https://www.beliefnet.com/inspiration/angels/2008/12/8-ways-to-recognize-archangel-michael.aspx

Book 3: Archangelology: Raphael

Abundance Attraction Secrets, & Emerald Flame Healing Power (Archangelology Book Series 3)

Angela Grace

Introduction

Have you ever felt lost? Truly lost? Many of us have felt this sense of being without a guide or purpose in our lives. I was certainly no different. Life can be brutal, and we often end up being hurt and wounded in ways that may not require a physical doctor, but these wounds threaten our existence nonetheless.

And so, we search. We consult healers and spiritual leaders, and we even try new and different concoctions from big pharma to try and feel better, when in reality, there are real and powerful guides out there who want to help you and to nurture you. Best of all, they can help you fill your life with abundance, healing, and courage. They can also give your life the direction to fulfillment. These guides are the Archangels.

From the many Archangels, there is a healing angel for every aspect of life. This book will introduce you to the healing, loving, and positively transformative powers of the Archangel Raphael.

While Archangels are divine beings, they possess an affinity for us humans, and they want to help us; all we need to do is ask them for assistance and guidance. Raphael is known for his kindness, healing powers, and guidance towards manifesting what you truly desire in your life. Your searching has brought you to this point, and your guide has arrived. Take Raphael's hand, and walk the path of angels as you create the life you've always wanted but could never have before.

Here, you will learn about the history of the Archangels, especially about the history of Raphael. This will help you understand his willingness to help you, which is essential to your receiving the gifts he wants to share with you. Next, you will learn how to communicate with Raphael. Being able to call him in times of need, to thank him for his blessings, and to clearly ask for what you need is essential to forming a harmonious relationship with him. This is also not a once-off deal; you will be forming a lasting relationship with Raphael, and he will become an integral part of your life. Therefore, you can expect to enjoy bountiful blessings, healing, prosperity, and kindness to appear in unexpected ways throughout your life.

Perhaps the most powerful of Raphael's gifts is his ability to transform lives through a glorious cascade of hugely positive energy. You can tap into this energy channel through techniques such as using mantras or affirmations, as well as other energy manifesting techniques such as meditation, reiki, chakra and dream work, and the use of crystals. For the uninitiated, this may seem overwhelming at first. **It isn't.**

Fate has made you choose this book, and here you will learn all the essential skills you need to activate the power of Raphael in your life. This is a guided journey into understanding, selecting, using, and benefiting a life enriched with Raphael. From the techniques, approaches, and methods of countless people who have called upon Raphael, you will also learn to experience great peace, bounty, and synchronicity.

Part one tells you my story, and like I did, you will also find your way towards a meaningful and fruitful relationship with the Archangel Raphael, and while you may also create such bonds with other Archangels, it is likely that you will always cherish your bond with Raphael.

Part two is all about how to begin including Archangel Raphael in your life. This section is loaded with information, skills, techniques, tasks, and healing activities to help you manifest the powers of Raphael in your daily existence. Once you have gotten to know Raphael, you will carry his emerald flame throughout your life, spreading love and light wherever you go. Let me be your guide, and let's discover Raphael together!

Part 1: Angela's Story

Welcome my brothers and sisters to the wonderful world of living with Archangels. You may already be familiar with some of the concepts involved in calling upon the angels for help or you may be a complete newbie—regardless, you are so very welcome to this space of learning, love, and light.

We all have a story, and like you, my story was not always the blessing it is now. I was searching for something more, even though I may not have known it at the time. Something was missing from my life, and I felt without a purpose as I struggled ahead. To those who didn't know me so well, I seemed to have everything working in my favor. I had a loving partner and a successful business. It seemed I was basking in wealth and adoration. What more could I possibly have wanted?

Some of you may find yourselves in similar situations to this. You have, like me, created a successful external illusion of perfection. When or if you ever mentioned not feeling complete, people may have looked at you like you were crazy. After all, what could you want when you already seemed to have everything?

However, as with all illusions, I had fooled others into believing a falsehood. I wasn't happy. I wasn't content, and I wasn't as blessed as I seemed. While I had some money, it wasn't enough for my lavish lifestyle, and I constantly worried about losing what I had. Even though I had savings, I didn't feel the real peace knowing abundance brought. You see, I had fixed my whole life around things instead of freeing my spirituality and embracing the awesome energies that surrounded me.

This journey into my spiritual nature would only start much later when I first encountered the powers of crystals and experienced first-hand their healing properties. I would love for you to read about this experience in *Crystals Made Easy*. My journey to angelology was a winding road, but I wasn't without guides on my inward journey. The angels were always there. Like a child learning to sit, stand, walk, and eventually run, I needed to learn how to tap into their powers, gifts, and guidance.

Have you ever had a moment of such pure and absolute otherworldly joy or tranquility that you thought you had imagined it? This was what my first experience with an Archangel was like. I had not intentionally summoned or communicated with him, but there I was, surrounded in complete and peaceful bliss. In the hectic world we live in, where we are told to harden ourselves and forge ahead, experiencing such a delicate and soft moment is not something we are programmed to process or understand. I certainly didn't fully comprehend what I had experienced.

The more I investigated the history and knowledge of Archangels, the more I began to understand how their presence in my life could channel energy and positivity to me. With these gifts, I could begin to manifest the changes I desired in my life. I could finally, and with intention, pray for the safety and health of those I loved. It was possible to even manifest healing and protection for my pets and for myself.

Best of all, I discovered the Archangels were not bound to a specific religious denomination. Believing in and connecting to the powerful Archangels didn't require me to change my faith or start subscribing to some alternative religion. I could start immediately. Using angelology in my life didn't require me to study for years or journey to some hidden temple. Everything I needed was within my reach, just like it is within your reach right now.

All I needed to begin was a little bit of knowledge and a small push in the right direction. Fortunately, my dear friend Linda had always been interested in and quite knowledgeable in all things esoteric, and when I one day raised the issue of angels with her, she immediately knew I had experienced a visitation. It was such a relief to know I hadn't gone mad, and there are actually millions of people worldwide who also interact with the Archangels on a daily basis.

Over several cups of herbal tea, Linda shared all she had learned about angelology, and I was instantly hooked. When I got home, I couldn't wait to begin my own research online or to contact the various internet-based communities who practice, discuss, and explain angelology.

Image 1: Archangels do not always appear in the typical or stereotypical form we see in Catholic architecture. They may appear as light, invisible presences or as normal people.

One of the first things I discovered was that each person experiences their angelic encounters differently, and while those of us from a Catholic background may see our angels as typical angelic figures who stand there with a set of shining wings and a burning sword, many other people see them quite differently.

Whichever way you see the angels, they have the power and ability to enrich your life, bring you much-needed guidance, and facilitate fortuitous changes in your daily living. For those who, like me, have been searching for a way to make sense of life and a way to move forward with light and positivity, meeting, knowing, and embracing your angel guide is the beginning of a life-altering path.

Like me, you too can experience freedom from worry, courage to step forward boldly, wisdom to choose wisely, and the love to believe deeply in your life. Where I had spent my whole life believing I was nothing and wouldn't be happy (and therefore, I had to accept what I had and be grateful), I realized I had been controlled by people who didn't really know me and didn't have my best interests at heart. By finding the Archangels, I discovered who I really am, and I have since begun to create the life I deserved, which is so much more than I could ever have dreamed possible.

This revelation is also within your grasp when you begin the journey towards angelology. Now, it's time to learn all about Raphael and his amazing gifts.

Part 2: Including Archangel Raphael in Your Life

Chapter 1: Introduction to Archangel Raphael

Chapter 2: How to Easily Call Upon Archangel Raphael

Chapter 3: Exercises, Mantras, and Affirmations

Chapter 4: Healing Animals and Loved Ones With Raphael

Chapter 5: Align Your Money Frequency With Archangel Raphael

Chapter 6: Archangel Raphael Meditations

Chapter 7: Archangel Raphael Manifestation, Chakras, Dreams, Crystals, and Karma

Chapter 8: How to Tell When Archangel Raphael Is Around

Chapter 9: Writing a Letter to Raphael

Chapter 10: Archangel Raphael Reiki

Chapter 11: How to Spend Time With Archangel Raphael

Chapter 1: Introduction to Archangel Raphael

As with all the Archangels, Raphael's name has great significance. It means "God has healed" in Hebrew and gives us a strong indication of what powers Raphael has at his fingertips. He is a magnificent healer, and we can easily turn to him to help us heal from illness and recover from energy-draining experiences such as death and grief. Throughout history, Raphael has made several

appearances in a great many diverse religions, making him easily accessible to people from all faiths.

Image 2: Whether you believe in Archangels already or are still unconvinced, the truth is that they are real, and they are powerful. Being aware of them in your life is one way to enjoy the blessings of divinity in your life.

Raphael Throughout History

Raphael is one of the three most prominent Archangels, and many who believe and follow angelology summon him as well as the Archangels Michael and Gabriel. In the Bible, Raphael is the angel who stirs the waters of healing at the pool of Bethesda as mentioned in the book of John. This links him to the great healing you can receive from him. You can imagine the great compassion he must have felt to stir the waters regularly to enable healing and physical revival for those in need. Raphael also appears in Islam as the angel who blows the trumpet, announcing the resurrection and

the last judgment. In the Torah, we learn that Raphael was commanded to heal Abraham from his circumcision, as well as to save Lot.

Image 3: When the waters at the pool of Bethesda was stirred, it was believed that an angel was near and the sick people who gathered at the waters would then be healed. It is believed that Raphael was the angel who would visit this pool and release God's healing on those gathered there.

Throughout history, Raphael has been a force for good, and a powerful healer and facilitator to healing change. In the Book of Tobit, we also learn that Raphael had come to earth disguised as a man and journeyed with Tobit. During this journey, Raphael was known to have protected and healed Tobit. Raphael also bound up a demon who had been possessing Tobit's future daughter-in-law (See U in History/Mythology, 2019).

Lot was also saved by an angel who warned him to leave Sodom, and Raphael is the angel who forewarned him. This has caused many of the faithful believers to assert that Raphael is not only a healer but also a savior and a guide to lead us away from danger.

Sufism encourages the faithful to aspire to be like Raphael as he is kind, compassionate, caring, and brave. These are considered to be the best qualities, and even today, these characteristics are widely held as being virtuous. If you can begin to be like Raphael in the way you care for others, help those in need, and offer kindness and compassion to all, then you will begin to see him showing up in your life more often.

Raphael is, therefore, capable of delivering great healing and liberation to those who ask for his help and guidance. If we consider what he has done throughout history, then we can easily believe he can help heal illness, bind addictions to no longer torture us, as well as alleviate mental illness, and he can lead us to a life of abundance and freedom.

Raphael's Healing Powers

Throughout history, we find many stories of mysterious healings and divine guidance. While most will not feature a typical angelic presence, we may need to look closer at them as Raphael is somewhat of a chameleon when it comes to his physical manifestations. In the book of Tobit, he appeared as a man. He is often described as an unseen presence in the Bible, where he is said to have stirred the healing waters at the pool of Bethesda. Knowing Raphael is close may be dependent on your perceptions and your spiritual awareness. However, his healing powers can't be doubted. Remember, he is the representation of God's healing on earth.

Being able to access his healing, request his assistance, and invite his presence is how you can begin to manifest healing and guidance in your life. Raphael is considered as the patron saint of travelers, healers, the sick, and the blind, and he is even attributed with the powers of matchmaking as he facilitated Sarah's first successfully consummate marriage by binding the demon who possessed her. Raphael is the manifestation of God's healing presence, and you can open the channels to that amazing healing and guidance in your life. So, how do you call on an Archangel?

Chapter 2: How to Easily Call Upon Archangel Raphael

Archangels have colors that are specific to each of them. For the Archangel Raphael, the color associated with him is a deep emerald green. While the Archangels are always around us, they do respond better when we are being specific in whom we are calling. Hence, when you start calling on an Archangel, it is a good idea to visualize the color of your chosen Archangel in the center of your forehead where your third-eye is situated. This is a powerful way to unleash your own energies and create a resonating call to summon Raphael into your life and into your mind.

Image 4: Emerald green is often associated with growth and healing, and it is the color sacred to Raphael. Visualizing this color can help you quickly and easily connect with Raphael.

Reaching out to Raphael is not a complicated process, and he is eager to help you. Like a dear friend who sees you suffering, he is only waiting for you to talk to him, to open up, and to let him in so he can help you heal.

How to Communicate With Raphael

You can instantly communicate with and connect to Raphael. When you are suffering a headache or the painful effects of an illness, all you need to do to reach out to him is to visualize yourself surrounded in an emerald green light. Some people prefer to see this light as a shower of emerald green sparks that settle on their body, melting into their being where these release Raphael's healing. You may even feel a tingling sensation in your body during this time. Whichever way you choose to see the light, you will be drawing from the Archangel's powers and, as you believe in his goodness and his willingness to help you, there will be an openness to healing in you.

This openness and belief in Raphael's powers are what will manifest the healing in your life. You can even imagine this like a friend who wants to help you. If you **believe** your friend can help you, and you **let** them help you, then they will quickly and effortlessly be **able to help** you. However, if you are constantly asking questions or doubting your friend's ability or their willingness, then you will delay and limit their ability to help you. To enjoy the full manifestation of Raphael's healing in your life, you need to accept and believe that he can and wants to help you.

Some believers choose to speak directly to the Archangel Raphael, and while there may not be a necessity for words, you can be assured that he will hear your call, and he will answer it. Raphael will not simply decide to help you on his own. He respects your right to choose, and he wants you to choose to call on his help. You may choose to call him by using some phrases such as these (below) to help you if you are unsure about how to speak to him in the beginning. What is most important is that you reach out (using whichever words you feel comfortable with); otherwise, Raphael will not be able to help you. You might say:

"Archangel Raphael, please help me."

"Holy Raphael, I call on you to be present in my life and to share your healing presence with me."

"Raphael, please manifest your blessings in my life today."

"Archangel Raphael, please answer my call and guide me through this painful time."

Archangel Raphael may also be called upon by using his sacred codes. Repeating certain numerical sequences channels the Archangels' energies. Calling Raphael may be done by repeating the following sequence, repeating each number 45 times: 157, 29, 125, 2129, 1577 (Purva Nimfa Magic, 2018).

Reaching out for Beginners

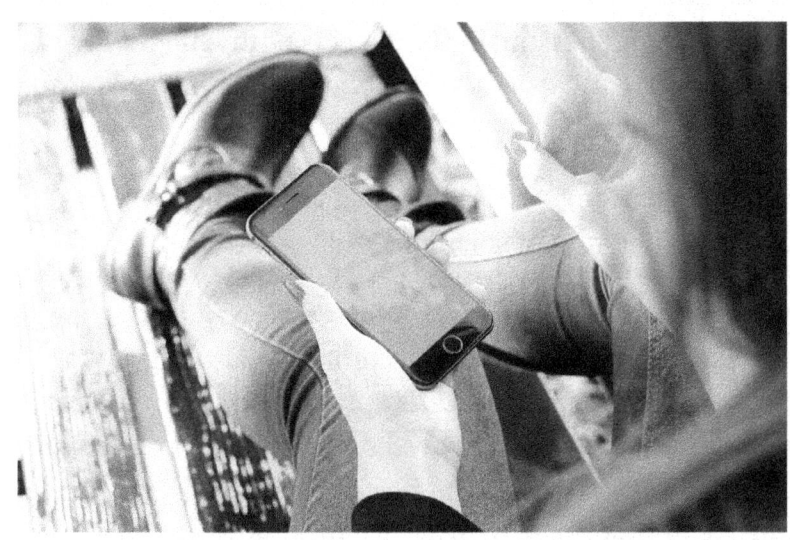

Image 5: Communicating with the Archangel Raphael is not exactly like hopping onto your phone and calling someone, though the connection may be even more instant than a phone call or message.

Connecting to the Archangel Raphael is about opening up, about receiving, and not just sending out a plea. So, like your mobile phone, if you are on airplane mode, you will not receive his guidance and healing if you are not switched on and fully present. It often comes down to whether you believe you are worthy of receiving his guidance and healing.

When you believe in your own worthiness and your ability to heal, you will be able to follow Raphael's guidance and increase your energy vibrations, which is how healing begins. Connecting to Raphael is about connecting to divine love. You are about to make the friend of a lifetime when you connect to the Archangel Raphael. Here are three ways to reach out and communicate with him:

1. Sitting quietly, imagine your body being showered by a bright emerald green light. Feel this light settle on your head, your brow, and your eyes, and feel it enter your crown chakra at the top of your head. As it soaks into your mind, you feel a wonderful and pleasantly warm sensation that slowly drifts downwards to rest over your heart. From here, you can feel this vibrant green energy pulse outwards to fill your body, raising your spirits and filling you with beautifully luminous emerald light. You can now speak to Raphael as he has felt your connection to his light and energy and has joined with you.

2. You may also choose to pray, invoking Archangel Raphael and the Almighty by whichever name you call on. Find a comfortable way to sit. You need not assume any specific prayer position, and you can even do this prayer while lying down. Now speak these (or similar) words of prayer:

"Archangel Raphael, I call on you to join with my life, to become present in my life, and to share your higher energy with me on this day. I ask that you fill me with your healing energy and your bright light of love and caring compassion. Let me feel the vibrations of your energy as it fills my body, gently reaching to the furthest corners of my physical, mental, and spiritual being. Today, I ask for your guidance and healing in the aspects of my life that have been weighing me down. Help me release the negative energies that have held me back from my divine destiny and limited the wholeness of my life."

You can then continue to ask specifically for the things you want, such as healing from a physical illness, relief from mental strain or tension, and spiritual guidance. It's not important how you ask, as long as you ask.

3. When you have a conversation with someone, you may notice the communication has two phases: talking and listening. You have spoken to the Archangel Raphael, and now, you need to listen for his reply. While some people function at a higher level of spiritual awareness and may hear the words of the angels, there are other ways to listen for the Archangels' responses too. You could start seeing signs, feeling a heightening of energy or vibrations inside yourself, or feeling a presence near you (this would be a kind presence that is guiding you in the right course of action for your request).

   You may think of the Archangel Raphael as a dear and wise friend; you have asked for his guidance and the gift of his healing. Now, you need to listen, watch, and receive that gift. Like with most gifts, you need to unwrap it. This means you need to accept the gift, decide whether you are going to place it somewhere so you can see and use it every day, or place it unopened in a drawer somewhere. Using the gift is up to you.

Communicating with the Archangel Raphael is not difficult. However, it requires your commitment to listen, to feel, and to receive the answers he offers you. If you are not open, you will not hear, feel, or experience him.

Image 6: If you are still struggling to connect with Raphael, you may be bogged down in negativity, and until you find meaningful ways to lift yourself out of that lower energy, you will struggle to communicate and ask for guidance.

One of the biggest reasons why beginners struggle to connect with the powerful presence of the Archangel Raphael is that they doubt he is real and they doubt they have the right to even call on such a powerful healer and guide in the first place. These are negative energies, which will drain away your ability to listen and receive.

Chapter 3: Exercises, Mantras, and Affirmations

Many of us feel negative about our lives. Things happen to challenge us, and we often suffer bouts of depression and anxiety due to negative experiences. However, by embracing the positive energy of the Archangels, we can begin to transform our life view and our perceptions and build a wellspring of positive energy in our lives.

As with acquiring anything else in your life, it does not happen overnight, though you may wish you can just snap your fingers and magically be healed of all negativity. Instead, it is a journey where you discover the power of the Archangels, become more aware of them throughout your life and your daily existence, and learn to incorporate their positive blessings in your whole approach to

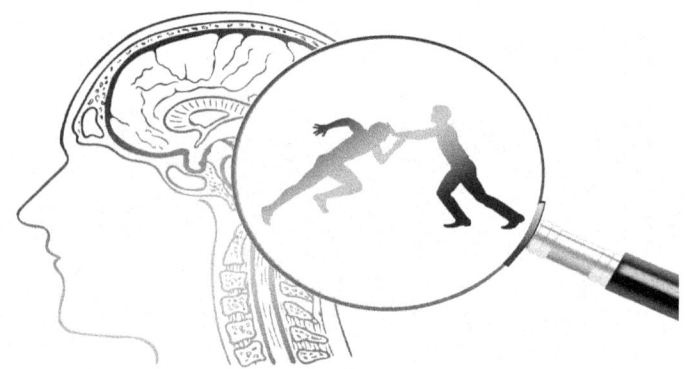

living.

Image 7: Negative beliefs can hold us back and prevent us from connecting to the Archangels or receiving their gifts.

There are many exercises, mantras, and affirmations that will help you attract the positive blessings of Archangels such as Raphael into your life. We will look at some examples of this here:

Transforming Negativity

When you actively become aware of the kinds of energy in your life, you can begin to choose which energies you will channel or increase and which you will release and let go of. There are several energy transforming methods you can use, and they are all really easy to do. You don't need anything other than the powers of your mind and your intentions.

- **Breathing Exercises**

Sitting calmly, allow your body to settle, stilling the chaos within you as you focus on your physical existence. Turn your attention to your body. Note any tension or tightness in your limbs. This is a sign of negative energies having caused you tension and worry. Negative energy is destructive and it can poison your body and your life.

As you inhale deeply through your nose, focus on the sensation of your body lifting and growing tall like a bright green fir tree. Feel your seat, the soles of your feet, and even your buttocks being gently anchored to the earth. You are comfortably held in this relationship between the heavens and the earth.

When you are ready to breathe out, simply let the air flow out through your mouth, neither forcing it, nor concentrating on it. Simply note how the warm breath carries away all of the negative thoughts, memories, and emotions you have been experiencing.

Inhaling through your nose, allow yourself to feel a bright emerald green light accompany that breath. As it travels down your nose, your throat, and into your lungs, you can almost taste a green and verdant earth in the breath.

Repeat this process of inhaling life and positivity with each green breath and exhaling negativity and heated thoughts several times until you feel wonderfully at peace and ready to receive the blessings of Raphael. This is one of the ways in which you can open your mind and your heart to receive him.

From this point, you may want to move on to the transformative meditations where you will learn to practice cord cutting, clearing, and shielding.

- **Transformative Meditations**

Having calmed your mind and your body with the breathing technique just described, simply let your mind open like a vast lake that stretches for as far as the eye can see. Now form the name of the Archangel Raphael in your thoughts, bringing his name to your lips as you speak out, calling on him. You may choose to call on his guidance and his wisdom in healing you from a presence in your life that has proven negative and destructive.

"Archangel Raphael, holy angel who brings healing and transformation, I call on your presence in my life today. I call you to help me heal from a negative energy that has arrested my life. Help me to move past this blockage in my mind and in my soul. Archangel Raphael, guide me on a transformation journey as I cut the cords to this negative energy, this destructive person or event in my life."

As you speak these words, do so with conviction, even allowing some frustration to come into your voice if this is how you are feeling. Raphael is a healer, and he will never judge you for being upset; instead, he will only seek to help you and heal you.

"Raphael, clear me of this negative energy. Let the last shredded garments of this negative presence depart from my mind and my spirit as I look forward with power, positivity, and an energy that is made to serve all that is good."

In your mind's eye, you may begin to see the negative person or event that has been holding you back being enshrouded in bright emerald green light. You may even feel a strange sensation of being pulled as this presence fades away or tears from your life. Having a strong emotional response to this severing of the negative energies is quite normal. Do not be concerned by this; instead, enjoy the liberating presence of Raphael's light and love as he creates healing in you. Now you can ask him to clear away the last blockages this negative energy had created:

"Raphael, help me this day. I thank you for the negative energy you have removed from my life, and I now ask that you clear away the negative beliefs I have created as a result of this presence. The negative energy is now removed, blessings be upon you heavenly angel for healing me. Now, I ask your assistance and protection from the limiting beliefs I have built. Guide me to break down these barriers."

At this point, you may feel a wave of light wash over your mind and heart. You may even feel slightly lightheaded as your mind is swept clear of old beliefs that held you back. In this deeply meditative state, you realize you are worthy, you are loved, you are enough, and you are divine.

The powers of Raphael have channeled the holy presence of your maker into your life, and you are now free from any barriers or obstructions of belief that had previously limited you or held you back.

Now, you may ask Raphael for his protection and shielding presence to keep you from slipping back into negative habits and falling prey to negative outside influences in your life.

"Raphael, I thank you for helping, healing, and guiding me. My life is now filled with light, love, and potential. Lastly, I ask that you shield me with your awesome powers. Build a wall of light around me, casting out any who would seek to harm me or lead me astray. I am made stronger by your protection, and your guidance leads me down the paths I am meant to follow. Shield and protect me with your favor, your love, and your power."

You may form a mental image of yourself wrapped in a protective shroud of a bright emerald green color. Some meditators see this as a set of powerful arms that wrap around you in a comforting embrace. You are fully protected, and any negative thoughts or events simply slide off this protective shroud. You are safe and healed.

Manifesting Abundance and Healing

As from our discussion in chapter 2, it is important to believe what you are asking, praying, or wishing for. When your belief is strong, you can do anything. If you live with positive energy and believe you are able to do something, then you can and will do it. This belief creates the power to manifest what you need or desire in your life. While you may not necessarily open your eyes and be the owner of a brand-new BMW, you can attract and manifest the things you need and believe in within your life.

Once you have cut the cords to things that hold you back or push you down, you can clear the doubt and self-defeating behaviors you have been struggling with. You can manifest your own abundance and healing through the powers now at work in your life. There are several ways to engage in manifesting things you want:

- **Affirmations**

With Archangel Raphael having cut the cords that bound you, it is now possible to draw in positive energy and words of power to help you reach your goals. Affirmations are power statements. They are written in the first person as if you have already done what you wanted. Again, you need to read or say these affirmations to help guide you and to draw the potential into your life. When you speak with power and conviction, you will be ready to draw on and manifest your dreams.

Image 8: Affirmations are positive statements that reinforce the great I am concept, which liberates you from negativity.

Initially, you may struggle to come up with your own affirmations. These generic ones are suitable for your first meditation sessions. Once you feel more confident, you will be able to make your own specialized affirmations.

"I am free from negativity."

"Raphael has guided me to this truth: I am free."

"Healed and liberated, I walk into the light."

- **Mantras**

Using a mantra during meditation is about creating a higher vibration to your energy. You influence the resonance or frequency of your spirit within your physical body. While affirmations are positive statements, mantras are power words you repeat at an increasing speed to help your body realign itself.

In Buddhist traditions, chanting "ohm" has the same effect, and it focuses the mind and brings clarity to your spirit or intention. While you reach periods of breathing in and out during your meditation, simply repeat these mantras, chanting them at increasing frequencies. You will feel an increasing building up of energy inside you, as if you are bursting to do something or say something. This indicates your vibrations have reached a higher plane, and you can now better receive the angels (Anglin, 2020).

Vibration increasing mantras include:

- ❖ Raphael's name
- ❖ Doing words such as "Heal" or "Lead" or "Guide"
- ❖ Angel words such as "Light" or "Love"

While there are many other techniques for communicating and experiencing the presence of the Archangels, these are some of the most powerful and easy to use. Through regular repetitions, you can build a foundation of knowledge and experience to help you regularly connect to and ask for the assistance of Archangel Raphael.

Chapter 4: Healing Animals and Loved Ones With Raphael

While we have spoken in detail about healing ourselves, invoking the protection and healing of Raphael to help heal our bodies, minds, and spirits, as well as manifesting what we desire or need, we are also able to share that healing and protection with those we love. By drawing the healing power of Raphael into ourselves, we can channel that energy to those who need it. This is especially powerful when it comes to healing our pets.

Some people may believe it is strange to seek energy healing and angelic interventions for animals; however, animals were made by the same mighty Creator who made you. They are as entitled to healing, peace, and love as you are. You can ask for Raphael's assistance in soothing an ailing pet with a clear heart and mind. The Archangels love and care for all of the Creator's works, including people, pets, spirits, and angels.

While animals and people who are ailing can't always speak affirmations or utter mantras, they can receive love, light, and healing when you channel the angels' powers to them. In essence, you become a conduit, calling for healing and guidance on their behalf, and then relaying the energy and power as you receive it.

Image 9: Our pets hold a valuable position in our hearts, and they help us heal through their offering of unconditional love. Healing them and comforting them when they are ailing is something Archangel Raphael can assist you with.

Visualizing Healing and Protection

Sitting quietly next to the person or pet you want to help heal or protect, you can gently touch them, or if you are separated from them, you may also use a photo of them to help you focus. Breathe in deeply, letting the restful light of the Archangel Raphael enter into you with your breath. Feel all worries slip from your shoulders like a scarf carried off on the wind.

As you exhale, you are aware of being held by the earth, and as you inhale, you feel yourself reaching up to the heavens. Draw the positive energies from around you, feeling them settle on your crown, then penetrate down into your body, easing down your neck, spreading out over your shoulders, and finally, resting in your heart. Become aware of how open and inviting your heart is. This is where all your good intentions lie, and this is where you reach from to call on Archangel Raphael:

"Raphael, I call upon you. Come guide my hand and my heart as I ask for your healing on this dear friend of mine. Let your power move through me and reach into this kind soul who is in need of your healing and protection. I ask that you strip away the disease and illness that has brought them low. My request is that you fill me with your powerful presence and let this energy of healing and light and love move from my touch into this dear soul, bringing relief and recovery."

As you hold the pet or person you are healing, you can visualize a faint green glow starting to form along your skin. This is the light and love of Raphael, and it is moving from you to them, growing brighter and stronger as you continue to communicate to and receive help from Raphael.

Again, your belief is what will determine the level of transformation and transference of energy you can channel. You may use your imagination to help you visualize healing happening in their bodies, and from your touch, whether on their bodies or on an image of them, the green light spreads to envelop them in caring protection and divine care.

Focus on remaining calm and centered as you continue speaking to Raphael and calling on his help and guidance. If you feel anxious, you are allowing negative energies to filter in from outside, and this will not help the healing process. Instead, increase your frequency by adding in mantras or affirmations.

"Raphael, Raphael, Raphael, Raphael … I call on you, Raphael. I plead your healing presence to be in attendance here as you heal this life. Heal. Heal. Heal. Heal. Heal. I plead for your healing and guidance. Let your light and love fill this being, this person, this animal with renewal of vitality and healing.

Let your power sever the ties of disease and illness which threatens this life. You have the power to release healing here and now.

This life is freed of illness.

This person, this animal is released from harm."

When you have completed your meditation, you may take a few moments to see the green light of Raphael's healing and love cover this life you hold dear. Feel the power of the Archangel move into them, protecting them from future ailment and a return of disease. You have shared the blessings of the Archangel Raphael with them, and you can believe they are healed and are now protected from harm.

Chapter 5: Align Your Money Frequency With Archangel Raphael

Image 10: Wanting financial wealth and security is a human instinct, and in a world driven by consumerism, this is easy to understand. Raphael can guide you to all the wealth you need and deserve.

Many of us want to have a financially secure life. Fearing we will not have enough money, we often become worried and stressed, which can lead to health problems. While Archangel Raphael is known as the angel of healing, he is also known as the angel of abundance. This means he can lead you to abundant health, abundant life, abundant resources, abundant opportunities, and abundant money as a result.

As with other requests you may make of the Archangels, you need to invite the Archangels into your life. You need to let them know you are ready to receive their gifts and energies. This is a powerful example of the law of attraction at work.

If you are talking about something, you will align your life towards that thing which occupies your time and energy. This repetition is what increases your vibrational frequency, drawing the angelic presence of the Archangels near.

While you may not necessarily wake up one morning surrounded by bags of money, asking for abundant wealth may be delivered to you in a range of ways. It could be in the form of a new job that pays you a better salary. It could also be in the way of inspiration that leads you down a path to financial freedom. Asking to become rich is not a request that comes from a place of positivity or higher vibration. Being rich is rather associated with greed, which functions at a lower frequency. If that is your desire, you will struggle to connect to the Archangels as they serve higher purposes, not base desires.

Asking for abundance with an open heart is about leaving the solution open to the Archangels to interpret. Raphael may guide you to the means to achieve your financial goals (if they are about freedom and betterment and not greed), or he may bring resources into your life to help you achieve what you seek. Being open and receptive to the Archangel Raphael's responses is what will determine your successful abundance journey.

Your thoughts of money should be of such a nature that you see it as a positive aspect of your life, even when you have nothing. Dwelling on how poor you are will only attract more poverty to you. However, believing you have enough and knowing you will receive heaven's blessings as you need it will open the golden gates of abundance into your life.

Once you let go of fears of not having enough, your vibrational frequency changes, and you start calling on positive energies instead of bogging yourself down in negative beliefs. Believe you will be taken care of, and you will. Have faith in the abundance of your birthright as a human being, and you will experience all the blessings and abundance you require.

Attracting Abundance

When you start changing the way you see money, you will begin the process of attracting abundance and wealth. Instead of looking at your bank balance and seeing zeros, you would rather look at all the things you do have, and imagine yourself having more of what you need. This does not mean you go on a shopping spree with your credit card and believe the Archangel Raphael will take care of the repayments. Instead, it is about opening yourself and believing you will be given all the opportunities and resources you need to make things happen in your life.

Abundance isn't a dollar sign. It is an alignment of factors, people, and places to help you achieve what you desire. Asking Archangel Raphael to bring abundance into your life may not result in you buying a winning Lottery ticket, but it may be a chance meeting with someone who becomes interested in an idea you have and that landslide series of events that lead to you owning a Fortune 500 company or landing the job of your dreams.

Therefore, when you visualize the opportunities you need and the roads to abundance you require, you will attract the powerful transformative energies and the flow of Archangel Raphael's energy into your life. Whatever you need, you will receive.

Doing daily meditations and prayers where you call on the Archangel Raphael is one of the pivotal steps in achieving the life of your dreams. We will look at specific meditations in the next chapter.

Chapter 6: Archangel Raphael Meditations

Meditating for specific goals where you seek the Archangel Raphael's guidance is within your reach now. In this chapter, you will be able to follow specific meditation scripts to help you reach your goals and achieve a greater connection to Raphael and receive his blessings.

Image 11: Meditations is another word for conversations. It is when you quiet your mind, your voice, and your attention, devoting it fully to the other person or being, and you listen to their responses to your requests. There is great power in meditation.

Abundance Attraction With Archangel Raphael

Sit comfortably, close your eyes, and breathe in deeply for five seconds. Hold for a moment, and then exhale slowly, letting the air pass over your lips for five seconds. Again, pause for a moment before inhaling for five seconds and then exhaling for five seconds. Do three more repetitions of this breathing in and out.

Once you have completed the pattern, simply breathe normally, letting your eyes rest comfortably as you let them close and open softly. Do not focus on anything in particular that may distract you. Instead, you turn your focus inward to the area over your heart (your heart chakra) and feel a warm presence there.

Rest your hands on your thighs or in your lap, making sure to relax them into an open and receiving position. Inhale as you begin to visualize a bright emerald green shower of light descending upon you. The light lingers on your body, clinging like glitter to your hair, skin, and limbs. You can feel an angelic presence, shrouding you in light, love, and abundant spiritual wealth.

Visualize what it is that you want. If you want to ask for something specific, you may. If you want to ask for abundance in general, you can also do so. Perhaps you want to ask for an opportunity or Raphael's blessings and presence for an important meeting today. Allow your mind to relax, slowly melting the tensions in your body as you open yourself to the abundance flowing from heaven and from Raphael into your life.

You receive this precious gift with an open heart, thanking Raphael for his guidance, care, love, and light. Allow yourself to experience an increased energy and vibration as if you know that which you asked for is about to happen.

"Archangel Raphael, I thank you for your presence today. Thank you for your care and love, your compassion and abundant guidance as I step towards my destiny under the protection of your wings."

Throughout your day, be mindful of the signs of Raphael's presence as he guides you towards achieving the abundance you asked for. You may see a neon green sign above a shop you frequently visit or you may be struck by the emerald green tie your new boss is wearing. These are all there to let you know you are on track.

Meditation for Healing With Archangel Raphael

Lying comfortably in your bed, close your eyes and allow your body to sink into the covers, softening and sinking ever deeper and deeper. Become aware of the earth below you and the heavens above you. Inhale deeply through your nose, letting the scents of the earth bless you and fill you. Draw the precious oxygen into your lungs, and when you exhale, imagine the breath you have just breathed being carried upwards to the heavens.

You notice a small firefly sparking above your head, gently flying lower and lower, and eventually it lands on your hand. The small body is flashing a brilliantly green emerald light. Soon, it is joined by other emerald green fireflies, and they all land on your body in a dazzling shower of light.

The fireflies have a soft vibration in their bodies, which they share with you. This energy fills you, sinking into every pore of your body and filling you with great calm and peace. You are aware of an angelic presence near you, and you say his name: Raphael. The bright emerald green light now covers, protects, and nurtures all of your body, mind, and spirit.

Can you feel the presence of Raphael next to, around, and inside you? Like a child, safely carried in the arms of their father, you are safely wrapped in the wings of Raphael. The pleasant warmth of his nearness soon travels through your body, and you can feel it gently vibrate whenever it encounters an ailment. If you have a headache, you feel the warmth fill your head, easing tension and pain. If you have a mental concern, you are made aware of his healing presence even there, soothing your troubled thoughts and bringing you peace and clarity. Healing is happening as you lie wrapped in his presence and peace.

Closing your eyes, you thank Archangel Raphael for his care, compassion, and healing. A warm tingling sensation in your body fills you and acknowledges the healing Raphael has shared with you this day. Breathing normally, you may find yourself drawn into a deep and peaceful sleep. Simply relax, knowing Raphael is watching over you, guarding and guiding you.

Meditation for Loving Your Body

This is a wonderful meditation to do in the bath or shower. Place your hands and arms in a warm self-hugging position. Feel the sensation of your skin touching skin. Close your eyes and let the water of the shower or bath cover your skin, tracing down the curves of your body and warming your physical existence.

Inhale deeply, feeling your ribs move, pushing outward against your self-hug. Exhale and feel the same sensation of being held on the outside of your arms now. The Archangel Raphael is holding you, protecting you, easing your worries and concerns, and connecting to your body. Breathing normally, allow yourself to luxuriate in this deeply nourishing and loving exchange as his energy moves through your skin in waves of green light.

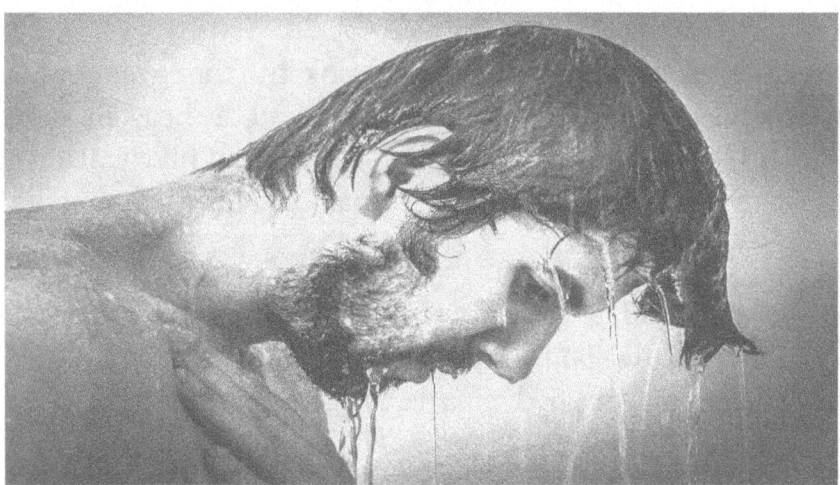

Image 12: Let the water run off your body in green waves of soothing, nurturing, and loving light.

Speaking aloud or in your heart, thank Raphael for his presence, for his nurturing of your body, and for his love of your physical presence. Express your own love of your body, telling yourself you have a beautiful and shining soul. Your body is the home of your spirit here on earth, and it is a temple. Archangel Raphael has shown you the virtue of your wonderfully alive existence, and you can feel inner peace overflowing in your mind. Thank Raphael for coming to visit you and promise to love your body from this day forward, treating it with dignity, respect, and compassion.

Meditation for Life Direction

Entering a meditative state, close your eyes and breathe in deeply, exhaling fully before inhaling again. Let the peace and radiance of the Archangel Raphael enter and sustain you. Feel an emerald green light glowing inside your mind, calming, soothing, and easing any mental tension and worries you may have.

Feel your mind expand as you allow the guidance and wisdom of the Archangel Raphael to fill your mind. Welcome his presence in your mind, your body, your spirit, and in your life.

Speak to him in the volumes of your spirit and mind as you ask him to guide you, to direct your path, and to lead you to the destiny you have been seeking. You may ask him to take your hand and to show you where your life is going, to help you understand the path before you.

Remember to listen to the responses and replies Raphael has for you. This is a conversation, and he will answer you in the most unexpected ways. Be open to receive his wisdom and guidance. Remember to thank him for any guidance he gives you, even if it's not what you had imagined or hoped for. Simply open yourself to accept that the Archangel knows your destiny, and while it may not be fully revealed in one meditation, you can always return to this safe and spiritual space and communicate with Raphael again, gaining further insight as your life direction is revealed to you.

Chapter 7: Archangel Raphael Manifestation, Chakras, Dreams, Crystals, and Karma

There are many supporting theories and methods to communicate with the Archangel Raphael, and these can help you to better connect to him, receive his blessings, and understand his guidance. During your meditations, being aware of your chakras will help you process the presence of divine energy in your body, as well as opening your perceptions by using your third eye or mind chakra to see and understand the messages and presence of Raphael.

When you are not fully open to receiving the wisdom and guidance of the Archangel Raphael, you may find that he approaches you in your dreams, which may require some analysis and interpretation. However, he will always find a way to connect to you when you have called on him. Sometimes, that calling need not be vocalized or even conscious. There have been many people who felt his presence and experienced his blessings in dream form as their subconscious or spirit called out to him.

Image 13: Crystals come in a range of colors, and their unique qualities allow for the refraction of light waves at different points on the electromagnetic spectrum. This light is energy and vibration. Holding an emerald means you are holding the vibrational energy of that part of the spectrum. This is also the frequency Raphael moves in.

Crystals are truly remarkable elements that can help you connect to the angels, and since they have healing properties too, they offer you a double benefit. Using crystals can help heighten your vibrational energy, opening you to the higher guidance of the Archangels. Malachite and emerald are the crystals most strongly associated with Archangel Raphael. Both are a wonderful green with malachite having darker swirls of green in it, and they are known to promote healing and can revitalize your body. Holding a malachite or emerald crystal in your hands while meditating will heighten your experience and draw the Archangel Raphael to you. Crystals, essential oils, and irises are a great way to strengthen your call (Acone, 2010).

Manifesting Abundance

To fully experience abundance in our lives, we may call on Archangel Raphael to help us heal from previous traumas, and using crystals can help facilitate this process. Emerald is known to align with our heart chakra and promote physical healing. Malachite also aligns with our heart chakra, promoting spiritual healing (Hibiscus Moon, 2017).

Placing the crystal on your body, where you feel a need for healing or on your third eye chakra can help channel the energy and vibrational presence of Raphael there. Using crystals helps you to increase and focus your energy for manifestation. The stronger your belief, the more powerful the results.

Manifesting Courage

Having courage in today's world is about being strong enough to persevere in the face of trials and challenges. In the Bible, we are told by God to take courage "for he has overcome the world," and this indicates how we too should manifest courage in our lives. Asking Archangel Raphael to help you manifest courage is one way to do just this.

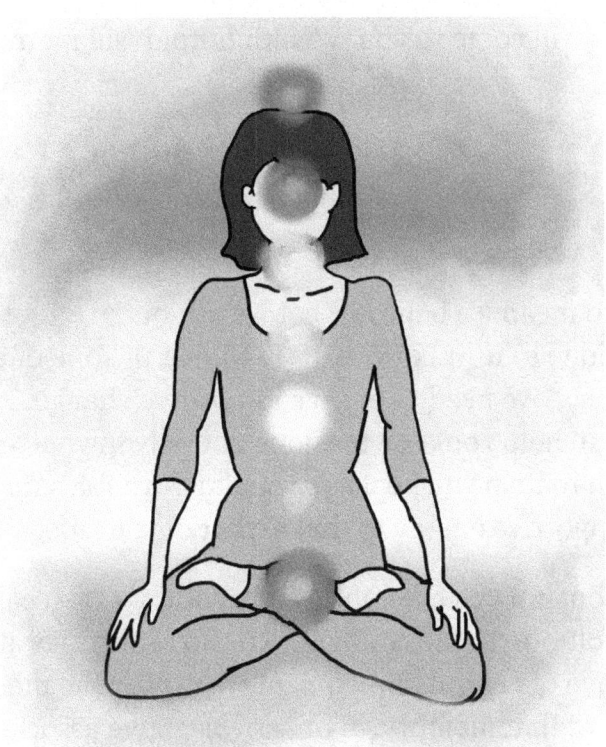

Image 14: The chakras are energy centers in the body. By releasing any blockages or channeling energy through different sections, you can open your body and spirit to receive energy and become a conduit to the powers of heaven. From your root chakra to your crown chakra, you are a connection between heaven and earth.

The solar plexus chakra is associated with courage, and by placing an emerald or malachite here while you meditate and call on Raphael, you will channel the powerful energies and guidance he delivers to the place where your strength comes from.

In your dreams, you may see an emerald green and golden light emanating from this area of your body, indicating Raphael is busy creating courage in you, releasing doubt, and healing your strength center.

Manifesting Wealth

None of us want to be poor. We cling to what we have, desperately seeking more. However, Archangel Raphael told Tobit that "Those who give alms will enjoy a full life," meaning that when we give, we receive. This is the law of karma and the law of attraction in action. Generosity of spirit will lead to a manifestation of wealth in all aspects of your life. This could be spiritual, physical, and financial wealth.

Talking to Raphael, you may find yourself asking for money, but this limits what he can do for you. Instead, ask for an openness and a manifestation of wealth. Remember, Raphael is the power of God's healing on earth, and he can perform miracles and wonders you can't even begin to comprehend. When you meditate on this and allow your hands and your heart to open, you encourage a flowing of energy and good things will come to you. Wealth untold will manifest in your life.

Manifesting Positive Change

Many of us use the term karma quite loosely to mean we believe what we put out, we get back. If we do good to someone, we believe good will be done to us. Likewise, if we undercut someone, we can expect retribution to occur. To correct our karma, we need to engage in positive change. Raphael can help you with this. His healing presence can help you ease tensions not only in yourself but also in the relationships around you. By asking him to help you heal a particularly troublesome relationship, you can draw his healing and supportive energy to that aspect of your life.

While you meditate about the person or relationship you are concerned about, you can call upon Raphael to guide you to finding a peaceful resolution to the conflict. You can replay the situation or past events in your mind, letting a glorious wave of emerald green light wash over the memory, coloring the people, places, events, and words of that memory. Soon, any negative associations you have with that person or event will be washed away and fade into the background of your mind. You may find the next time you meet that person, they behave differently, and you will also act with a different energy towards them as Raphael guides you in peace.

Calling on the Archangel Raphael to manifest wealth, healing, and guidance in your life may seem like an illusion to the newbie. You may think it's just your imagination when you see green light or feel his presence. However, imagination is the freeing of your mind, and only when you open your imagination can you begin to communicate with the Archangel Raphael. Use your imagination; don't hold back.

You may see the crystals that you use glowing or casting brilliant green light on your body, and you may wonder if you are imagining their vibrations or heat. Do not let doubt drain the energies from these moments; instead, go with it. Use all the skills you can to manifest the presence and gifts of the Archangel Raphael.

Chapter 8: How to Tell When Archangel Raphael Is Around

While Raphael appeared as a man in the book of Tobit, he does not need to physically appear to guide and influence us. There are a range of signs to help us experience the loving compassion of Raphael. When we see these signals, we can be assured Archangel Raphael is close and his gifts are flowing through your life.

The Signs

The signs range from thoughts, feelings, colors, images, and experiences to words that suddenly enter your mind. Look for these signals in your day as you pass through life (Virtue, 2010).

- **Sparkles of Emerald Green Light**

People have reported seeing a bright light of emerald green color, announcing the presence of Raphael. This light can be in your mind as a vision or it can be sudden signs or places that have this light quality.

Image 15: Seeing incredible green light is a sure sign Raphael is nearby and working his awesome powers for your healing, compassion, and protection.

You may be sitting in a verdant garden, or you may be traveling to a place where you find yourself in green surroundings. Raphael is letting you know he is present.

- **Messages**

Raphael may leave you messages in anything from the headlines of newspapers to license plates. Be alert to messages from him telling you he is near, he has healed you, or he is helping you. Once you see this message, don't forget to thank him for his intervention and intent towards you.

- **His Name**

When we need a little reassurance, Raphael is quick to step in and let us know he is near and he has his guiding and protective wings over us. Many people have reported seeing his name or words of comfort when they needed a sign most. This can be in signs, names of places, and even in newspapers again.

- **Appear In Your Mind**

Many people who have been ill reported seeing Raphael in their minds, and while doctors would write this up as delirium, these people can clearly describe seeing Raphael. The presence of him in our minds is not a product of an overactive imagination—he is real. Seeing him in your mind can be incredibly soothing, and people speak of his larger than real presence, which fills them with healing and peace.

- **Tingling and Vibrations**

Many of us have suddenly experienced a vibration or tingling sensation before when we call upon Archangel Raphael. We may also feel a sudden sense of warmth as if someone is hugging us. Others report feeling the hair rise on the back of their necks as they sense his power. It could also be a sign of his healing in your body as his energy penetrates into your cells, organs, and limbs.

- **Suddenly Finding Resources**

Raphael wants us to learn and to heal, and while he is eager to give us his energy, he also wants us to use it in our lives. He will often guide us towards the healing we need. This may be suddenly finding the doctor you needed or discovering a book on spiritual healing that resonates with you. Either way, Raphael is guiding us towards healing.

- **Singing and Music**

All of heaven is singing. We are quite familiar with the concept that the angels sing, so it isn't much of a stretch to believe that the angels will also communicate with us through music and songs. When you need a special message, Raphael may suddenly speak through a song on the radio, or you will discover an album that soothes you in your time of need. Even birdsong can bring you an easing of tension and lessening of your physical and emotional burdens.

Image 16: The sound of singing, music, and the lyrics of songs can be the way in which Raphael communicates with you. Be alert to the messages of these cheering you up, showing you compassion, and helping you heal.

- **A Gut Feeling**

Many people have done miraculous things simply acting on their gut feeling. They have saved people and avoided disaster, and they have found prosperity in just listening to their instincts. When they think back on these events, they might even say that something told them to run, to invest, to go for a meeting, to make that appointment, or to change their habits. This "something" is Raphael. He whispers hints and suggestions into our ear, and this leads us where we are meant to be. He will never force us to choose something, and we need to really listen to that inner voice to fully benefit from his guidance. We have free will, and we need to choose what will work for us.

Chapter 9: Writing a Letter to Raphael

Image 17: Letter writing has traditionally been how we communicate with friends, reach out to them, get to know them, and share with them. Raphael is your friend, and you should show him the same care and friendship as you would a dear friend who helps you without any thought of return. Writing a letter is one way to do just this.

Your Close Friend

Start by writing a letter by hand to Raphael. Take care in selecting beautiful paper, and perhaps use a special pen for this. You are showing your attachment to and love for your dear friend, Raphael. In your letter, share your hopes, wishes, desires, and dreams with him. Express your gratitude for what he has already done for you.

This letter is a great way to communicate with him about those you wish to heal or help. You might write something like:

"Dear Raphael, thank you for being my friend and guide. I value the healing and prosperity you have brought into my life. Today, I wanted to tell you about my dear friend Lisa who is struggling to make ends meet. She is a kind and dear soul, and I wish her health and abundance. Could you please work the energies of abundance in her life and could you help me to assist her?

Thank you for your presence and support.

Love

Rachel."

This letter need not be miles long, and it need not be filled with academic language or poetry. Simply write to your friend, Raphael. Talk to him, tell him about your wishes, share with him your challenges. When you open up your communication to him, he will also maintain a more constant presence in your life.

Read Your Letter

Image 18: Lighting candles is about bringing light and love into your life and the space where you meditate. The elemental flames light more than just the candle; it also lights up your spirit.

Let your letter sit in a special place in your home for a day or two, then have a candle ceremony where you read the letter aloud to Raphael. You may choose to combine this with a meditation or mindfulness session, perhaps having your emerald or malachite crystals near, burning some incense, or lighting aromatherapy candles.

Read your letter aloud, letting it become a conversation between you and your dear friend, Raphael. Speak it like a plea, telling him more about your desires and wishes. There is no need to be formal, though you should be respectful. Remember to listen and wait for his responses. Over the next several days and weeks be aware of signs of his presence in your life as he begins to answer your requests and guides you towards the abundance and healing you asked for.

You may also receive visions or dreams in which you see the solutions or healing you requested. Write these down as soon as you have them. Later, you can reread these, and if there is anything that is unclear, you can always meditate and communicate with Raphael. He is patient and kind, and he will always clarify what he meant and guide you to a better understanding of his energy and how this will manifest in your life.

Importantly, when you receive feedback from Raphael, thank him for his attendance to your needs and wishes. A grateful heart is an open heart, and this is what you need to receive the guidance of the angels.

Chapter 10: Archangel Raphael Reiki

Reiki is energy healing where the practitioner channels energy by raising their palms. The presence of crystals can amplify this technique and channel the energies towards specific body parts where ailment exists. Light or energy workers use this method to communicate with and channel the healing powers of the Archangel Raphael to those in need. While this method may be quite foreign to you, you can use it successfully when you communicate with Raphael and receive or transmit his energies. Whether you want to heal yourself, a loved one, or a pet, this method is very adaptable and effective.

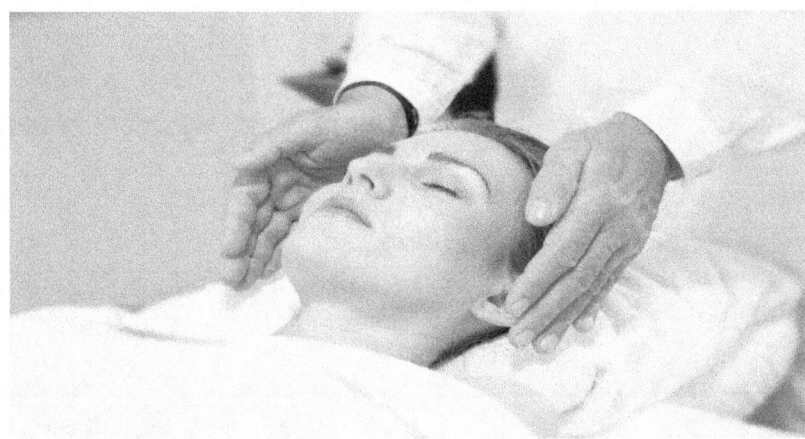

Image 19: Reiki is about transmitting energy, encouraging energy flow, and dissolving blockages that affect your health, your chakras, and your spiritual well-being.

Archangel Raphael Reiki Meditation

Sitting comfortably, allow your body to soften and gently find the most natural position for you. Breathe in the vibrant energy of the Archangel Raphael and breathe out the negative energies of a day of toil. Feel the bright emerald green light of Raphael enter your body, bringing energy and transformation to every cell of your being.

Raise your palms, facing them towards the person or beloved pet you want to help and heal. In your mind, you may call on the assistance of Raphael; however, it is important to be still, to allow yourself to empty as you open, and to allow the healing energies of Raphael to pass through you and into the subject of your healing.

Be mindful of the living world around you. Draw those powers and verdant energy into you, letting it flow through your palms like the mouth of a river to cascade down on the one you love.

Let your mind be still as you channel the love, healing, and inner bliss you feel to those who need it. You are now a still point that shares positive energy and compassion with those who are in need. Let them drink the energy, divine mercy, and guiding presence of the Archangel Raphael from your hands.

Like watering a garden, you shower down blessings to the pet or loved one you care about. Allow your energy to move outwards like ripples on a clear pool of water. You are part of an ever-expanding wave of energy that heals and protects those around you.

If you become distracted, simply focus on the surface of your palms. Let the tingling energy and vibrational frequencies settle on your body, move into your cells, and circulate through you. Then allow the channels to open from your palms, sharing the divine blessings of Archangel Raphael with others.

Chapter 11: How to Spend Time With Archangel Raphael

Archangel Raphael is known to be a compassionate healer. This means he knows our weaknesses and our flaws, but he loves us nonetheless. Since he is such a wonderful friend and powerful presence, many of us choose to make him a part of our daily life. He is not simply a presence we turn to when we have nowhere else to turn. Instead, his guidance can and should become a daily exchange of energy and wisdom.

Image 20: Having Raphael in your life is a constant stream of positive and healing energy. He becomes an integral part of your life and habits. Having him near allows you to channel divine energy on a daily basis, and we need never feel as if we are asking too much or receiving more than our share. As long as we are grateful and express our gratitude, as well as share our energy with the world around us, we are more than welcome to take Raphael's hand.

Daily Life While Carrying the Emerald Flame Everywhere

Archangel Raphael is not only there for the big stuff. He wants to help you with all aspects of your life, from the tiny headache you have to the doubts that you have before going on a date. If you let him, he will even guide you to your soulmate, like he did for Sara and Tolbit's son.

You can speak to him on a daily basis, and he will never tell you "go away, I'm busy." Instead, he wants to help you, and he is all around you, waiting to share his guidance, love, and compassion. How wonderful is that!

Some believers carry an emerald or malachite pendant around their necks to remind them of Raphael's nearness, and they keep a constant channel open to him. Experiencing real health, well-being, and compassion for others is not something you only dream of. It is something you live daily by including Raphael as part of your everyday life. Thanking him constantly and carrying his emerald flame of light everywhere with you will make you a lightworker who shares their blessings, love, and compassion with those around you.

With the daily guidance of Raphael, you can transform your life and lead others to this awesome friendship and wellspring of healing energy. Raphael wants to share, and by showing your gratitude to him and sharing his gifts, you will become a blessing to others.

Conclusion

The road stretches before you, but you no longer walk it alone. You never did. Now, you simply know this irrefutable truth. The creator has sent his Archangels to hold you, keep you safe, heal you, guide you, and befriend you. Archangel Raphael is here, now, and he is at your side through this life. It is within your power to connect to him, to call on him for guidance, healing, and counseling when you are struggling and even for the small steps you take through life every day.

Having learned how to call Archangel Raphael and how to meditate on his guidance, presence, and caring, you can now boldly reach out to him whenever you need him. His presence in your life will continue to help you be a more grateful, energetic, and spontaneous being filled with light and love that will attract abundance, friendship, and love to you.

I encourage you to share your journey and the protection of Raphael with those in your life, to make his presence felt, and to continue to develop as a worker of light, whether you practice this as a career or simply as your contribution to the human race.

Lastly, I would like to leave you with this prayer:

May light and love travel with you on this day,
I pray for the protection of Archangel Raphael to guide you
to carry you on his wings and to bring you solace
for any hurts you may have suffered.
I ask that he lead you to the abundance your life deserves
and that he holds your hand in friendship
and in love as he holds mine with his other hand.
I pray for light and I pray for peace to comfort you
in darkness and in doubt
as I reach out to you my brother, to you my sister.

References

Acone, S. (2010). *Crystals to Help Connect With Archangel Raphael*. Healing Crystals. https://www.healingcrystals.com/Crystals_to_Help_Connect_with_Archangel_Raphael_Articles_1791.html

Anglin, E. (2020). *How to Raise Your Vibrational Frequency: Channeling the Angels*. Learn Religions. https://www.learnreligions.com/raise-vibrational-frequency-1729268

Hibiscus Moon. (2017, February 22). *Crystals for Working With Archangel Raphael* [Video]. YouTube. https://www.youtube.com/watch?v=7aOAuOkj-7c

Meditatia. (n.d.). *Guided Meditation Reiki*. Meditatia. https://www.meditatia.com/guided-meditation-reiki.html

Peroshini. (n.d.). *Archangel Raphael. About The Angels*. http://peroshini.com/peroshini/About_The_Angels.html

Purva Nimfa Magic. (2018, September 22). *Raphael-Archangel Raphael-157,29,125,2129,1577* [Video]. YouTube. https://www.youtube.com/watch?v=kPiHXGj7XVQ&list=PLCMPRCPVXHGcmAYIIO2MjkDs_Dc4EECkb&index=4&t=0s

See U in History/Mythology. (2019, October 21). *Archangel Raphael: The Angel of Powerful Healing - Angels and Demons* [Video]. YouTube. https://www.youtube.com/watch?v=7kdipeG-IZU

Virtue, D. (2010). *8 Signs from Archangel Raphael*. Beliefnet. https://www.beliefnet.com/inspiration/angels/2010/06/healing-miracles-of-archangel-raphael.aspx

Virtue, D. (2016). *Archangel Raphael 101. You Can Heal Your Life*. https://www.healyourlife.com/archangel-raphael-101

Illustrations References

Image 1: ptra from Pixabay https://pixabay.com/photos/angel-castel-sant-angelo-rome-wing-2677047/

Image 2: Dimitris Vetsikas from Pixabay https://pixabay.com/photos/archon-michael-angel-archangel-2086750/

Image 3: Mark Hultgren from Pixabay https://pixabay.com/illustrations/portal-gateway-pool-door-exit-454462/

Image 4: Thomas Wolter from Pixabay https://pixabay.com/photos/green-leaf-gem-emerald-plant-4928714/

Image 5: Jan Vašek from Pixabay https://pixabay.com/photos/iphone-template-mockup-mock-up-500291/

Image 6: Lirinya from Pixabay https://pixabay.com/photos/watts-mud-dirty-foot-feet-1012402/

Image 7: Gerd Altmann from Pixabay. https://pixabay.com/illustrations/brain-think-thoughts-psychology-4065092/

Image 8: John Hain from Pixabay. https://pixabay.com/illustrations/woman-power-glory-affirmation-2128020/

Image 9: No-longer-here from Pixabay. https://pixabay.com/illustrations/dog-paw-hand-love-friendship-2383071/

Image 10: S K from Pixabay. https://pixabay.com/photos/money-dollars-success-business-1428594/

Image 11: Okan Caliskan from Pixabay. https://pixabay.com/illustrations/meditation-spiritual-yoga-1384758/

Image 12: Olya Adamovich from Pixabay. https://pixabay.com/photos/man-male-model-person-young-979980/

Image 13: Aloysius from Pixabay. https://pixabay.com/photos/gems-stones-crystal-gemstone-836763/

Image 14: LillyCantabile from Pixabay. https://pixabay.com/illustrations/reiki-alternative-yoga-healing-4133336/

Image 15: My pictures are CC0. When doing composings: from Pixabay. https://pixabay.com/photos/meadow-bokeh-nature-dew-dewdrop-4485609/

Image 16: Dieter_G from Pixabay. https://pixabay.com/photos/birds-swifts-singing-twitter-music-2672101/

Image 17: stempow from Pixabay. https://pixabay.com/photos/hands-writting-invitation-typography-2110452/

Image 18: Pexels from Pixabay. https://pixabay.com/photos/ash-candlelight-candle-christmas-2179184/

Image 19: Jürgen Rübig from Pixabay. https://pixabay.com/photos/wellness-massage-reiki-285590/

Image 20: Aaron Cabrera from Pixabay. https://pixabay.com/photos/worship-singing-inspiration-church-4088561/

Book 4: Archangelology: Metatron

Well-Being, Angelic Alignment & the Gift of Accomplishing Wonders

(Archangelology Book Series 4)

Angela Grace

Introduction

When I first began my journey with crystals and Reiki healing, I had no idea what opportunities would be opened up for me to grasp. Nor did I realize just how much more there was for me to learn about healing myself, the wisdom of the universe, and how to make it all happen on my own terms.

I had nearly been consumed by my depression. It had led me to one of the darkest places I had ever been to. After losing my partner, struggling with my job, and feeling alone and isolated, I began turning my life around by studying and practicing Reiki. With the use of Reiki and crystals, I felt as though I had finally found myself again, but it was my *true* self. I was no longer the superficial social butterfly who surrounded herself with meaningless friendships, who hid from her past and trauma, and who drowned her sorrows in vodka. No, I was becoming the person I always knew I was meant to be but had never known how to become.

It sounds like a dream come true, right? It was like I was finally on the path to positive transformation. Looking back now, I can definitely say I was. At the time, it didn't seem so clear cut, though. I felt myself changing a little bit every day. My moods, emotions, thoughts, and how I perceived myself and the world were all slowly shifting. The part I struggled with was how my relationships began to change.

Coming from a family that never believed in me and having based most of my adult friendships off of menial connections determined by social status, the list of people who I could talk to about my personal transformation was very short. I couldn't imagine bringing up how crystals made me feel to the friends who I got manicures with. The thought of reaching out to my family and discussing energetic healing was too strange. As effective as it is, there are still a lot of people who consider Reiki and crystal healing to be pseudoscience, witchcraft, or just nonsense.

Feeling like I had so few people to talk to aside from my friend Linda (who I am eternally grateful to for supporting me and helping me on this path), I began to feel alone again. It was at this time when I began to think that I wasn't the only energy worker or healer that felt like they were alone on their chosen path. So, I dove into the worldwide web, and I started to look into ways to ease this loneliness I was experiencing.

This is when I stumbled across the notion of spiritual entities who exist to guide humans and offer them strength and healing—more specifically, archangels.

Call them spiritual, energetic, miraculous, or anything else that feels right to you, but it is hard to deny the existence of such benevolent, guiding entities. A lot of people associate archangels with religion, but the notion of angels, miracle workers, and spiritual guides has been around a lot longer than any of today's religions. Many different interpretations of archangels have been found all around the world, and they encompass thousands of years of history. For that reason, archangels have now made a name for themselves among spiritual healers and energy workers, separate from their religious affiliations.

I began to study up on how to work with archangels for personal and spiritual growth. It was very comforting and intriguing to think that there were archangels that could become energetic companions for me and offer guidance and understanding when no one else in my life could.

One of the archangels I discovered—and who has been a powerful catalyst for change in my life—is Archangel Metatron. Metatron as an archangel initiates transformation and change. He helped remind me that the path I was on was the right one. I was already going through so many personal and spiritual transformations, but having Metatron remind me that I wasn't alone and that I had protectors and guides to see me through gave me the strength and courage to keep going.

Even though I have settled into a place in my life where I am happy with my successes, comfortable with who I am, and have reached a state of inner peace, I still work with and confide in Archangel Metatron. He is by my side when I want to bring about change, big or small. Metatron stands witness to the miracles that I see happening in my life. He is the angel I turn to when I need to clear my mind of cluttering thoughts.

Since discovering Metatron's power and invoking him as an archangel in my spiritual repertoire, I can honestly and confidently say that I have taken the right steps and made the right choices to change what I needed to in my life. Through change comes growth, and I have grown into someone who is willing and able to spread my knowledge and experiences to people like you—people looking for a little guidance.

Maybe you already know the basics of working with the archangels, or maybe working with spiritual entities is a new concept to you. Either way, this book offers you the information needed to connect with Archangel Metatron in order to help and change yourself. By invoking Metatron, you choose to transform your existence, just as I have.

Perhaps you are feeling like I did when I first stumbled into energy healing—lost, alone, scared, isolated, and depressed. Maybe you are lacking joy, passion, and fulfillment in your life. You could be simply looking for answers or for a voice and a hand to show you a new direction. The idea of angels and archangels have an almost universal impact, filling people with hope and warmth. That is what I am here to offer you.

Through my experiences and practices, and through the journey I have taken with Metatron, you can also experience profound change, bring fulfillment to your life, and make your own success. I can teach you how to work with Metatron in a variety of ways, such as by using meditations and affirmations. I can teach you how to sense when Metatron is present and also how to combine Metatron's power and gifts with other types of energetic healing. Empower yourself with my wisdom and Metatron's energy.

Chapter 1: Introduction to Archangel Metatron

When discussing archangels, it is important to make the distinction that they are individuals in and of themselves. You can call upon different archangels for different work you do for yourself and others. Archangels have histories that span thousands of years across many cultures. They each have personalities, special powers, and associations.

Archangels are more than just icons, though. They are beings who have each contributed in their own way to human evolution and societal growth and change. Metatron is the bringer of change, and as such, he can be called upon for transformation. Transformation and change are incredibly broad terms and can be applied to many different aspects of your life and what progress you want to see.

Metatron is considered the most powerful angel and the prince of the seraphim. He has the power to command other heavenly beings and all the other angels. From a religious standpoint, Metatron is said to be the only angel with access to the Creator, or God, and is rivaled only in power by the Creator.

Aside from this religious affiliation, Metatron's power is unparalleled in the realm of archangelology and spiritual healing. This divinity and power is respected and appreciated by those who seek to work with Metatron.

Unanimously, across all faiths and spiritualities, angels are considered divine beings who serve a purpose. Whether this purpose is connected to a God or Creator or exists separately from religion is going to be a topic for your own faith. In terms of this book, references will be made to religious connotations, but working with Metatron and the other archangels is not contingent on religious belief.

Angelologists, who don't necessarily have a religious affiliation, have been inspired by, interested in, and drawn to Metatron and his existence for many years. He has become a favored archangel in many angelology and archangelology studies and practices.

Metatron's History

Historically, Metatron is a unique and mysterious angel. This is primarily because he is never referred to by name in the Bible. However, historians, scholars, and those who analyze religious texts have often postured that Metatron is represented by a lot of the unnamed angels in the Bible. Furthermore, Metatron is the only archangel currently known whose name does not end with the letter "L". Michael, Raphael, Gabriel, Uriel, and the other known archangels have a specific cadence to their names that Metatron lacks.

It is speculated that the name Metatron is derived from ancient words from Hebrew or Greek. These words range in meaning from "keeper of the watch", derived from the word *mattara*, "to guard and protect", derived from the word *memater*, and "the one who serves behind the throne/the one who occupies the space next to the throne", which is derived from the Greek words *meta* and *thronos*. There is another Latin word, *mitator*, meaning "leader" that has also been suggested as a source for the name Metatron.

Metatron appears by name in the Book of Enoch, the Talmud, the Kabbalah, and in some Islamic texts. He has been described as an angel who records the word of God and also events that happen on Earth. Meaning, he is always watching Earth and humanity.

The various religious references to Metatron reflect different views of the archangel and what he is supposed to represent. However, they do have some congruence in how he appears as a favorite of God or the Creator and that he has elevated power and status over the other angels.

In the Book of Enoch, 3 Enoch, Metatron is said to be special because he is the only angel who was born a human. He was Enoch in mortal form, but God ascended Enoch to heaven after the great flood to show he was merciful. Upon his ascension, Enoch was transformed into a powerful archangel and given command over the other angels. This was because God trusted Enoch and was very proud of his transformation from human into angel.

In the Jewish Talmud, Metatron is described as being seated beside God. This is another display of how important and respected Metatron is by God. All other beings have to remain in a bowed position before God. The Talmud suggests that Metatron is allowed to sit because he is a scribe and sitting is a more comfortable posture to record all of the heavenly and earthly events. In this text, it is also believed that Metatron is given temporary rule when God is occupied, absent, or busy.

In some Islamic beliefs, Metatron is considered the Angel of the Veil and the only being who truly knows what lies beyond. He is also regarded as the angel who is called upon to fight dark spirits, demons, and other dark magics.

Archangel Metatron isn't a well-known figure in religion, despite his association with power and elevation above the other angels. However, in archangelology and spirituality, he has become a prominent figure who is looked to for guidance and healing.

Signs of Metatron's Healing Power and Influence

Spiritualists, healers, and archangelologists say that Metatron serves humanity in many ways, including in healing. They have reported seeing bright flashes when Metatron is near, the flashes being representative of the glorious crown bestowed upon him by God.

Other archangelolgists say that positive thoughts presenting themselves during periods of depression are a sign of Archangel Metatron communicating directly with an individual. It is his way of guiding humans into positivity. He records events pertaining to each individual human; thus, he wants them to be happy rather than consumed by sadness.

Metatron is known for a geometric shape referred to as "Metatron's cube". Later chapters will go into more detail about sacred geometry. However, the presence of recurring geometric shapes in an individual's life is said to be indicative of Metatron's influence. Those recurring shapes are considered to be offsets of Metatron's cube, a very powerful geometric shape when it comes to spirituality, healing, and transformation.

Archangel Metatron has also been said to be related to numbers—more specifically, to the number 11. If someone sees the number 11 consistently, it can be a sign of Metatron's influence. Perhaps Metatron has been in contact with you already, and you just didn't know how to read the signs.

Chapter 2: How to Easily Call Upon Archangel Metatron

Archangel Metatron helps guide people through ascension, which essentially involves raising their energetic and spiritual levels to a place of divine transcendence. He is devoted to creating paradise on Earth and is willing to aid those who seek his wisdom and guidance. Like with most spiritual practices and healing, Metatron needs to be invoked. Archangels have great power and will use their influence when possible, but unless you contact them directly, they are unlikely to intervene.

Whether you are new to archangelology or already have some experience with it, knowing some easy ways to invoke Metatron will help you open the door to spiritual and energetic transformation.

By inviting Metatron into your life, you open yourself up to receive spiritual and energetic healing, you can begin clearing away negativity, you gain protection from disease and corruption, and, of course, you are pushed toward transformation.

While there are some more advanced and in-depth techniques to invoke Metatron and to seek specific guidance, you can also easily call upon him for beginner practice or at times when you might not be able to use a more in-depth method.

Archangel Metatron has a very intimate understanding of humans and their problems. This might come from the notion that he was once a human or from the historical idea that Metatron watches and records everything that happens in the world, including the lives of individual humans. As such, this angel is uniquely qualified to be a personal support system for you.

Meditation

Meditation is a well-known practice for anyone who is studying or participating in spirituality and energetic healing. It has been used for centuries to raise the level of consciousness and allow practitioners to receive divine messages and knowledge. It makes sense that the practice can be used to connect with Archangel Metatron then, doesn't it?

While you can use guided, complex meditations to connect with Metatron, in terms of an easy connection, you don't need a big ceremonial meditation. Rather, all you need to do is close your eyes, take a series of long, deep breaths, and let all thoughts, worries, and anxieties leave your mind. While you are breathing and relaxing, set the intention that you are looking to connect with Metatron.

Once your mind is clear and your intention is set, you will be open to receiving and listening to messages from Archangel Metatron.

This is a very quick exercise that can be done just about anywhere at any time. The more you practice it, the quicker you'll be able to clear your thoughts and listen for your answers. If you have a specific question, you might want to set an intention like, "I am asking for guidance from Archangel Metatron on [insert question or topic here]". That way, the message you receive can be more focused.

This quick invocation can help you during particularly stressful times when you need to take a moment for yourself and clear the clutter from your thoughts. It can also be done in a room full of people, even though you might need to practice tuning out other noises before you have the ability to do so.

Meditations don't need to be long and ritualistic to yield results. Simply by relaxing your body, clearing your mind, and setting your desired intention, you can invite guidance from Metatron. Since he is a light and upbeat energy who resonates on a higher frequency, the clearing of your mind is essential to raise it to a state that can receive messages from him.

Activating Your Pillar of Light

Every person has within them what is known as an "Ascension Pillar of Light". This pillar is a core of light at your center. It is the center of your being, but it also expands around you. The Ascension Pillar connects you to the ground and the crystalline core of the planet. It also travels up your spine, flows through your heart, and expands out from the crown of your head, connecting you to the cosmos and the divine.

Archangel Metatron can be called upon to activate this pillar within you. By activating your Ascension Pillar of Light, you empower yourself to serve yourself and others at a higher level for the interest of all. You ascend to greater consciousness.

Calling on Metatron to activate this pillar is not complicated. It can be done simply with little practice or prior experience. It is a good step to take if you are new to spiritual work and energy healing. If this isn't your first time working with archangels but you haven't activated your Ascension Pillar yet, you might find it helpful on your own journey.

To activate your pillar, you'll want to focus on the energetic space above your head and tune into the energy of Archangel Metatron. As a divine being, he is always within reach. You might resonate with Metatron's energy in the form of a glowing orb or a pink and magenta crystalline structure.

Once you have aligned yourself with Metatron's divine light energy, allow that light to shine down through you. Think of it as a spotlight bathing you and the pillar of energy around, above, and below you. This light will flow through the crown of your head, into your heart, down your spine, through your abdomen, and down into the crystalline core of the planet that centers you.

While the light flows through you, it opens up all your energetic channels and pathways, clearing out negativity, energetic clutter, and spiritual junk that creates obstructions.

Please remember to ground yourself after this kind of energetic healing. You can do so by drinking a glass of cool water, placing your palms and forehead on the floor, or touching and holding a rock, tree, or wood.

While this exercise to call upon Archangel Metatron is specific to your Ascension Pillar of Light, it can also be used as a way to open up your energetic channels. It might sound complicated, but it is another quick and easy method to make a connection with Metatron and gain some light, healing energy from him.

Chapter 3: Exercises, Mantras, and Affirmations for Transformation

There are many different ways that you can call upon Metatron's power in your everyday life. These methods of invoking power are meant to clear negativity from your thoughts and your life. With Metatron's ability to transform and clear negativity, you can change yourself and also your life.

Affirmations and Mantras

An affirmation is a mindful and meditative practice that is meant to change your thought patterns. Your brain is trained to think a certain way. The more you have those thoughts, the easier your brain defaults to them. For example, if you think negatively about your job, over time, those reactions become natural. Every time you think about your job, it can create negative thoughts and feelings. However, if you retrain your brain to think positively about your job, then you won't feel stressed out or anxious when the topic arises.

Affirmations are how you can rewire your brain. Using ones associated with Metatron will help you embody his powers of positivity, clearing, and transformation. An affirmation can become a part of you by speaking it aloud each day. Try writing it down on a post-it note and putting it on a door or mirror that you look at often. Whenever you see the written note, speak the affirmation aloud, or say it in your mind again.

With each utterance, your mind will start to believe what it is you are affirming, effectively changing your thought patterns. Using affirmations that invoke the power and traits of Metatron will extend beyond your own thoughts and include your actions and the world around you, as well.

Mantras are sacred sounds, words, or phrases that are meant to help with focus and concentration, especially during meditation. Using a mantra that is aligned with Metatron's power helps you to embody his teachings and wisdom when you meditate. You can also use those mantras as a way to keep yourself focused on a certain goal or task.

The meditation exercise from Chapter 2 can be enhanced further with a mantra that is meant to help you concentrate on Metatron and his gifts. You can write down mantras, as well, or keep them in the back of your mind, especially when meditating and invoking Metatron.

Some examples of affirmations that you can use to invoke and align with Metatron include:

- "I align with Archangel Metatron now."
- "I align myself with Metatron's power of transformation."
- "I fill myself with Metatron's healing light."

You can use pre-written affirmations, but the best ones to use are those that you come up with on your own. They can be as vague or specific as you want. If you have a certain goal, such as changing your job, clearing your mind of negativity, or transforming something within yourself, you can use more specific affirmations.

Some specific affirmations for you to take inspiration from include:

- "I align myself with Metatron's mind-clearing abilities."
- "Metatron's power transforms my career path."
- "Metatron's light clears and transforms [say what you want to clear and transform]."

When using affirmations, it is important to remember to word them as though what you want is already happening. This is the power of positive thinking and how using Metatron affirmations can cause shifts in how you think and how you perceive the world.

Mantras aren't necessarily specific words. They can be as simple as sound utterances that you feel connect you to Metatron more closely. Sometimes, during meditation, you might receive a sound mantra that you'll feel compelled to repeat when working with Metatron.

If you are new to mantras and using them in meditation, start simply by intoning Metatron's name during meditation as it holds power on its own. As you work more with him, you might come across other mantras that will aid you in your work with archangels and Metatron.

Some good mantras to begin working with Metatron include:

- "Metatron"
- "Transformation"
- "Powerful change"

More advanced mantras can include:

- "Archangel Metatron is always with me."
- "I carry Archangel Metatron's light inside of me."

Like with affirmations, the best mantras are the ones that you come up with yourself. They will be imbued with your personal power. If you are at a loss for where to start with mantras and affirmations, there are some great YouTube videos that can offer you guidance. Doing a search for "Metatron Affirmations" or "Metatron Mantras" will lead you to videos that can help guide you.

Prayer

Prayer is similar to affirmations and mantras as they are intended to invoke the power of spiritual beings and entities. However, they differ in that they are a request to a spiritual entity or meant to express thanks. When working with Archangel Metatron, it is important to give thanks for his help and guidance. Additionally, prayer can be used to ask for specific outcomes.

Some prayers that you might use for thanking Metatron can include:

- "I give thanks to Metatron and his awesome power, guidance, and knowledge."
- "I am grateful to Archangel Metatron for his participation in my transformation."

You can use prayers like the following to ask Metatron for specific guidance or help:

- "Metatron, I ask for your healing light to clear the negativity from my home."
- "Beloved Archangel Metatron, walk with me as I transform myself inside and out."

When you offer prayer to Metatron, it doesn't have to be ceremonial or ritualistic. You can end or start each day with a prayer or use one every time you call on Metatron. Prayers can also be used as a way of invoking his power in more advanced ways.

Cord-Cutting and Energetic Shielding

We will end this chapter by going over the cord-cutting and shielding prayers. These are two very powerful healing methods that can be enhanced by the archangels. Since these prayers are transformative, Archangel Metatron is perfect to call upon for these processes. They can be used as a way to invoke his power for the specific purposes of shielding and cord-cutting.

If you'd like, you can empower these prayers with a mediation session. Perhaps dim the lights a bit and take some deep, calming breaths to settle your mind and clear away thoughts. Once you sense Metatron's presence or feel your mind opening, you can proceed with either the shielding or cord-cutting prayer.

Energetic shielding is the process of protecting yourself from unwanted thoughts, feelings, and energies. Cord-cutting is when you sever the energetic ties between yourself and events, memories, people, or other aspects of your life. Each time you have an interaction with someone or something, an energetic cord is made between you and that thing. If these cords are negative, they can hold you back and cause other problems for you, so severing them can set you free.

Shielding

Here is the shielding prayer:

"I ask for Archangel Metatron's healing, shielding light. Metatron, lend me your light to shield me from negative energies. Lend me your power to open up my energetic channels and receive your wisdom while blocking out the energies, thoughts, and feelings that no longer serve me and that could hurt me. Protect me from outside thoughts, feelings, and energies that do not serve my highest good."

Cord-Cutting

Here is the cord-cutting prayer:

"Archangel Metatron, with your shining spear, please sever the energetic cords that no longer serve my highest good. Cut the cords that hold me back, that keep me from my greatest potential, and that bring negativity to my life. Release me from the energies that harm me and keep me from progressing. When I count to three, the cords will be released. One...two...three."

Chapter 4: Metatron and How to Use the Power of Sleep and Astral Time

Sleep is considered to be one of the most beneficial remedies for the mind and body. All through childhood, if you get sick with a cold, it is recommended that you rest as much as you can to help fight off the virus. Whenever someone is stressed out or has had a bad day, getting some quality sleep can completely change their attitude. Have you ever heard the phrase "you'll feel better after a good night's sleep?"

There is some science behind that. There are aspects to sleep that help the mind recover, like the phases of sleep. Most importantly, REM sleep is imperative for the mind's recovery, but also for emotions, spirit, and physical recovery. It is during REM sleep that you dream. Without dreams, the mind literally loses its cohesiveness, leading to hallucinations, illness, madness, and, eventually, death (if proper sleep is not resumed).

During sleep, the brain falls into a deep and slow brainwave pattern. This is how dreams happen. Dreams can involve messages from spiritual entities and, when in the dream phase, your mind is incredibly receptive to spiritual information and knowledge.

By understanding this openness, you can use the time when you sleep to receive incredibly vivid and profound messages from Archangel Metatron. By having a healthy sleep cycle, you fortify your mind, body, and spirit.

When you want to call Metatron to you during your sleep state, he can bring you greater youth and vitality. Through sleep, you can manifest changes in your life, which is another way Metatron can assist with his great power of transformation.

You should think about setting up some kind of small altar or honoring space that you can use to summon or invoke Metatron for your dreams. Once the space is set, before you go to bed at night, sit there and say a prayer to Metatron, or give an offering that will invite him to join you in sleep. Offer things that are gold or orange in color. These can be flowers, candles, and even decorated cloth. You can even offer orange crystals like calcite.

By placing these offerings in this intention space, you send out the invitation to Metatron. You can also use a prayer to further initiate contact with him in sleep. Use a prayer like these:

- "Metatron, I invite you to walk with me in my dreams."
- "Archangel Metatron, I am ready to receive your visions of youth and vitality in my sleep state."

When you set your intention to accept Metatron into your dreams, you can utilize his powers for manifesting the life you want. When you are asleep, your mind has incredible power and continues to remain active. Your subconscious and your intuition are at their strongest while you are asleep. As such, they have the power to manifest what you truly want in your life. This manifestation power is amplified by Metatron's gifts and presence in your dreams.

The more you call upon Metatron to join you in sleep, the more his power will combine with yours and transfer into your everyday life, allowing you to manifest your own desired reality. By learning to use the same dream visualization as a form of visualization in your awakened state, you can further practice manifestation and achieve even greater goals.

Visualization is a very powerful form of manifestation by which you visualize what you want and transform it into what you have. Metatron, the archangel of transformation, can definitely aid in making your visualizations a reality. Sometimes, it has to start in the dream state for your heart and mind to truly show you what you need to manifest.

The unconscious mind and heart know what they want and need. That is why, in sleep, you can find strong and vivid visions to guide you. Trust yourself and the knowledge you receive in those visions, and carry them into your waking life to change your reality. Let Metatron guide you, and accept his gifts to help you manifest what you want in both your sleeping and waking states.

Chapter 5: Aligning Prosperity, Abundance, Love, and Well-Being with Archangel Metatron's Frequency

When working with archangels, you can call on their power for a lot of different purposes. Some of the greatest gifts in life that people seek are prosperity, abundance, love, and well-being. These gifts are achievable with the help of Metatron and with the use of spiritual energy and magic.

When it comes to prosperity and abundance, some of it comes down to mindset. One of the greatest skills this book is meant to teach you is how you can change your own reality by shifting your mindset. With the transforming powers of Metatron, you can truly transform the way you think.

A simple shift in consciousness can really alter how you see yourself and your life. The concept of prosperity is often lined with money, success, and material wealth. Sometimes, if you dig a little deeper, you can find prosperity without the ties to physical wealth and success. Or, more importantly, you can see prosperity in what you already have.

The same is true of abundance and love. There are a lot of different ways you can find abundance and love all around you. Asking Metatron through prayer, affirmation, and mantra isn't always enough, though. When you can make these shifts in your thought process, you can turn yourself into a magnet for confidence, inner peace, and prosperity. In the laws of physics and spirituality, you attract the energies that you put out into the world.

While it can be a good starting point for changing your mindset and creating a more positive reality, you can use other methods, too, such as candle magic and the combination of Metatron's power with other archangels.

Candle Magic

Candle magic is a powerful form of visualization and manifestation. It combines meditation with manifestation. In conjunction with divine angelic power, candle magic can be a very effective tool for you to use. While it might sound a little hocus-pocus, the goal of candle magic is to amplify your focus on your goals and intentions so that you can give them more power and more of a chance to come true.

Using candle magic also dives into the spiritual essences of some everyday tools like the power of colors. Different colors can correlate to various desires. Therefore, you'll want to use a color that corresponds to what it is you want. For instance, pink is a color associated with love.

The basic colors that you might find yourself working with and their meanings are as follows:

- Red: passion, seduction, and love
- Orange: creativity and confidence
- Yellow: abundance and joy
- Green: earth, growth, luck, and money
- Blue: peace and protection
- Purple: intuition and motivation
- White: purity and a blank slate (can be used as a substitute for any other color)
- Black: protection and banishing
- Pink: love and self-care

Candle magic itself is a fairly simple test of focus, concentration, and personal power. Before you begin, you'll want a goal or aspiration in mind. It might help you to write this down and keep it with you. Include your invocation for Metatron in your goal.

Choose a candle that is color-appropriate, such as one that is associated with your goal. You might even want to carve symbols into the candle wax, like a heart to represent love or a dollar sign to represent money. You can choose any symbols that resonate well with you and your goal. They don't necessarily have to be a "normal" symbol that is used to represent a certain concept or idea.

If you do have an altar or intention space for Metatron, setting up your candle in that area and also sitting before it while performing candle magic is going to strengthen your connection to him. You might want to include another offering like orange calcite or a crystal that matches the color of your candle.

When you're ready, light the candle and begin to meditate on the goal that you wrote on the paper as well as the traits that Metatron can provide you with to make it a reality. That being said, you might want to pick goals that Metatron's powers can really assist with, such as clearing and transformation.

While meditating on your goal, feel free to read aloud what you wrote on your page. This is also a good time to practice manifestation and visualization. This kind of meditation isn't going to be focused on the verbalization of an affirmation or mantra. Rather, you'll want to use your mind to fully visualize what your goal is and how it would look or feel to have that goal become a reality.

If your mind begins to wander or the visualization fades at all, look at the candle flame, and let the light be your focal point for maintaining your focus on manifesting your desire. Let the candle burn through your meditation, and then blow it out. For a truly strong manifestation candle magic, repeat the exercise with the same candle for three consecutive nights. You might want to close each meditation with an additional prayer to Metatron, as well.

Archangels Metatron and Haniel

Sometimes, it can be beneficial to combine the gifts of two different archangels. They are all-powerful and have their own associations, but you don't need to limit yourself to the company of just one archangel. One who works well with Metatron's power is Haniel.

Haniel is an archangel that can mend bonds and familial relationships. When combined with Metatron's powers of transformation—healing, clearing light and ultimate change—the two archangels have the power to fill you with celestial light and love.

Not only does Metatron gift you with the healing, clearing light, but Haniel fills you with self-love and universal love. Together, that creates celestial light and love. This is a very warming, healing light and love. This practice can really open you up, clearing away negativity and spiritual blockages. Feeling like you are loved by a divine source, and also by yourself, is an irreplaceable feeling.

You can utilize candles of orange for Metatron and blue for Haniel, and you can use prayers, affirmations, and mantras to call upon them both. Rather than using one affirmation or prayer to invoke each separately, use one prayer, affirmation, or mantra that calls on both of them. That way, it will be even more powerful and specific for what you want.

Other archangels of well-being that can be called upon with Metatron include:

- Michael, archangel of protection and defense
- Raphael, healer of physical and spiritual ailments
- Uriel, who helps with loneliness and personal strength
- Gabriel, archangel of creation, ideas, creativity, and belief in oneself

Consider taking a look at my other books, *Archangelology: Michael, Protection & Angelic Codes* and *Archangelology: Raphael, Abundance & Attraction Secrets*, for more information on working with other archangels.

Chapter 6: Archangel Metatron Meditations

In the previous chapters, we discussed different kinds of meditations that can be used to connect with and invoke Metatron. From simple, mind-clearing meditations to candle magic with enhanced focus meditations, you've already gotten your feet wet with the possibilities. Meditation can become much more intricate, and when you follow a guided meditation, you can be led on some amazing spiritual journeys.

Every person has a spiritual body. Whether it is referred to as an aura or energetic field, or even as a spirit, this part of you can become sick and damaged, just as your physical body can. The spiritual body is energy. Energy has a current—a flow that is smooth and fluid like the water in a stream. Just as the flow of water in a river can get hindered by the build-up of rocks, leaves, and other natural gunk, the energy flow of your spiritual body can get sluggish when it becomes overencumbered with spiritual junk.

Spiritual junk is essentially emotional and spiritual negative garbage that builds up in your spiritual body. It can lead to physical illness and disease. Through guided meditations and with the aid of Metatron's clearing abilities, you can maintain your spiritual body, clearing it regularly. Even when not dedicated to cleansing, guided meditations are such a profound journey that they can act as spiritual cleansing techniques.

Follow the guided meditations in this chapter to obtain a stronger connection to Metatron and to clear your energetic body.

Metatron Meditation for Clarity and Focus

This first meditation is for clarity and focus with Archangel Metatron. When you participate in a guided meditation, consider setting yourself up in a calm, relaxing environment with dim lighting, soothing music or sounds, and maybe some candles and soft-smelling incense. To strengthen your meditation, sit near or in front of the honoring space or altar that you have set up for Archangel Metatron.

To begin, sit comfortably in a chair or on the floor. Sit with your spine straight, and if you are in a chair, place your feet flat on the floor. If you are sitting on the floor, cross your legs and fold your hands in your lap. Close your eyes.

Take a deep breath in through your nose. Inhale until your lungs are fully inflated. Feel the breath entering your body, filling you with life. Exhale out from your mouth, feeling as your chest contracts and how the air leaves your body. Breathe in again through your nose, and breathe out through your mouth. Continue this breathing pattern.

Let your mind open, and seek the connection you have with the Archangel Metatron above your head, hovering around your crown chakra. Sense his presence with you and his light and energy flowing down into your mind and into your body.

Feel as Metatron's light clears the pathways and connections through your mind. As it does, your thoughts become less foggy. Let that clarity spread into your third eye chakra at your brow and into your eyes. Feel the cloudiness from your eyes clear, enhancing your focus.

Slowly start to release Metatron's energy and light. As you do, breathe out deeply, and release any negative energies and blockages that hinder your clarity and focus. Breathe in the love and light that Metatron bestows upon you, empowering your spiritual and physical body with the means to resolve difficult situations. Breathe out deeply.

Begin to become aware of your surroundings again. Wiggle your fingers, and blink your eyes a few times. Give thanks to Metatron for his wisdom and guidance during this meditation.

Light Body Meditation with Metatronic Energy

To get started, settle down in a calm, quiet place where you won't be disturbed. For this meditation, lie down and close your eyes. Let your mind and body relax with a series of deep, calming breaths. Feel your thoughts and your muscles unwind with each deep breath.

Find your connection to Metatron above your head at your crown chakra. Sense his presence there, and open your crown chakra to receive Metatronic energy, lighting up your crown chakra.

Feel that energy tingle through your scalp and into your mind, spreading down into your brow. There, imagine it lighting up your crown chakra.

Feel the tingling energy entering into your spine. Let it light up your spinal column, traveling into your throat and illuminating your throat chakra. Everything the energy touches inside of you opens and is cleared of blocks.

Lower, let that energy travel down your spine, settling in your chest and lighting up your heart chakra. Feel the way your heart flutters with life and Metatronic energy.

Traveling down your spine, the energy tingles lower to the base of your sternum. Envision it lighting up your solar plexus chakra before it travels down below your navel. In your belly, imagine the Metatronic energy clearing your sacral chakra, opening and illuminating it.

Feel the light travel all the way to the base of your spine, bringing energy to your root chakra, energizing your entire being, but also rooting you to yourself and to the earth. Visualize the light exiting your body from the base of your spine.

From a distance, envision all seven chakras and your spine lit up with Metatronic light energy. Feel how it creates tingles and flutters through your whole body, expanding your consciousness and opening you up to spread that transformative Metatronic energy into every aspect of your life.

With a deep breath, release the Metatronic energy from your chakras and spine. Intend the energy to travel through your physical and spiritual body.

Begin to come back to yourself and your physical body. Open your eyes, and refamiliarize yourself with your surroundings and your body. After this meditation, it would be a good idea to ground yourself by drinking a glass of cool water or by holding a rock or a piece of wood. Remember to give thanks to Metatron and his energy.

Divine Protection and Abundance Meditation

Get yourself settled in a quiet, relaxed space where you can be alone and uninterrupted. Sit in a chair or on the floor with your spine straight. If you're in a chair, press the soles of your feet firmly to the floor. If you are on the floor, cross your legs, and rest your hands in your lap. Close your eyes and relax.

Begin to breathe deeply, letting go of the physical world and opening your mind and body to Archangel Metatron. Become more and more relaxed with each long inhale and exhale.

Sense your connection to Metatron, opening you up and surrounding you with a bright, crystalline light that protects you from negative energies. With each breath, you're feeling safer and safer within your crystalline shield.

Now begin to imagine the forms of your friends and family surrounding you. Take a deep breath in, expanding your crystalline shield with more of Metatron's loving, protecting energy. Breathe out, extending that shield around your friends and family to protect them from negative energies.

Hold that safe space for all of them, feeling the love you all share and the power of Metatron connecting you on a spiritual level. With another deep breath, envision the crystalline light casting out negative and unneeded energies that no longer serve you or your friends or family.

Breathe in through your nose, spreading Metatron's crystalline light across your skin and through your body. Let it open your energetic channels and release old habits—bad ones that hold you back from your highest potential. Breathe out, releasing the light and your energetic shield.

Open your eyes, and begin to come back to yourself. Take your time reorienting with your surroundings and your physical body. Make sure to thank Metatron and his protection. Also, give thanks to the abundance of your friends and family.

Chapter 7: Chakras, Karma, and Crystals with Archangel Metatron

Aligning with Metatron's power and using it to change your life can also spread beyond just shifting your mindset and changing your own reality. You can focus this power more precisely through meditation and through the use of tools and spiritual devices that amplify it and that also resonate specifically with Metatron's energy.

More than that, you can target certain areas of your life—and your past lives—as a way to clear away karmic negativity and to further open your chakras. The spiritual body extends far beyond your current incarnation; it includes both past and future lives.

Chakras

The seven chakras that are most widely known in the human body rest along the spine. They are three dimensional, swirling pools of energy that are conjunction points for the physical body, emotional body, and spiritual body. They are where all the energetic and physical connections within you join and flow. When one chakra is blocked, it can throw the entire body out of balance and lead to illness and disease that can affect you physically, emotionally, and spiritually.

The seven chakras that are commonly associated with western spiritual practices are as follows:

- Crown Chakra - This one is situated above the head and associated with the cosmos, the color violet, and spiritual enlightenment.
- Third Eye Chakra - This energy point is located at the center of the brow and is associated with the color indigo, intuition, and clarity of thought.
- Throat Chakra - The throat chakra is located at the base of the throat, and it's associated with the color blue, communication with oneself and others, and truth.
- Heart Chakra - This is located at the center of the chest, directly on the sternum and is associated with the color green; it is the center of compassion, love, and acceptance.
- Solar Plexus Chakra - Located below the sternum and above the belly button, this energy point is associated with the color yellow and is the creative center of passion; it's the source of your personal power.
- Sacral Chakra - This chakra is situated below the belly button and above the pubic bone and is associated with the color orange; it is the emotional center and the center of passions and desires.
- Root Chakra - Situated at the base of the spine, the root chakra is associated with the color red and with your foundation, your survival instincts, and your connection to the material world.

The chakras are all connected to make up an energy network. When one is blocked or misaligned, spiritual garbage and energetic build-up can cause the others to become blocked, as well. When specific chakras are blocked, it leads to ailments that are associated with the source power of the chakra spiritually, emotionally, and physically. For example, a blocked root chakra can result in issues with the legs and feet, and also with eating disorders and paranoia.

By locating the root cause of an ailment and symptom, you can direct Metatron's clearing light to the chakra that is blocked. Sometimes, unblocking one will then lead you to others that are also blocked. Through different meditations, you can target a specific chakra for clearing, or you can clear all of them.

Chakras have to maintain balance, though. They can become blocked or underactive, and they can become overactive, as well. Metatron's power of clearing and transformation can keep your chakras balanced and aligned, helping you maintain optimal physical, emotional, and spiritual health.

If you are struggling with your mood, a physical injury or illness, or if you have any kind of stress, you may want to call upon Metatron to clear your chakras. You should try to refresh your chakras with vibrant energy and vitality.

Karma

Karma is the idea that whatever you put out into the universe—both positive and negative—returns to you threefold. This can be in the form of thoughts, emotions, actions, desires, goals, judgments, or anything else. All of these processes involve energy; they are produced by energy, and they send out energy. It is that energy which karma reacts and responds to.

Energy doesn't have the same limitations or boundaries as physical flesh or materials do. This means that it can often transcend space and time. As a result, karma can follow you from one incarnation to the next.

Sometimes, negatively-acquired karma from a previous incarnation can lead to struggles in your current life. The karmic balance can become so disrupted that it carries over, and you end up dealing with the consequences of negative karma from a past life in your current one. This can be incredibly frustrating, as no matter what you try to do in your current life, it may never be enough to balance the karmic scale.

There is a scientific explanation for this transfer of energy. The law of conservation of energy states that energy can be neither created nor destroyed—only transformed. So, when karmic energy is thrown out of balance in one life, it then transfers to the next until it can be changed into a less negative and harmful energy.

By entering a deep state of meditation with Metatron guiding you, you have the ability to channel his powers of transformation and clearing to help you shift the energy from your past karma. You can then stoke the revitalized energy with youthful, vibrant energy to make it purer and more lively.

Deep meditative states take time to practice and achieve. They are best done by listening to a repetitive sound, like a rattle, drum, or gong sound. By listening to a repeating tone and focusing on deep breathing, your mind can enter into that deep, deep state. Before you begin such a meditation, you'll want to invoke Metatron's power and set the intention to heal your past life karma through transformation.

Some of the visions and experiences you have in this deep meditation can even give you insight into what happened in your past lives or who you were.

Crystals

Crystals are some of nature's most stable structures. They are amazing catalysts for energy; they can refract, absorb, transform, transmute, and reflect it. Crystals are natural healing aids due to these abilities, and each crystal has a vibrational resonance that interacts with other energies.

Divine beings like angels are pure energy. Therefore, they also have an energetic resonance. These energy frequencies can coincide to work together, making each other stronger. There are hundreds of kinds of crystals, but there are a few that resonate strongly with Metatron.

Archangel Metatron has associations with watermelon tourmaline and with orange calcite.

Orange calcite is an orange-colored crystal that is associated with connecting the spiritual body and the physical world. It also enhances creativity and helps with emotional problems. Orange calcite also brings positive energy into areas of will and sexuality. It resonates with the root and sacral chakras.

Watermelon tourmaline is a green and pink stone that is closely connected to the heart chakra. It is exceptional at removing blocks and cleansing. It is a balancing stone that also aids in removing insecurities.

When working with any crystals, there comes a time when they need to be cleared. Just like a person's spiritual body can become gunked up with spiritual and energetic junk, a crystal can, too—especially ones used for healing and cleansing. There are a lot of ways to clear crystals, such as putting them under the sun, a full moon, or with another crystal, or by running them under water.

As a clearing and cleansing archangel, Metatron can also be called upon to cleanse crystals of built-up energy. You can ask him to cleanse any crystal; it mustn't only be one of the stones that are associated with him. To have Metatron clear a crystal, place the one in need of clearing on his altar or intention space. Invoke Metatron, and say a prayer to ask for his cleansing power on your crystals. You can even draw Metatron's cube on the crystals to help clear them.

Due to the balancing, cleansing, and spiritual nature of the stones, you can see why they are close to Metatron and his powers. Offering these stones to Metatron on your altar or in your intention space can connect his power with yours and with the stones. Using these crystals in meditations for karma and chakra-balancing is another way to enhance Metatron's frequency and use crystals in combination with his gifts.

Sacred Geometry and Metatron's Codes

All throughout history, the study of numbers, shapes, and mathematics has been a focal point for philosophers, scientists, and mathematicians. It has also been an important focus of spiritual study and archangelology. Sacred geometry is the study of these shapes as they occur in nature, like the spirals of a seashell and the hexagons in a honeycomb. Some of these natural shapes are found all the way down at the molecular level. They are often considered to be the keys to unlocking the secrets of the universe.

There are five shapes that are known as "Platonic solids", coined during the era of Ancient Greece and Plato. These sacred geometric shapes are the four-sided pyramid, six-sided cube, eight-sided octahedron, twelve-sided dodecahedron, and the twenty-sided icosahedron.

These platonic solids make up the Metatron's cube. This sacred geometric symbol is linked directly with Metatron and his powers. Along with the Platonic solids, Metatron's cube has thirteen circles in its composition. These circles are then interconnected with different straight lines. It is a complex geometric shape.

Metatron's cube represents the journey of energy through the universe and the balance within the universe. The lines through the circles represent the intimate tie between the feminine and the masculine. The lines show that everything in the universe is connected. If one string is tugged or flicked, that ripple effect reverberates through the entire shape.

You can use Metatron's cube as an aid for meditation, especially in practices that involve Metatron and his power. To use Metatron's cube during a meditation, you start at the center and follow the flow of energy through the entire shape. This can be soothing and unlock a lot of energies inside of you. If you imagine the cube rotating in a clockwise direction, it can become a cleansing energy that can be applied to anything, including your chakras and karma. This rotation also repels negative energies as well as promotes the flow of positive energy.

Along with its power to repel negative energy, Metatron's cube is also a very strong protective symbol. Painting it on walls or windows, and even wearing it as jewelry or getting it as a tattoo, can create a protective barrier or shield for you.

Chapter 8: How to Sense and Feel Metatron's Presence

When sensing Metatron's presence, you'll have to feel it out for yourself. A lot of angelologists and spiritualists have described their experiences with Archangel Metatron and other divine beings in great detail. Sometimes they are incredibly vivid. Other times, the visualization isn't as clear, but the feeling is still strong.

In the beginning, you might only get a sense of light or warmth when Metatron is around you. This can be a spontaneous feeling, or it can occur when you specifically call upon Metatron. Some people never consider working with archangels or with Metatron until they first feel his presence.

We did touch on what Metatron can feel like once you've contacted him or how he might send messages utilizing numbers and geometric shapes. However, there are more definitive ways to sense his presence.

The more you work with Metatron, the stronger your connection will be and the more vividly you will feel and sense him. The way archangels choose to reveal themselves varies from person to person. There might be some similarities to how Metatron appears, but spiritual entities can change depending on your energetic state and mindset, as well. It is possible that Metatron's appearance could even change over time as you progress on your spiritual journey.

If you are new to working with angels and spiritual entities, the presence of Metatron might not be as clear or obvious in the beginning. Often, Metatron can be seen as bright light. Sometimes, the light is white, but other common colors that Metatron's light appears in are orange, gold, and magenta.

Some spiritualists that work with Metatron describe seeing him in his angelic form with long, flowing hair in armor of silver and violet and also with big, fluffy wings. There is no right or wrong way to see angels.

Sometimes, it isn't so much about seeing Metatron as it is about feeling his presence around you. Metatron can be felt when you call on him with prayers, affirmations, and mantras. You can feel him when meditating on your own or when doing a guided Metatron meditation.

Getting familiar with knowing how you feel and sense Metatron is important, because then you'll be able to sense him both within and outside of meditation. You'll be more open to receiving wisdom and guidance, and you won't need to focus as much in order to sense when he is around you. This way, when his presence is spontaneous or he comes to you without being invoked first, you will know right away and be ready.

To familiarize yourself with how you can sense Metatron and how he presents himself to you, do a simple breathing meditation like the exercise from Chapter 2 in the "Meditations" section. By deep breathing and relaxing into your meditative state, you'll be able to reach out with your mind and feel for Metatron.

When you are beginning to contact and work with Metatron, keep a notebook with you. Write down whatever thoughts, feelings, and sensations you experience when reaching out to him. When you go back and analyze your notes, you can determine what seems right in terms of what Metatron feels like.

Working with divine entities is incredibly intuitive. When you sense Metatron, you'll know what he feels like. Having notations can really help you release your own inhibitions and trust your intuition. When you trust yourself, you'll also trust what you feel from Metatron.

Chapter 9: Write a Letter to Metatron

Since Archangel Metatron is a companion and guide, there are some exercises you can do that will bring the two of you closer together on a more personal level. Even though Metatron is a divine being, you should still build a relationship with him, both a working and personal one.

The simple act of writing letters to Archangel Metatron is a good practice for getting to know your angelic companion better. This is also one way to feel like you have a friend who listens to you. When you write to Metatron, it is important to approach it as if you were writing a letter to a friend of yours. You'll want to get comfortable with the idea of Metatron being a friend, not just a guide or helper. If you enjoy writing letters to Metatron, you might even want to reserve a journal or notebook for them.

What you'll need for this activity is a blank piece of paper (lined or unlined), an envelope, a pen, and sealing wax (optional). If you write lengthy letters, you might want to have some spare paper on hand in case you run out of space on the original sheet.

Write your letter like you are addressing it to a friend or loved one. Not only is this a chance for you to contact Metatron as a companion, but you can also use it for prayer requests for yourself, friends, family, and even pets. Try to balance a more casual nature with your prayer requests. This exercise is a healing one, but it is also meant to strengthen your relationship with Metatron, so try not to cram in every request you have. Write other things to your archangel companion, as well.

Let yourself get creative, and don't limit yourself to a single page. While Metatron might not write back, this is at least a way in which you can tell him more about yourself. The more he knows about you, the more your energies can align and you can do some incredible things together.

Once your letter is written, fold it up and put it in your envelope. Seal the envelope with the sealing strip, and then address it to Archangel Metatron. For an added flare and touch of magic, use sealing wax and a seal on the backside of the envelope.

Set the envelope on your altar or intention space for the remainder of the day or even overnight. Then, when you sit in the space, open the letter and read it aloud to Metatron. You might want to say a small prayer or do a quick meditation before you get started in order to invoke him and invite his presence.

While you are reading, don't just reiterate what you've put on the page. Give it life; give it tone, emotion, and style. Speak as though you are carrying on a conversation with a friend. This genuine communication will be another energetic exchange between you and Metatron as it reveals more about your personality.

After reading your letter, fold it back up and keep it, or fold it up and burn it. If you choose to burn the letter, do so in a contained, fireproof container, and make sure you have the necessary safety measures in place to prevent the fire from getting out of control. Also, don't hold the letter while burning it.

Over the next several days and weeks, keep an eye out for subtle changes that relate to your letter and the requests you made in it. Any time you notice one of these changes, make sure to say a "thank you" prayer to Metatron, or have a small "thanking ritual" to honor his participation.

Writing letters to your archangels is a good way to keep in communication with them. Between people and divine beings, sometimes the messages can get lost in translation, (literally). By writing somewhat regular letters to Metatron, you keep the line of communication open, and you might even notice that he starts to contact and communicate back.

Chapter 10: Metatron and Reiki

Did you know that Reiki healing can also be combined with angelic power, like with Metatron's power? If you're not familiar with Reiki, we strongly urge you to check out our book *Reiki Made Easy*. It will help introduce you to the healing power of Reiki. If you're already familiar with Reiki, some of this chapter will be a review for you, but it will still be good to learn how to combine Reiki and Metatron.

Reiki originates from Japan and is a traditional energy healing method that utilizes static hand positions, power symbols, and universal energy to heal intuitively. The word Reiki, when translated, means "universal energy". A Reiki practitioner receives attunements from their Reiki Master to become more aligned with the energetic frequencies that Reiki exists on.

There are a lot of different Reiki traditions and paths to follow. The most well-known tradition is Usui Reiki or traditional Reiki. This tradition was practiced for thousands of years in zen monasteries and then made more prominent and available by Dr. Usui in the mid-1800s. Dr. Usui elaborated on the then-known Reiki methods and made them available to the public. He also taught the practice, and one of his students brought Reiki healing to the US in the 1920s.

Reiki practitioners channel universal energy through their bodies and into the body of a client, patient, or even into themselves. Unlike other energy healing modalities, Reiki is intuitive. It goes to where it is needed; the Reiki practitioner doesn't direct the energy. However, practitioners can amplify the energy through the use of Reiki power symbols, crystals, and even with the archangels.

On the flip side, your work with Archangel Metatron could be enhanced with the use of Reiki energy and Reiki power symbols. Depending on what level of Reiki you're attuned to or your interest in the practice, you might never get to the point of using the Reiki power symbols. Depending on the tradition you follow, getting attuned to the symbols usually happens around Reiki level II.

Metatron's cube is a powerful geometric shape that also resonates with Reiki. You can draw the symbol (or Metatron's cube) or trace an already-drawn symbol three times while saying its name. This will infuse it with Reiki energy, enhancing the cube's already potent qualities.

The crystals that resonate with Metatron are also tools that can be made stronger with Reiki, thus bringing out the archangel's qualities.

Crystals used to invoke and work with Metatron will also respond favorably to Reiki energy. Draw a Reiki symbol on them, or infuse them with Reiki before or during a meditation/ritual in which you are working with Metatron.

To combine Metatron's power with Reiki during meditations for an enhanced spiritual experience, invoke both Reiki and Metatron during meditations and prayers. If you perform Reiki healing sessions, invoke Metatron with a prayer or mantra to join you and guide you. Your healing will be stronger, and you might even receive divine messages from Metatron to pass along to your client or whoever you are performing a healing session on.

When you learn and understand different methods of spiritual healing and the application of spiritual energy, you'll discover different ways of combining them for a more powerful experience. It isn't always about power, though. Sometimes, you will want to combine spiritual energies to utilize different qualities and characteristics.

Chapter 11: Spending Time with Metatron

When you choose to walk a spiritual path that includes the companionship of archangels, you have the option to truly transform who you are. A lot of spiritualists will call upon the archangels when they need them, but to truly gain the gifts and benefits of Metatron, you need to fully embody him in your everyday life.

While a lot of the exercises and meditations we discussed in previous chapters were targeted toward healing or other specific goals like clearing negative energy, you can also call upon Metatron and his divine light in every other aspect of your life.

There are many ways to incorporate Metatron's guidance into your daily life, such as by infusing your food with positive, divine light from Metatron. Not only does this cleanse any potential toxins from your food, but it helps ensure you gain the maximum nutrition possible. It also gives you a positive energy boost from the food you eat. Infusing food with Metatron's power can be done through meditation, prayer, and the use of Metatron's cube.

The lessons that Metatron teaches about karma, positivity, and transformation should also be carried with you throughout your daily life. The concept of perception and how your perception can shape your reality is really going to aid you in transforming your own world.

So, when you think of Metatron being a part of your life, don't think of how his wisdom can change you; rather, think of how you can change your thoughts and actions to embody his wisdom. Then, make the conscious effort to transform yourself into someone who lives by Metatron's teachings.

If Metatron becomes an archangel who you have a close connection with, we definitely recommend making an altar or intention space dedicated to him as it will be easier to connect and commune with him regularly. Furthermore, carrying a piece of that altar with you, such as a crystal offering or a picture of Metatron, will help keep him close to you at all times. Keep the altar object in your pocket, in your purse, or in a backpack. As long as you know where it is, then you will be able to feel his presence and power.

Affirmations are a good way to include Metatron into all aspects of your life, but you should also practice reaching out and sensing him nearby during any event. If you ever find yourself in a situation that is uncomfortable or confusing, reach out to Metatron for guidance. Whether it is a problem at work, an issue in your romantic relationship, or problems with your family, look to Metatron to light the way for you. He can be great at offering transformative ideas to resolve issues and clear away negativity.

That being said, there doesn't need to be some kind of conflict or issue for you to call upon Metatron. Just having him around you during your day-to-day activities can empower you, giving you strength and hope.

As an archangel, Metatron wants to assist humanity. His divine light is all around you, and with some practice, you can learn to feel it in everything you do. This is what it means to spend time with Metatron and carry him with you on your spiritual journey. He can assist with the big and the small, and he can be by your side through everything. This is the kind of divine spiritual relationship that will forever fill you with light and give you the guidance to become the best version of yourself that you can be. In doing so, you can achieve all your goals and conquer some amazing new feats.

Conclusion

Working with any of the archangels is a great gift and venture into your own spirituality. Spiritual entities and divine beings have vast knowledge and wisdom that we are only just starting to understand and grasp. Metatron is an archangel who stands out from the rest in many ways. His powers of clearing negativity, balancing, and transformation have become great assets to spiritualists and angelologists.

By unlocking Metatron's gifts, you can free yourself to explore new options and opportunities that can change the life you live. Metatron works hard to transform energies and circumstances in your current life and even in your past lives. Inviting him in as a divine entity for companionship and guidance will give you a friend to walk this spiritual path with.

Now that you have finished this book and you have all the tools you need to get started working with Archangel Metatron, begin simply by using some of the easier meditations and by looking for signs of divine presence in your life. Even if you have experience working with other archangels, when you begin working with Metatron, start slow and with clear intentions.

If your mind and spirit are already aligned with other archangels, it can be hard to focus on a new angel with whom you have yet to align. Therefore, start out slow regardless of whether archangels are new to you. As you get more immersed in working with Metatron, you'll be able to align with his energy more readily.

Just for taking an interest in archangels and what Metatron can do for you, you're well on your way to transforming your life. You're ready to clear away the negative energies that hold you back. Take Archangel Metatron with you into your career, personal life, goals, dreams, and desires.

Change the reality of your dreams and your everyday life with Metatron's powerful manifestation and visualization abilities. Let him be your guide and companion on this journey into a new life and a new you.

If you enjoyed this book and found the information helpful, please leave a favorable review so that other people can find this book as well. Make sure to check out some of the other books I've written that elaborate on crystals, Reiki, and other archangels so you can continue to expand your horizons and spiritual ventures.

Good luck with your endeavors and transforming your life and well-being!

References

Amira Celon oracle card readings. (5, July 2017). *IMMEDIATE cord cutting & shielding ***POWERFUL HEALING**** YouTube. https://www.youtube.com/watch?v=8m1qBRLHdik

Archangel secrets. (2020). *5 steps to get angelic shielding connecting with Archangel Metatron.* https://archangelsecrets.com/connect-with-archangel-metatron

Ask-angels.com. (2020). *The ultimate guide to archangel Metatron | angel of life.* https://www.ask-angels.com/channeled-messages/archangel-metatron/

Cooper, D. (2020). *Angels with Diana Cooper: Archangel Metatron.* Soul & spirit. https://www.soulandspiritmagazine.com/angels-diana-cooper-archangel-metatron/

Guided meditations by Lisa Beachy. (17, July 2011). *Archangel Metatron - receive focus and clarity meditation video.* YouTube. https://www.youtube.com/watch?v=MbwXf2wOENo

Healing crystals. (2020 a). *Calcite - orange calcite natural chunks.* https://www.healingcrystals.com/Calcite_-_Orange_Calcite_Natural_Chunks__Mexico___Canada_.html#:~:text=Orange%20Calcite%20helps%20integrate%20the,of%20the%20will%20and%20sexuality.

Healing crystals. (2020 b). *Watermelon tourmaline.* https://www.healingcrystals.com/Watermelon_Tourmaline_Articles_22.html#:~:text=Watermelon%20Tourmaline%20works%20with%20the,Yang%20together%20in%20one%20crystal.

Hluchan, K. T. (2018, March 21). *The archangels and their divine responsibilities.* Patch. https://patch.com/pennsylvania/horsham/archangels-their-divine-responsibilities

Pictures sourced by: https://pixabay.com/

See u in history/mythology. (15, November 2019). *Archangel Metatron - the lord of angels - angels and demons - see u in history.* YouTube. https://www.youtube.com/watch?v=obnUL892zGw

Soul flower. (2020). *Chakra chart meanings.* Soul flower: finding soul. https://www.soul-flower.com/blog/chakra-chart-meanings/

The legends of history. (8, May 2020). *Archangel Metatron: the prince of presence [Book of Enoch] (angels & demons explained).* YouTube. https://www.youtube.com/watch?v=j5vyXx7YSys

The secret of tarot. (2020). *Archangel Metatron.* tsot. https://thesecretofthetarot.com/archangel-metatron/

Thomas, S. S. (25, September 2018). *Color magick: A beginner's guide to harnessing the power of every color.* allure. https://www.allure.com/story/color-magic-witchcraft-meanings-guide

Book 5: Archangelology: Jophiel

How To Burst With Creativity, Grow From The Past, & Skyrocket Your Beauty

(Archangelology Book Series 5)

Angela Grace

Introduction

In the busy and bustle of my day, I realized that I needed to figure out some of my burdens. This would not only improve my mood, but it would help me to shed the weight of the modern and often frantic world.

With my mind calm and my incense burning, I reached out, and in my mind I was now in a field and surrounded by yellow and pink flowers, the smell of lavender and roses swirling in the air. I am standing alone, but only for a moment, as a divine woman arrives with brilliant wings of light, a sight of purity, bathed in a beam of golden yellow.

As I stand before her, the beauty of God, I must admit that I am in awe of this divine being so graceful, yet so powerful. She is so beautiful and serene, but the truth is that I know her, I feel her power in myself and in the very beauty all around me, and it is all as it should be.

She is both an angel, an old friend, a companion, and a confidant.

Her eyes have a radiant glow, clear and strong, and they shine like marbles of the finest glass and resonate with strength and love that enlightens my soul, my energy.

She is the one who brings to us all the messages that can heal our confidence, our magnificence, that can guide and empower, that can heal and help us rediscover our truth.

As I stood there basking in her magnificent garden of pink and yellow flowers, she is bathed in glorious light. Her presence alone makes me feel refreshed, revitalized as if I have rediscovered myself after a long absence, as if the pains and wounds of the world have been washed away in a gentle stream.

She is the most beautiful sight I have ever beheld, and I am humbled in her grace, yet she makes it clear to me that I am worthy of sharing this moment with her.

But who is the glorious, beautiful being? Who is this winged muse whose simple presence inspires in me the confidence to write a grand opus?

Jophiel is her name, and she has filled my life, my soul with energy that has revitalized me, redirected me and allowed me to grow beyond the limitations I had placed on myself in the past. She has taught me to trust, to love, to show compassion, and to understand that even in negative situations there is a positive opportunity to learn and grow.

And this is where we begin, by sharing the wonder of her light, the teachings of her energy, and how she can help us, guide us to better places in our lives, how she can teach us to better love ourselves and heal our souls of any wounds.

Jophiel is an archangel, and by channeling her we can grow, by communing with her we can learn to love ourselves, and by enveloping ourselves in her wisdom we can begin to really see our true selves.

How is all this possible? How can you draw on her teachings and her divine power? That is what I am here to help you to see. That is what we are going to uncover and learn together.

As surely as she speaks to me, and I receive her messages both in the everyday world and the dream world, she is surely reaching out to you as well.

We are going to look at how she is already with you, sending you messages every day, and all the little things you can do, change, and adopt to build a better divine connection to this most beautiful of archangels.

And when we reach the end of the journey, we will reveal a bigger truth, the answer to the question, "How can archangels bring us closer to the divine?"

Chapter 1: Jophiel the Beautiful

She is the archangel of beauty, of wisdom, of understanding, and of judgment. Her name is Jophiel.

Quite literally her name means the Beauty of God, and in her presence, it is easy to see why, and like most angels, she is able to manifest in a number of forms. She is always beautiful, radiant, kind, and enchanting.

Jophiel is not just beautiful, though. She is, in fact, paradise in the physical form, a beautiful and radiant being. She is an angel about whom poets have written, and in our dreams of beauty, we see only a glimmer of her grace.

She is breathtaking and awe-inspiring, yes, but she is also more than just her beauty. She is the feeling of inner beauty and inner clarity in all of us. She is the moment of seeing the beauty around us and understanding them on a spiritual level.

She is the calm and the quiet confidence we each have the potential to discover, and she is always there gently encouraging us to pursue the best version of who we are.

Yet unlike so many of the other archangels, she does not have to be heavy-handed. It is that soft whisper, the gentle assured touch that she wields to help us on our path, where her strength comes from.

Jophiel and Wisdom

Jophiel is a wise and creative archangel, an ally who can help us to focus, showing us the path that is most kind to our souls, allowing us to grow, and teaching us the ways of interpreting the world and its energies as we may not have done alone.

She also uses her calming wisdom to show us how better to understand ourselves, our friends, partners, and relationships as she is compassionate and loving. And this is what she can help us with, our own compassion not just for others, but for ourselves and our surroundings.

Kindness begets kindness, even when the act itself may seem cruel, such as walking away from a relationship. We all know too well how a relationship can turn toxic, and in her wisdom, Jophiel will send us signals that a relationship is not serving us and can be harming our souls, and at this point, the kindest thing to do for one's self is to walk away.

Because we must remember that if our compassion is not sought, it may be met with resistance, and while we must remain compassionate and available as much as possible, it is OK to walk away as we can always reunite later.

Jophiel and Language

It is said that Jophiel was there at the beginning of all creation. She was there to bless us with love and integrity, but there was also another gift.

You see, Jophiel was there with the first people and gave us all our language. And as language is such an important part of our knowledge and our identity, this is a gift we must always cherish.

In this way, it is only too clear why this task would have been held in such importance to Jophiel. Through language we learn to speak, then to write, sing, create, play, and also to love and respect, care, and communicate.

This is a powerful gift we received, and this is such an awesome level of energy that she affects. She is in the very songs we sing, in the very beauty of words themselves.

This is why her wisdom and knowledge of our realm cannot be denied. She is the one through which song and story draw all meaning, and through which she connects with all aspects of who we are.

This is also why music is considered a universal language. Jophiel has influence over the creative aspects of our world, bringing inspiration into us, and making music resonate with us all. Even if the music is different or in a different language to the audience, it will still resonate.

Jophiel's Creativity

Jophiel is the patron angel of artists, and the creative part of ourselves can help us to become closer to her, to really begin to feel her in everything we do. From scrapbooks to paintings, books to songs, Jophiel is that compassionate and creative muse in our souls.

By creating and embracing that artistic side, we can begin to build that relationship. Try to make time in your life to draw, write, take beautiful photographs, and embrace little moments of creativity that can help you to see the world as beautiful as she wants you to see it.

Throughout our growing understanding of her love for us, we will come to see how important art and creativity are to Jophiel and to our relationship with her.

We can also begin to use creativity as a way of reaching out to her, asking her for divine inspiration and her blessing in the very things we are creating.

And by creating something with love and beauty, we are embracing her and allowing others to share in her love.

Little Projects

You may think that you don't have a creative bone in your body, so it is fortunate that creativity comes from the soul. We are all capable of creating; we just may not realize where our inspiration is drawing us.

Scrapbooks are a great mini-project to start on your quest to be creative. These make great gifts for a friend or loved one, especially as these can be used to trigger and envelop an emotional connection.

If scrapbooks aren't quite right, there are a great many other projects you can begin to really get the most out of the creative energy of the soul. I'll cover a few suggestions here that anyone can try, which in turn encourage that creativity.

One easy project would be to start a journal. This is a great idea for all kinds of reasons, but mostly because it is so flexible. Whether it's part scrapbook, part recipe book, or part outline for a memoir, this could very well lead you to find the truest form of your creativity.

Another favorite among creative people is cooking. Simple recipes are good and do the job, but trying new foods is a creative endeavor that really suits those with more analytical souls. As we look at flavors we liked and didn't like, that then can lead to creating new dishes.

Try drawing, more specifically doodling, idly allowing the pen to make a shape, then adding to it, then adding around it, now a different pen. Not only can this end up being quite artistic, but it can also be very relaxing indeed.

I, of course, write. It is a way of channeling my energy, and therefore the energy of the divine Jophiel, who is a muse, into the words I write.

With her inspiration, a great many grand tales have been told, and storytelling has become one of the most important parts of how we as people both interpret and deal with the world around us.

Every film, television show, book, or legend started with written words, and words carry immense power. This is especially true when we are writing about our emotional and spiritual truth. This helps us to purge our souls of bad energy, and this, like all creative endeavors, allows us to channel that into a good vibration.

Chapter 2: A Flash of Color

As we come to understand more about Jophiel and her influences in our everyday world, we will want to know how to read the signs she is sending to us, the vibrations and energies she is sending through our divine spark, that energy that links us together.

All angels resonate with colors, smells, and sounds, which in turn resonate with us on the spiritual plane.

Jophiel vibrates with the color magenta, and shades of pink and peach that are vibrant and beautiful, but her fire is yellow. This combination of vibrant and beautiful colors is why she is represented in our world by the smell of flowers.

This, with her gentle nature, can make her the most calming force among the angels, but she is still a strong and empowering influence. Her signals are all around us, and once we begin to understand what they are, we can start to see what they are telling us.

We'll look at some of the things that indicate her presence, and some of the things that we draw from her presence, without even realizing it.

Colors and Smells

She is the beauty of flowers, so the sighting of a rose may be what is telling us Jophiel is sending us a message. This is an important part of our journey, to understand the messages we are given.

She is the light smell of flowers in the air, of jasmine, lavender, and oranges. These smells tell us that she is nearby. These smells and the colors that go along with them mean that she is sending you her love and her energy.

Enveloping ourselves in these things is a great way to leave her messages and to invite her into your life more.

The colors of pink and yellows can also show us that we are receiving messages from Jophiel. Bright sunrises or sunsets, colors that invoke reactions like flowers, could be telling us to watch for an opportunity or a change.

She communicates to us in these and many other loving and beautiful sensations, such as feelings of intense inner serenity and moments of profound calm.

Confidence

Jophiel wants you to be happy, and she wants you to pursue the things that make you happy. Part of that is that she can make you feel more confident, more empowered in yourself, and in your abilities.

She can help you realize the potential in yourself that you never realized you had, a creative and compassionate potential, a calm and assertive potential. Jophiel is sending you the signs to see where these energies and skills exist.

This can be an enticing smell, a familiar song, a day where the sunrise is a soft pink, or a cool breeze on a day filled with stresses. These are all signs that you are doing the right thing, that you are on the right path.

Feeling suddenly calm and confident is Jophiel holding your hand and helping to guide you through the thing you once feared. And as with everything, practice will help, but those first feelings of sudden confidence are energy she is sending you.

Inspiration

Confidence is only part of the creative process. Inspiration is another part of what Jophiel sends to us. Sometimes when dreaming or daydreaming, our best ideas ignite as if from nowhere. This is the gentle hand of Jophiel pulling back the curtain on what we yearned to see or say.

By revealing something that our souls wanted to express, something that was locked away, she is showing us that it is the right time to begin that project or lifestyle change.

Inspiration can also be to physical, to get fit or go for a jog. Inspiration is a message from "the unknown" to pursue something we realize we want. Of course, there is no mystery; the "unknown" is Jophiel.

The gentle and assured strength of conviction you feel when you realize that yes, you can do it, is her speaking to your soul.

Quiet Strength

There will be times in life where we are feeling the pressure of dealing with often chaotic amounts of information and noise. In these times we can begin to really see how much Jophiel supports us.

Jophiel is love and wisdom, and she is the feeling of hope we begin to feel when we are overwhelmed. She is the strength that quietly tells us that it is going to be OK.

Every time we are struggling, something will whisper to us that we are able to handle anything the world throws at us. This gently reassuring, almost motherly voice is Jophiel.

Hers is a strength that is understated and controlled. It is a gentle reassurance, and unlike many more forceful archangels, Jophiel is more drawn to help you to heal and benefit the self while also embracing and giving love to others.

Adopting this Strength

One thing we can learn from Jophiel is how to adopt a calmer, more composed strength. Believing in your convictions should be front and center, and being fearless is also important. However, being calm is of utmost priority.

Speak softly, calmly, openly, and with love. Allow yourself time to breathe, to dispel emotional reactions, to weigh the various parts of the message you need to convey, and to decide how you want it to be heard.

This is how Jophiel speaks to us, and it is born of her love, so using this with those around us is an important skill we can learn from her.

Chapter 3: Serene Grace

Jophiel is always around us, and we are always linked to her. We can see her message even in times where our situation may not feel blessed. She is there gently holding our shoulder or hand, gently guiding us.

We can look closer at our situations and really begin to understand the almost motherly love that she is sending to us, telling us that it is OK. All we must do is begin to look at what she is teaching us. We also can begin to change things in our every day, to begin embracing the ideas of beauty that she is channeling into us.

This is Jophiel's grace, the true core of her power, and the thing that sets her apart from other archangels. Many arguments can be won by the compassionate, using logic and wisdom to counter aggression and anger.

This quiet strength that I have touched on is evident time and again in how Jophiel communicates with us and her influence on us.

Calming

As we may find confidence in times of uncertainty, the same is true of a sudden calm in times of upheaval. This is all a sign that she is aiding us when we need her grace.

Jophiel is calm, gentle, kind, and compassionate. She is the inner voice telling you that what you feel is wrong needs to be discussed, and she is showing you how with her calm and compassionate being.

You will feel her in a soft breeze, whispering to you that you can talk to your colleague, friend, or even lover about something bothering you. By embracing her calm and compassionate manner, we too can learn to deal with any issues with her gentle strength guiding us.

She is the sudden, undeniable calm that washes over us in moments where all the noise has grown a little too loud. We feel the air enter our lungs and slowly exhale. That is her calming influence doing its work over our physical stresses.

What we need to do now is consider how we can build on this calming influence by doing things in our lives to encourage calm.

Tidying

An old adage that I want to bring to your attention, as it seems important here, "a tidy house is a tidy mind." I not only believe this is true, but I know this is one of the messages we are receiving.

Clutter can lead to feeling overwhelmed, and Jophiel may be telling us that it is time to tidy and remove that clutter, to reorganize our lives not just with the physical clutter, but also the mental clutter.

We may receive this message through smells and colors around us, through hints in our lives that we have come to understand. Jophiel is a gentler archangel than most, and her way is not as brash as others. It is through that subtle manner that she is able to teach us grace.

And in this grace, we may realize that a pile of old letters or that bookshelf needs to be organized, tidied to help us clear our physical space, and that burdens of negative emotion can be tidied in the same way to help cleanse our minds.

Reorganizing a book or DVD collection, dusting our shelves, throwing open the window, and throwing out the excess is a great exercise. It's one that many people already do once a year, usually referring to it as spring cleaning.

This act of ridding ourselves of clutter is something that we have needed as people for a long time. This is a message from Jophiel.

Honesty

Jophiel represents not just beauty, but also honesty. Integrity is as much of what defines her as the love and compassion she shows us. This is one of the core lessons we can learn from her, one of the core messages she wants us to understand.

If we are to clear our minds of the burdens of negativity, we have to realize that it is OK to let go as that energy does not serve us, does not matter to us. And this honesty is one of our most important tools. It is where we decide what is important to us, what we can embrace, and what we are cast off.

This can be done with compassion and love. And with this honesty, it will bring us closer to Jophiel.

Embracing this honesty can also allow her to show you the things you are yearning for that you may not have even realized. Be it something physical or spiritual, she can show us through her love what we are missing in our souls.

Grace

Grace is more than just the way we move. Grace is a concept of how we walk, talk, and think of ourselves, but also how we treat others.

It is calm and composed, kind even in the face of difficulty. It is composure and honesty. This is an important part of building the best connection to Jophiel as we can.

It can be the grace to know when to try or to say goodbye. One of the most important ways we can better ourselves and connect with Jophiel is to have the grace to be kind to those who are not kind to us.

Banish Ignorance

A big part of Jophiel's messages of love and reassurance is that she knows that we are all equal, all our bodies and souls are loved the same by her and by God. Being ignorant of another person's feelings and beliefs is not what Jophiel sends in her divine message for us.

She is telling us to love all those around us, even when it may seem that the person does not deserve compassion. The simple truth is that we are not to judge others. That is not our job. Our role in this life is to help bridge the gap between the divine and the human.

Even those who do not want to see the truth of archangels need our love and support, possibly most of all.

Chapter 4: Blessings and Healing

Jophiel is beautiful, honest, and a beacon of integrity. She is also a being of healing, and this is an important part of the process.

You may have had low self-esteem, but suddenly found yourself washed over with positive thoughts and energy. This is the word of Jophiel; she wants you to see the blessings in your everyday life.

She wants you to marvel at a painting or book, to envelop yourself in the things that make you happy. She is the moment of sudden calm, of peace in our minds. In those moments, Jophiel is sending you messages that it is OK to relax, to let the energy go.

This, the state of healing, is one of her many blessings to you. It is OK to have hardships and stresses, we all have them, but all that time Jophiel was giving you the strength to persevere, to endure. She is the one who helps you rest and heal when you need it.

And not just in the physical sense, but in the emotional sense, too. When you have had times of sadness bookended by a moment of profound clarity and joy, that is Jophiel speaking to you, whispering that it is OK and that you are going to get better.

Her blessings are the calmness and grace with which we discuss a disagreement with a lover or let go of an old friendship that has grown sour. It is the casting out of all that negative energy from pain and sadness and replacing it with fresh and new hope, love, and calmness.

Her healing can help us relax our minds and our bodies, removing our spiritual clutter in much the same way we have begun to remove the physical debris and embrace our new start, our new chapter.

A great way of understanding the many blessings we are receiving is to write a journal, to commit positive thoughts to a positive place so that they are there as a reference. Once we have embraced our creative energy from Jophiel, we can begin to do this in a powerful way.

Committing these positive thoughts to a physical and creative outlet will let us heal and help us to see better how Jophiel communicates not just to us, but through us.

In this way, we will come to realize that we are, and always have been, worthy of the love and happiness we seek in others and in ourselves.

She will show us that by seeing our inner beauty and waking an outer beauty, it will affect the positive energy of others around us. This is her greatest blessing.

Making Space for Love

Self-love, and the love of those around us, is a big lesson that Jophiel is trying to teach us, and it is something critically important to our ability to heal. Jophiel wants us to heal and to love. To do that, we need to make room for these things in our lives.

We need to see that toxic people in our lives take up more room than those we love. By making the decision to put ourselves first and cast these people out, we can make more time for the good and loving influences with less negativity and drama.

Not only is this what we may need, but it could also be the trigger for those negative individuals to change. As we begin to see Jophiel as being as wise as she is, she may be using us to help bring her messages to those unwilling to accept them.

Pets

While this is not a requirement, I find that pets are a great source of healing energy and calm, where they can love unconditionally. In building this bond we can really begin to understand what true connections are.

I think rescue pets are especially good for the soul if you consider that you are helping that pet to heal from untold emotional distress. The journey to your bond and companionship is one that will help you understand the world and see the beauty of all things, even when hardship had to be experienced to get there.

If you have a local animal shelter, volunteering your time to help can be greatly satisfying work. It certainly is worth exploring since compassion is such an important part of our connection with Jophiel.

Again this is by no means a requirement, but when we learn to love and heal others, both humans and our animal friends, we learn to better love ourselves.

Healing

When we hurt ourselves, wounds need time to heal. While this is something we can see in the physical sense, it is something we cannot see, but feel, when we are healing emotionally and spiritually.

Jophiel is a healer. She is there beside us helping us in the time we are resting our souls, be it through meditation or cleansing our space and energies.

It cannot be stated enough that we also need to introspectively allow ourselves to be loved, to forgive mistakes we've made, to let go of the negativity, and to begin to rebuild ourselves in a purely positive light.

Part of healing is letting go of the past, and this is daunting at first. Jophiel will help you, filling your life with confidence and hope as you begin to let go of the old wounds and baggage.

Misery Loves Company

One of the great pitfalls of being a spiritual being is that our energies are affected by those around us, and at this moment I just wanted to talk about the adage that "misery loves company," and explain how we should deal with it.

When we say that misery loves company, we are actually saying that those who feel sad or angry may feel better by bringing down the moods and energies of others around them. They are happy to make others feel as low as they do.

It is something we see time and again as a society, and as spiritual beings, it is a delicate balance to strike, both trying to help others and to avoid allowing people to bring our mood down.

What I would always suggest is to try to help the person in the first instance, but gently and with compassion. Upon rejection, take a step back, re-energize and then return later to this person. Offer that individual an open door should he ever want help.

At this time, I would then always advise you to put yourself and your energy first. You can't help those who aren't ready to accept your help. By making it clear that you're ready when they are, you can take your energy and keep yourself at a distance.

Toxic situations are going to exist, but that doesn't mean we have to allow them to affect us. It is true that we could be exposed to negativity, but learning to heal is learning how to handle situations like this.

Think about it like this: Sometimes we have to remove a meal out of the ovens, and you may accidentally burn your finger. The next time you approach the same oven, you make sure you are protected. This is much the same as what we need to do to help those who perhaps do not want our help.

Chapter 5: Beautification

Our home is the physical representation of our true selves, and sometimes clutter can get in the way. This isn't the only thing in our lives that we may need to change in order to feel calmer and more enveloped by Jophiel's love.

Beautification is the act of making something more beautiful, making it more individual, or just removing the clutter from it. The act of beautification is one that we can undertake to bring us closer to Jophiel.

This could be something as simple as moving our furniture so it lets air and energy flow easier through our homes. It could be redecorating, reorganizing, or even restoring.

Taking something old, and loved, and breathing new life into it is the same as healing. By embracing an act like this, we can bring Jophiel more into our lives, to give ourselves more of an understanding of the beauty she sees in us.

It could even mean dressing in a way that is a better indicator of the true self, embracing the confidence which she has begun to bestow upon us and the grace which we can draw from her energy.

Little Things to Try

One of the greatest soothing acts is the act of restoration, the healing of an object. I know Jophiel likes both to heal and to inspire creativity, so one thing to try would be to buy an old desk, sand it down, and repaint it, or to buy an old chair and recover it.

Incorporating those vibrant pinks and bright, beautiful colors can draw Jophiel's energy into the object, into the room it inhabits. This restoration will allow you to bless that thing or place with her love and her energy.

Take old books and recover them, or repurpose old items for a new life, like turning an old garden watering can into a plant pot. All these small creative outlets that beautify your home and your space will help you get in touch with Jophiel's positive energy.

There's a practice from China called feng shui, in which the homeowner arranges the home in such a way that energy can flow through it easily. This is done using maths, angles, and a special compass.

Laying out your furniture in a comfortable way is one of the things you can do to make your home beautiful or inviting, so researching feng shui could be a fun way of broadening this knowledge.

Beautification of Self

You are beautiful, you are as intended, and most of the world looks upon you as the beautiful person that you are. While I know that you may not always feel beautiful, the truth is you have not learned how to embrace your beauty.

Perhaps the confines of the normal dress make you uncomfortable. Jophiel is drawing you to a style you are too shy to try, but embrace it, lean into what makes you who you are. Be the beautiful and empowered version of yourself that Jophiel sees; she will send you the signs.

You may feel a tingle in your back at the sight of certain shoes or perhaps a coat. This is Jophiel telling you that it is OK for you to buy this item, to embrace this part of you.

Another thing to consider is that others may only see how you hold yourself, how you hold your energy. Nervous, chaotic energy is like being near roadwork. All that noise and energy is unflattering and causes those around that energy to not appreciate what is happening.

Calm and quiet confidence is the embodiment of Jophiel, and learning how to channel nervous energy into a calm and peaceful aura is a powerful tool. All the while, this is what Jophiel is encouraging you to do.

Once a day, stand before a mirror and tell yourself that you are strong, you are calm, and you are beautiful. Own it, and soon you will know how you feel, the way others respond to you will begin to change.

Beautification of the Home

Keeping a house tidy is one thing, but making a house beautiful is an entirely different undertaking. Making the space calm with easy energy and airflow is just Step One.

Adding plants that bring color and decorating with stones and colors that brighten and energize the house will make your home bristle with positivity.

Removing unrequired furniture, bringing in candles, softer lights, lighter curtains, and repapering or repainting the walls are little changes to the way a home looks and feels. They can, however, draw beauty into the home and make it more relaxing, which is when we are more susceptible to positive vibrations.

I mentioned feng shui earlier, but another home improvement style I wanted to touch on is minimalism. This is the idea of only keeping things that are essential, having as few colors and items as possible in the space you are using. In this way you are reducing the noise and clutter of the space, allowing the energy and air to move around it more freely.

This approach is visually simplistic, however, I know that this kind of approach to decor is not for everyone. It is certainly something that can be looked at and researched by those looking to improve their home, especially if they feel crowded.

The Things We Say

Being beautiful is one thing, but being kind is something else entirely. One of the core concepts of angelic love is that it is unconditional and is for everyone. So speaking to or treating someone with anything else is not the divine intent.

The way we speak and the words we use are how people will come to know us. If we are dishonest and cruel, it will show just as surely as the reverse is true. If you are saying positive things and you mean those words with your very soul, the energy of those words will ring true.

This is the truth of receiving messages, too. We can only accept the truth if we are ready to hear it. This is why whenever Jophiel speaks to us, we know that she is telling the truth because all of her messages are wrapped in love and compassion.

Love and compassion are the way we should treat others and the way we should speak to them. Once people come to realize that this is simply who you are, they will become more receptive to the positivity around you.

Choosing When to Say

One of the things that happen all too often in our modern world is when a kind person tries to help someone who needs help, but is too eager to help. This is a truth we must be ready to understand, that not all people are truly ready to accept the help of others.

Sometimes, our best intentions can lead to negative reactions from those who are simply not at the right stage of their journeys to accept our help or to even know that they need it.

Offering someone an open invitation to a chat or a sympathetic ear should they need it is fine, but make sure you take from Jophiel's lead. Wait for the right moment, and then approach the moment with the right energy.

One thing to keep in mind is how emotional the person is. Extremely angry or sad people can react badly to offered help even if it is what they need.

It's Not What You Say

Jophiel is not heavy-handed with her messages, and there is a reason for this. Sometimes you can say something that is true, but it's said too bluntly, leading to the adage "it's not what you say, but it's how you say it."

This is to say that while what you are saying is correct, the individual you are speaking to may not want to hear it in that way. Much like how Jophiel is gentle with us, guiding us to the answers on our own terms and in our own times, we must learn to guide others to their own truth, without being too forceful.

Even if what you wanted to say is the truth that they need to hear, we must always understand that sometimes the truth can hurt.

I'd liken it to drinking coffee when it is too hot. Sure, you're still going to get the coffee, but you might scald your tongue. However, by waiting for the right time, or preparing the coffee and giving it time to cool, you will get a better payoff from that cup of coffee.

Chapter 6: Magenta Meditation Moments

Our physical world is not the only consideration when we think about how we are tired or stressed out.

Sometimes our clutter is coming from inside ourselves, and the only way to tidy this is to center our energy, to find moments in meditation where we can draw on Jophiel's power and grace. Once we have, we can really begin to call on her, making space in our lives for more of her positive influence. But how can we do this, you ask.

We can do this in a number of ways, and I want you to take these methods, little ways of building that energy both as a shield and as a settling beacon, into your every day.

The first way we can begin to make our meditation practices work is to fit the space with things that we will need such as a comfortable space to sit and a comfortable cushion or mat, preferably in those shades of pink or yellow that we have discussed.

We then want to bring incense, sandalwood, roses, even jasmine or lavender. These soothing and beautiful smells are indicators of her grace, so by using them we can feel closer to Jophiel in our meditation.

By making ourselves space and time for these meditations, we can begin to make this part of our routine of self-improvement and contemplation. Using mediation to consider things we want and removing the negative from our lives is important, but how can we maximize meditation?

Rubellite Reiki

The stone most associated with Jophiel is rubellite, a vibrant pink stone imbued with an energy that can pass into you.

Making you feel more energized isn't all these stones offer as they have the power to improve our moves by being charged with positivity and love. Whenever we look at reiki as energy healing, we must consider the kinds of energies involved, and these stones are the ideal counterpart to Jophiel.

Having the right room and the right stones are one part of the healing and meditation process, but the most important is the mindset and the understanding of how we can affect that.

The first thing to do when clearing our minds of clutter ahead of meditation is to breathe. Jophiel is calm and gentle, so slow, calming breaths through the nose and out through the mouth with eyes closed will help.

Calming ourselves before we start playing music or lighting incense is best as it will allow our minds to declutter and be more receptive to new love and energy.

Music

Taste in music is a very individual thing, and this is OK. Music should soothe you. While classical and instrumental music may be more calming to others, you may need vocal harmonies and upbeat tempos. This is totally fine, and Jophiel does not judge as she understands the creative part of our souls is all a little different. She knows that one person's wine is another's vinegar and loves us all equally.

Find the music that resonates with your soul, listen to it, sing along, or sit with your eyes closed and soak it in. Let the vibrations in the music resonate in your soul.

If the music makes you cry, let yourself cry. Even this fleeting sadness is a moment of intense beauty. It is something your soul needed to experience, and it's an experience that will draw you and Jophiel together as she is the archangel of love and beauty and compassion.

Talk

One of the best ways to expel any negativity, be it from a partner, colleague, or a situation, is to talk about it or to write it down.

Getting the negative energy out of your body is such an important part of healing and meditation that finding a way to express this in a positive way is only going to help you to feel better.

This will also help your partners, co-workers, and friends to better understand themselves. This offers the opportunity for them to vent their own toxic baggage in a safe and loving place which will help them to embrace their own healing.

Walk it Off

One of the simplest, and yet most effective, ways for us to unburden ourselves is to walk. Plan a visit to area parks or animal sanctuaries. By taking the time to remove yourself from the rigors of modern life by walking is immensely rewarding.

Exploring the world around us is a great way to enjoy all of the beauty, smells, and colors we experience with Jophiel as our guide.

This can be a great way to both physically get fit and mentally shed the weight of modern stresses, especially if we are walking to allow our souls to unburden all of our tension, if we are able to talk with a partner or friend, or if we listen to relaxing music.

Hobbies

Hobby groups are a great way to meet people with the same passions and energy as you. The hobby itself can also be therapeutic. allowing you to focus on one thing and put all the other thoughts to one side.

This is exactly the kind of skill that could be being inspired by Jophiel's influence. Her inspiration could be leading us to find companionship in like-minded others and to become more open to the world around us.

Hobbies can range from collecting stamps to classic baseball cards, from painting a canvas to stitching a blanket. Embracing something that will make you happy is all that Jophiel will want for you.

If you want to tie Jophiel into a hobby, collect either pink or yellow objects or rubellite stones. This would allow you to have new things to explore and gather while also showing a profound appreciation of Jophiel.

Chakra

Our bodies have numerous chakra seats. These are the areas where we draw energy, be it our hearts, minds, or even our voices. These parts of our souls draw power, confidence, and energy from the world around us.

Of the points of chakra in our being, the two that resonate most with Jophiel are the 1,000 petal lotus chakra and the crown chakra, which is the chakra of the mind. The liberation the Jophiel can bring to this part of us illuminates and enlightens, allowing us to understand things more clearly.

The other part of our chakra she can affect is our solar plexus, the energy in our core and in our breathing. This allows us to calm down, and by being so, it allows our body and mind to be open to Jophiel's message.

In this way, she helps to see our best self, our higher self, the form of us that is ignited by her flame of wisdom. This part of ourselves allows us to feel more clearly the intent of her message and to understand more profoundly our truest desires.

Our chakras are the very energy of ourselves, and coming to embrace this energy is incredibly important. And as Jophiel is a healer of the spirit, her ability to heal our chakra cannot be emphasized enough.

Meditation How-To

Here we will look at how to meditate with Jophiel, and how through meditation you can be closer to her. This is going to be a short and gentle meditation that will allow you to feel much calmer, centering your energy and soul.

The first stage always is to make space for your meditation. This can be a specific room in your house, but it must be clutter-free and with fresh air able to pass through.

To set the room, we will want essential oils or incense. Either rose or lavender is ideal as these are scents we associate with Jophiel time and again.

Soft, relaxing music should be played at below speaking volume. Something soothing and instrumental is ideal, but calm vocalizations also are fine.

What we want is to keep the mind clear, free of clutter. A scented candle with golden leaves or a pink color can also help to encapture the energy of the room.

Once these adjustments are made to your space, it is time to begin. First, either sit cross-legged on a mat or cushion with your back straight. Draw in long and deep breaths through the nose to draw in the fragrances.

Exhale slowly and calmly, out through the mouth, and close your eyes with your hands open, palms skyward.

Allow your rib cage to fully expand and contract. Remember to draw in deep cleansing breaths and exhale slowly, almost through pursed lips. Slow your breathing and take in nothing but the soothing music.

In a calm whisper, speak softly to Jophiel. Thank her for the beauty she shares and for her love and wisdom. Ask her to join you and to allow you to bask in her love and guidance.

Take slow and deep breaths in, slow and calming breaths out, eyes closed but not pinched, forearms rested on your folded legs.

Repeat softly and calmly: " Thank you, Jophiel, for your kind beauty, honest wisdom, and gentle guidance. Thank you, Jophiel, for your love and allow me to share your light with you."

With your eyes closed, again take slow, deep breaths, in through the nose to draw in those scents of her grace, and out slowly through the mouth. Allow your energy to pass out of your physical body.

Repeat once more softly, calmly: "Thank you, Jophiel, for your kind beauty, honest wisdom, and gentle guidance. Thank you, Jophiel, for your love and allow me to share your light with you."

When you are calmer, reach your arms forward, and on your next breath bring your hands together. Draw them in, palm to palm, bending at the elbows until your thumbs reach your chest.

Exhale slowly, moving your hands away from your body. Slowly allow both the physical and emotional energy escape.

Once your arms are fully extended again, slowly inhale and then return your arms palms upright and repeat softly, calmly: "Thank you, Jophiel, for your kind beauty, honest wisdom, and gentle guidance. Thank you, Jophiel, for your love and allow me to share your light with you. I am ready to be one with your grace."

Now slowly, calmly open your eyes, relax your shoulders and back, and slowly breathe in through the nose and out through the mouth.

Allow your mind this moment to refocus as you unfold your legs and stretch your fingers towards your toes. Blow out your candle, turn off the music, and return to the regular parts of your day revitalized and with Jophiel's love fresh in your soul.

Chapter 7: Dreams and Vibrations

Dreams are a very deep and incredibly complex part of who we are. They serve as part message from the spiritual world and part our interpretation of events, and as such, they are an endlessly powerful part of our minds.

They are something that we don't fully understand and contain information about us we may not even realize.

Jophiel is known to hold influence over our dreams. You may be having difficulty figuring out something, be it a personal relationship or an issue with study or work, so naturally, when you dream, you are trying to make sense of these worries in the dream state.

This is normal and good for you. This is the mind connecting with the archangels and taking on their messages.

If you have hues of pink and yellow in your dreams, that is Jophiel's message telling you that what you are seeing is something you need to learn, gently drawing you to your realization of how to move past this roadblock.

If you are seeing a mountain bathed in a brilliant magenta or gold, this could be Jophiel telling you to make the journey, to literally walk the path, and reassuring you that the destination will be worth the steep climb.

If you dream of something that makes you feel calm and confident, that is Jophiel telling you that it is OK to pursue and want that thing, it is OK for you to put yourself and your needs first. This is about self-love, which is a big part of Jophiel's message to us.

Dreams are such a massive and important part of our minds and souls that keeping a dream diary may help you to see patterns and unravel their meanings.

Lucid Dreaming

Lucid dreaming is the act of meditation before a dream, a way of reprogramming our minds to allow us to control and interact with our dreams.

Using the techniques of lucid dreaming, we can send messages in a dream state to Jophiel, asking her questions for guidance or advice. She then can show us things in our dream that we may not be expecting.

In lucid dreaming, we can conjure memories and smells, tastes, and colors. These things can allow us to enter a place in our minds where we can begin to address Jophiel directly with our questions..

Once we have asked the question, we then must not resist what it is we are being shown. This will be a divine message from Jophiel herself, a gentle and calm guide by which to find our path or to seek out something entirely new.

This is something that sounds daunting, but is not only possible but is something that has a lot of modern science research behind it.

Daydreamer

Some of the people around you may be telling you not to daydream, but these dreams are messages. They are important to our souls, and they are, much like our regular dreams, filled with messages, especially when these moments are followed or preceded by moments of calm or smell like rose and lavender.

These are messages from Jophiel, who is reaching out to us, asking us to listen and to pay attention to what is around us. She is urging us to take that moment, that opportunity, or even that relationship and run with it.

This is Jophiel telling you in her wisdom that it is all going to be OK. You just have to trust her and the messages she is sending you.

Vibrations

The energy of all things vibrates with us, and this can lead to a lot of positive effects, improved energy as well as emotional and spiritual healing. If we can surround ourselves with the right energy and vibrations, we can really maximize this.

Part of this is looking at the energy of other people. If you see a person who is combative and negative, the best approach is to distance their influence and to counter this energy with love and understanding.

We need to understand, you see, that even when we feel that there is the potential for negative influences, we can turn this to a positive if only we are prepared to remove ourselves from situations that do not serve us.

These negative and toxic vibrations can hurt our energy, and we need to protect ourselves as best as possible. If it is not possible to protect ourselves or to change the energy by helping that person, we have to remove ourselves.

We are blessed with the gift of love every day, and we are bathed in light from Jophiel, who is always assuring us that the act of removing the negative is a good thing as it will help us to grow.

Chapter 8: Communication and Patience

We receive messages all the time from the archangels around us, including Jophiel, who may be drawing us to notice specific colors or smells. Is that communication between us a two-way street?

There will be times we will want to communicate with Jophiel to ask for her help and guidance, to ask her questions directly, and to ask her to come to us.

We will take some time here to look at how we can communicate with her, how we can draw her into our lives, and how to draw on her grace and energy. We will also come to see that she is already there, ready to gently guide us and offer us help and advice.

And the amazing part is this process isn't as complicated as you may think. As we will come to see, not only does she want to commune with us, but also she is always ready to receive our message. Our understanding of this is an important part of embracing her love.

Writing a Letter

When we want to give thanks in the modern world, we send an email or an e-card. In times gone by, we would have sent postcards or letters. For staying in touch with angels, there isn't an email we can use, but we can still write a letter.

When we write a letter to an archangel, it is worth keeping their element in mind, Jophiel is an air element. We'll come to why that is important shortly, but first, how do we write a letter to her?

This may sound like an odd place to start, but it is important that you use paper and pen, or pencil if you'd prefer, and it must be handwritten.

We hand-write letters for archangels to show that we have written it with sincerity and care. We must sit in a space we have calmed, using rubellite and lavender or rose scents to channel all of that beautiful energy we have.

We then clear our minds entirely and introduce ourselves, state who we are, our full names, and say our hellos. We must then thank Jophiel for her blessings and her love.

From here, the letter can be written as you would talk to a friend or family member with love, compassion, and sincerity. The letter may contain a request for help for ourselves, for guidance, or for help for someone else.

We ask this favor politely as you would a sibling or parent, not begging, not pleading, Jophiel loves and cherishes you, and she asks for nothing more than respect, so this doesn't have to be a complex, pleading letter.

We then thank Jophiel for helping us and those around us and thank her for our letter and the inspiration she gave us to write it. We thank her for her gifts of love and compassion. The letter then is burned. And lastly, because Jophiel is the element of air, we find somewhere we can release the ashes into the air.

In doing this, we are asking for Jophiel's help, but also showing our appreciation for the gifts of beauty and love we receive from her in our day-to-day lives.

We should not worry, however, if we do not see an answer right away. It may be that the question we are asking is always being addressed. It could be that in her wisdom, Jophiel has a bigger plan, a plan we may be unavailable to see just yet.

If we do not want to discard the letters, another thing to do, and this can lend itself to a creative exercise, is to buy a sandalwood box. Inside this box, keep some dried lavender, line the box with yellow, pink or maybe even peach felt, and paint the outside of the box the same color.

You can even decorate the box with Jophiel's name or with a rubellite stone, and then simply place your letter in this box. This will draw her to the letter and will allow you to keep the letter if you wish.

Conversation

Writing a letter is one thing, but a conversation is another way we can open up that communication, most specifically through prayer.

Jophiel is love and integrity, so prayer to her with a fire in our hearts and an honest desire igniting that flame will make it easy. Unlike a letter, we just need to speak clearly with conviction and address her directly.

"Beloved Jophiel" is a good way to start such a prayer, and with that fire of pure desire in our hearts, we can show Jophiel that we are speaking to her. In these moments, we will begin to feel her grace and her message.

Patience

There will be times when we won't be seeing messages from Jophiel, and this is completely normal. The truth is we are not always ready to see the messages being sent to us.

I liken this to trying to convince individuals that they are wrong about the "best album ever" when they are simply not open to that discussion, shutting down any conversation you try to have before you can make your point.

When we feel as though we are not receiving messages, it may be caused by our minds and energies being closed to the divine. We could be meditating and following all of our usual practices and routines, but just not receiving. In these times, it is important to remain calm, positive, and receptive.

There is likely an influence we haven't seen or some subconscious stress that we haven't managed to clear. Be open, and Jophiel will be there, helping us to clear out this blockage.

Patience and calm will then lead to the healing we need to start receiving those messages again.

This is perhaps the reason we all say that "patience is a virtue" and, of course, the adage that "good things come to those who wait." We know that in this world, there is a time to wait and a time to act.

Understanding the power and importance of patience is only ever going to benefit us. And by understanding the right time will come when it really is the right time, we can take happiness and run with it.

Chapter 9: Outer Beauty

If you have ever heard the adage to "stop and smell the flowers," this is such a good way in the reality of showing appreciation to the angel Jophiel.

Beauty is not just within or the realm of the human form. It is all around us. Even now our sky is a brilliant blue, and as the sun sets we get brilliant pinks and yellows on occasions.

We get the bloom of beautiful flowers in the spring, the bright and brilliant colors in summer, the autumnal oranges and browns, and even pristine snowfall in winter.

There is beauty everywhere, and part of making time for love is to make time to visit the outer beauty that is all around us, from zoos and beaches, from Christmas fairs to flower-rich fields.

Jophiel wants us to soak in all the natural beauty of the world around us. She wants us to embrace it, to love it, to care for it.

She wants us to visit ancient buildings and murals and attend concerts and performances. Art is as much about an expression of love for Jophiel as is the budding of a rose.

I wrote earlier about taking a walk, and this is very much the right time in which to undertake this journey of discovering outer beauty. We can visit nature reserves and old libraries. We can visit and photograph endless beaches and as many sunsets as we can.

The night sky is full of endless stars and the big bright moon, all of which are moments of beauty we can use to embrace calm and peace.

Churches

While it might seem obvious, the need for our souls to visit places of worship is profound, especially in times when there is upheaval in our lives.

Going to a place of divine worship is something that can bring us closer to that divinity, but also gives us the time and a place to reflect.

Churches are houses of the Lord, and of archangels, and they can allow you to pray with the energy of the divine around you. They are also places with a quiet reverence afforded by those who are in attendance. This calm and quiet is also far removed from the hustle and bombardment of the everyday human experience, and often it is that noise and chaos that dampens our energy.

So it is only logical that coming to places, like churches, that are filled with the energy of the divine and allowing ourselves to switch off and cast away those excesses will help us on our journey of clarity and healing.

Churches are a good place to listen, whether it be to the divine words of God or the hymns and joyousness the divine blesses us with. This sharing in the divine messages can help us remember what is truly important and to clarify what we are searching for in our lives.

Making a Place of Beauty

One of the great things about the energy of an archangel is that we can really begin to incorporate ways of drawing them in, using things that they are drawn to.

With Jophiel essential oils and scented sticks are a really great way of drawing her energy into space. This is one thing we can really begin to do by making a place of beauty.

Yes, flowers and scents will make up some of this area, but photographs of loved ones, or even framed ticket stubs from a memorable event, will be a welcome addition to this space, making it both personal and reflective.

And these memories should all be positive, should all be of love and happiness, all be of joy and beauty. In this way, we have a place in our homes that is brimming with that positive and beautiful energy.

If this is somewhere near a window, it will allow the light and breeze that passes through it to energize the house with the energy of love and positivity, making it a place where Jophiel will be and easier to communicate with.

Places of Power

Churches are not the only physical places we can visit that will allow us to feel closer to the divine.

Henges and other such places of power are great places to visit. This is because they already are charged with powerful spiritual energies. These are places of worship and peace, calm and understanding, and they are attended by many people from all walks of life who are on their journeys to understanding themselves and the world.

The power of love and the divine is abundant in these places, so visiting them, and experiencing the energy of the place and the people, is a really good way to embrace the beauty of our world.

Places of powerful beauty also can have the same kinds of energies, such as large rivers, waterfalls, vast canyons, beautiful woodlands, and fields. Places like these are great places to go and unburden the mind. Walk and listen to the silence, to the air, and to the chirping birds. Listen to the gentle trickle of the stream, breathe in the clear air, and disconnect from the chaos that sometimes clouds our minds.

Chapter 10: Time With

Part of our journey in life is to find time to spend in the presence and light of archangels. We have come to know those feelings of beauty, and being surrounded by beauty, are signs that Jophiel is near to us.

But what can we do when we want to invite Jophiel to spend time with us beyond these messages? Or to ask in a broader way, how do you spend more time with Jophiel?

This is actually a simple question because in many ways we have already answered it. In many ways, we have discussed drawing her near and listening to her. Meditation, love of self, love of others, and visits to divine and healing places make our world such a beautiful and wondrous place.

In doing these things, we are calling to her. In the moments of joy and bliss we feel in these experiences, we are feeling her presence, and we can conjure and call on her by embracing these experiences.

We can draw her to our hearts by visiting an art gallery, by painting, by carving, by drawing, by writing, or by singing. In all of these small artistic moments, she is with us, she is by our sides.

We can feel her love by loving ourselves, by embracing the things we love, and by doing the things that make us feel joy and completeness.

This is because these are the elements of our emotional spectrum that she is tuned to. These are the feelings and sensations we can use to communicate with her both directly and indirectly.

Understanding the Messages

We will begin to see flashes of yellow and pink and smell roses and sandalwood when she is nearby, but there is so much more than that. Now that we are seeing and experiencing these divine messages, we need to understand what they mean.

The messages could be leading you to a new career, a new relationship, or a new form of art to pursue, but they will always be there.

I cannot tell you what *your* messages mean. All of the messages we get are so different, but that is OK, Jophiel is a patient and gentle archangel who will always be gently reassuring you in her messages.

You'll come to realize the meaning when it is the right time to do so. Jophiel knows this, and she would not put any pressure on you, would not want you to stress.

Then when you realize the message's meaning, you will be able to embrace that lesson, that new relationship with open arms, thanks to the divine messages and assurances we are receiving.

One of the most interesting things to keep in mind is that messages of love and beauty may be around us all the time, but it is for us to understand what this message is telling us. Divine clarity will only ever come when the time is right and when we are ready to accept the message.

Our minds and hearts must be open to Jophiel's messages all the time, otherwise, we could be missing important messages in our every day where we least expect them.

Paying It Forward

I discussed volunteering at a pet shelter earlier, but I wanted to return to that idea here and to expand on it. Homeless shelters and charity organizations need our help, and dedicating even a little time to these places can help not just us on a personal spiritual level.

By paying our blessings forward, we will be helping those who need our help, who need our compassion. This could be by serving food in a shelter during cold winter months or hosting a games night for the disenfranchised. We can do so much to help heal those around us, which in turn can help us to feel more complete, more loved.

We could help run community events, ones with a theme of repairing the old, beautifying it, or creating something entirely new, allowing others to engage their creative souls and allowing us to embrace ours.

And in moments like these, Jophiel will be there with us, showing us how much our efforts mean to her and showering us in her love.

Time For Prayer

When it is time to pray, be it before bed or first thing in the morning, one of the core things to include is that you are welcoming Jophiel into your life.

Welcome and thank her, and allow her into your dreams and your waking moments where she can stand by your side, speak to you, and guide you. When we pray and we reaffirm this connection through prayer, we are allowing that influence and energy into our hearts and souls.

With Jophiel, this is especially prudent as she is the embodiment of love and beauty. By showing this acceptance of her love as part of our daily routine, we will show Jophiel that we are grateful and welcoming of her love.

Prayer doesn't have to be long, drawn-out, or complicated. It just has to be honest and felt in our hearts. Jophiel will feel our honesty and love and repay it with her love, integrity, honesty, and guidance.

A prayer before bed, with an invitation for Jophiel to speak to you or to guide you in your dream, and allowing your heart and mind to remain open to her message is one of the most important parts of our lives.

Conclusion

Dearest reader, dearest friend, our time on this journey of understanding has almost come to an end, and as we come to the end of our time together, we have to ask two final questions.

First, what have we learned? We now know how to draw Jophiel to us and how to communicate with her. We know that she holds influence over our dreams and that through meditation and lucid dreaming we can summon and converse with her.

We know that her presence is felt in places of power and in moments of beauty. We know that she sends us messages through this beauty, and we know we can see her influence in beauty. We have come to recognize some of the smells that encourage her presence, and how her vibrations affect our daydreams.

We have discussed finding time in our lives for prayer, for creative pursuits, and meditation. We know this is important as Jophiel is a calming and peaceful, loving influence on our souls.

We have looked at removing the clutter and the noises that overwhelm us from our everyday lives, and when it is time for us to walk it off or walk away.

We have talked about Jophiel's wisdom, creativity, and power over those feelings within ourselves and her influence over our chakra. We have looked at how she influences our hobbies, and how embracing these things help us to build those bridges of communication.

We have talked about her flames of wisdom and how embracing her messages can help us to contact our higher selves. We have learned that we may see messages showing us to pursue desires that we didn't know we had.

We have seen how she is always encouraging us to embrace love, embrace beauty, and behave in a sincere and honest way, paying our positive and loving energy forward. We have looked at how to understand the messages we are receiving, and how to see that even in times of great stress we can see these messages, reassuring us that is going to be OK and that we are never alone.

We have learned that volunteering and helping those around us are part of our role in this world and that in these moments we will feel a closer connection to Jophiel and her beautiful grace.

We have discussed the importance of communicating with Jophiel, be it through writing a letter, starting a conversation, or making time to pray. But we have also learned that sometimes we will not be ready to accept the messages we are being sent.

We have learned the importance of patience, the importance of allowing ourselves the time to heal and reflect, and that with patience we can begin to understand and learn things about ourselves that we otherwise wouldn't know.

Yes, we have learned and taken a lot of new strengths and understanding into the world, that we now can begin to live as the best, most divine version of ourselves, and that is what we wanted to achieve.

We know that archangels are the embodiment of one of the aspects of God Almighty. We know that by building these bigger and more profound connections to Jophiel and her beauty, there is a profound truth we can begin to understand. Yes, that is the same truth I asked you to consider at the start of our journey.

Our last question is the one I asked at the beginning of our time together.

How Can Archangels Bring Us Closer to the Divine?

When we begin to feel the love of Jophiel in our everyday life, we begin to become bathed in her golden shower of light, and we begin to feel closer to the divine.

This is because growing closer to archangels is to become closer to God. Each archangel is a reflection of part of God's power and grace, so while Jophiel is the archangel of beauty, wisdom, and enlightenment, she draws this energy from God.

In this way, we are becoming closer to God, closer to the divine, so that we may ascend to higher places of understanding.

By embracing and being embraced by the archangel Jophiel, we are allowing ourselves to become more than we were before, purer and more enveloped by God's grace.

We have now learned all that there is to learn about the divine being known as archangel Jophiel, her compassion, and her magnificent beauty. Surely as her hand is on my shoulder now, she gently is encouraging me to embrace my love and beauty.

She is in your dreams, in your hopes and loves, in your moments of inspirational clarity, and in your plans. She is also there for you, waiting to envelop you in love and grace beauty, so take a deep calming breath and invite her into your soul.

References

Aroche, Cristina (2018, Feb. 28). *Archangel Jophiel: What you need to know about her* (video). YouTube www.youtube.com/watch?v=nxf5GOdTZV0&list=WL&index=2&t=0s

Beckler, Melanie (2015, July 9). *Archangel Jophiel of beauty, creativity, and insight.* Ask-Angels.com. www.ask-angels.com/spiritual-guidance/archangel-jophiel/

Hopler, Whitney (2018, June 26). *The Archangel Jophiel's gifts include inspiring beauty and creativity.* Learn Religions. www.learnreligions.com/how-to-recognize-archangel-jophiel-124276

Houston, Diana (2019, May 11). *Rubellite: Meanings, properties, and powers.* CrystalsandJewelry.com. https://meanings.crystalsandjewelry.com/rubellite/

The Black Feather Intuitive (2019, June 26). *Who is Archangel Jophiel? The archangel of beauty.* www.theblackfeatherintuitive.com/archangel-jophiel

The Secret of the Tarot (2017, Oct. 29). *Archangel Jophiel (complete guide).* https://thesecretofthetarot.com/archangel-jophiel

Chakra (2019, March 20). Wikipedia Foundation. http://en.wikipedia.org/wiki/Chakra

Feng Shui (2019, Nov. 29). Wikipedia Foundation. https://en.wikipedia.org/wiki/Feng_shui

Jophiel (2020, Feb. 8). Wikipedia Foundation. https://en.wikipedia.org/wiki/Jophiel

Minimalism (2019, April 26). Wikipedia Foundation. https://en.wikipedia.org/wiki/Minimalism

Book 6: Archangelology: Uriel:

How To Tap Into Divine Wisdom, Boost Inspiration, Skyrocket Productivity, & Manifest Your God-Given Purpose
(Archangelology Book Series 6)

Angela Grace

Introduction

Our world is difficult to navigate alone. We often receive mixed messages, confusing energies, and troublesome negativity from both ourselves and others. We face hard choices and struggle to live the life we were created for. And, although we may listen for God and try to follow His instruction, His voice is hard to hear.

Luckily, God has created beings specifically designed to help us find our way. Angels exist everywhere throughout our world, often just out of sight, and carefully guide us. The word "angel" translates to "messenger," and that's exactly what they do. They carry messages from God and communicate them to us in a way that we're capable of understanding. Whether or not we choose to listen to these messages is our prerogative and illustrates the gift of free will, but angels truly want the best for us and have good intentions. They recognize the value of our lives as individual Images of God and work with us individually to achieve a better world.

Among the angelic hierarchy are the Archangels, the princes of Heaven who hold special roles among their peers. They are looked to as leaders and as powerful influencers, and they are always available to you! Many people believe that they are restricted to communicating with their individual Guardian Angels and aren't worthy of an Archangel's time, but that's far from the truth. Archangels such as Michael, Raphael, Gabriel, and Uriel would all love to meet with you one-on-one and help you create a life of peace and productivity.

This book will be focused around creating a meaningful relationship with Archangel Uriel. Uriel is a lesser-known angel who often works behind the scenes to reveal truth, light, and help lift our earthly plane into the angelic realm. He is the angel of wisdom and knowledge, and he can help you if you're feeling lost in this world or need some extra help being productive, inspired, or finding your God-given purpose.

Although he isn't mentioned much in the canonical Scriptures, Uriel is still eager to chat with you and work through whatever is on your mind. Thankfully for us, he's very good at offering explanations and his voice is easy to hear! After a few simple exercises and meditations, you will be able to interact with Uriel on a daily basis and feel his influence in everything around you. You will be able to channel his dynamic, plentiful energy into your work and career in order to accumulate more wealth and abundance. You will also be able to use his eloquent nature as a way of finding your life path and determining exactly what steps you need to take in order to reach your full potential! After Uriel dispels the confusion that plugs your mind and energy, you will undoubtedly find more satisfaction in multiple areas of your life.

Through this guide, you will learn to:

1. Understand Uriel as both a symbol and an independent entity.

2. Communicate with Uriel and recognize his voice.
3. Perform daily exercises, affirmations, and cord-cutting that allow you to achieve more throughout your day.
4. Hire Uriel as the personal guard of yourself and your pets.
5. Align your frequency with Uriel in order to manifest more positivity in your life.
6. Complete a variety of meditations that allow you to hear Uriel in different ways.
7. Utilize dream-work, crystals, and karma as a means of connecting with aspects of Uriel's being.
8. Recognize the signs that Uriel is present in the world around you.
9. Write a letter to Uriel as you might write to a friend.
10. Perform the basics of a Reiki healing with Uriel's guiding hand.
11. Spend time with Uriel in your daily life and include him in your heavenly domesticity.

If this is your first time doing energy work or engaging in esoteric work, don't worry! This guide is meant for beginners as well as people who have spoken to angels in the past. Even if you've contacted Uriel before, you'll find that you'll be able to deepen your connection with him after you're done reading. Whatever your skill level is, you'll be able to communicate with Uriel with very minimal supplies. You may be interested in investing in some crystals, candles, and oils in order to connect with his energy, so keep that in mind as you proceed, but they aren't necessary if you're looking for a profound relationship with the Angel of Wisdom.

If you're ready to change your life for the better, go on and turn the page!

Chapter 1: Uriel the Wise

Archangels are beings of incomprehensible complexity and intelligence. We have no idea what angels see when they look at us, how they experience time, and how they exist outside of our physical world. For many of them, we're even unclear about the exact role they play in God's Creation. In fact, the sight of an Archangel is assumed to be terrifying or at least awe-inspiring, as seen in the ways people have responded to them in Scripture (The Legends of History, 2020).

However, this doesn't mean that Archangels are completely unapproachable! Because people often respond to their image with fear, many Archangels have introduced themselves with the phrase "be not afraid," (*Al-tirah* in Hebrew) to emphasize that humanity should not be fearful of their presence (Luke 2:10, 2 Kings 1:15). In fact, "be not afraid" is the most repeated commandment in the Hebrew and Christian Scriptures, appearing 144 times total! The second most common phrase, "Love God," appears only 72 times (Be Not Afraid: Luke 2:1-20, 2018). It's clear that the Heavenly Host does not want to inspire terror in our world; the angels are a source of peace and guidance.

Uriel, the powerful Archangel of Wisdom and knowledge, is also easy to talk to. Let's examine a few verses from 2 Esdras, where he comforts the prophet Ezra:

> Where is the angel Uriel, who came to me earlier? It is his fault that I am so confused. My prayer is useless, and I have nothing to hope for but death." I was still speaking when the angel Uriel appeared again. He saw me lying there unconscious like a corpse, so he took hold of my right hand, gave me strength, and stood me on my feet. Then he asked, "What's the matter? Why are you so disturbed and confused?" I answered, "You abandoned me completely! I did as you told me and came out to this field, but I cannot explain what I am seeing." "Stand up straight," he answered, "and I will explain it to you." "Sir," I answered, "please explain it to me. I will die in my frustration if you leave me, for I cannot understand what I have seen and heard. Or is my mind playing tricks on me, and is this just a bad dream? I beg you, sir, tell me what this vision means." The angel said, "Now listen closely, and I will explain the meaning of these things that you fear (2 Esdras 10:28-38).

Uriel did not simply make a command and leave. He came when he heard Ezra's distress and helped him with his physical exhaustion before asking questions, listening to the complete answer, and beginning a patient explanation to help relieve Ezra of his confusion. As the angel of wisdom, this is his specialty; relieving us of the confusing thoughts that cloud our minds and judgements so we can move forward in a way that is more deserving of our ultimate purpose.

However, as with all other Archangels, it's beneficial to have a deep understanding of Uriel before trying to communicate with him. Knowing his history, personality, and energy will help you recognize his voice when he speaks to you directly and will even help you see his influence in the world around you! In order to understand Uriel, we will first examine his role in Scripture and then look at symbols that are typically associated with him as well as other people's experiences with him.

Uriel in Scripture

The verses we just looked at were excerpts of 2 Esdras, a text written by the prophet Ezras somewhere between 70-218 CE. It's part of the Apocrypha (also known as the Deuterocanonical texts), meaning that although it's highly respected and often referenced for specific insights, it is not considered a part of Biblical canon (What are the Catholic Apocrypha, n.d.). The canon texts only mention three angels: Gabriel, Michael, and Raphael. However, Jewish texts such as the Talmud include Uriel as the fourth angel that stands by God's throne in each cardinal direction. Here, Uriel is said to stand to the North, the direction associated with mindfulness, thought, and the third eye. In a similar manner, the name "Uriel" translates directly as "Light of God," referencing how he illuminates our minds with the truth (Chaignot, n.d.).

However, while his name is not mentioned directly in canonical texts, many theologians believe that Uriel is the angel referenced in Isaiah 63:9 who is called the "angel of God's presence," as well as one of four angels who asked for divine intervention for the Nephilim in Genesis 6:1-4 (Chaignot, n.d.). The rest of the knowledge we have about Uriel comes from legend, interpretation, and from direct interaction with the angel himself.

Symbolism and Associations

Uriel is often cited as the Angel of Earth, whereas Michael is the Angel of Fire, Gabriel is the Angel of Water, and Raphael is the Angel of Air (Hopler, 2018). It's sometimes a bit puzzling to think of Uriel as both Light and Earth, but try thinking of it in this manner: he exists in our Earthly plain in order to raise it into the Light. Therefore, his influence can be found in the studies that help humanity to progress and realize divinity, such as the arts and sciences. He's the perfect angel to talk to if you're a student, teacher, or just someone who wants to see society improve. Uriel lives in the hearts of all social activists, regardless of their faith. Because of his Earthly connection, he is also adept at navigating humanity, explaining abstract concepts in a succinct way, and giving grounded advice (Hopler, 2018).

In the same way, Uriel can be approached for personal development. Whether you're at a crossroads in your career, making a difficult decision, or struggling to better yourself in any way, Uriel can give you the direction you need to move forward. Think back to the text we examined in 2 Esdras. Uriel was eager to explain and to answer questions, making him a great fit for Ezra! Similarly, he will work with you in a patient, non-judgemental way that makes your life path clearer.

Perhaps his work through the arts and sciences is the reason why he doesn't appear as much as other Archangels in the Scripture. His hand is present in our own works as he leads us through our projects, so he sometimes steps to the side and doesn't get credit for all of the work he does! He is a humble Archangel who exists to lead us to the truth while making us believe we discovered it on our own (The Legends of History, 2020). However, like Ezra, we can learn to recognize him, call upon him, and listen for his direction. We can even begin to think of him as a friend who we can turn to for advice!

Uriel's feast day is July 11, and some have said that his energy is stronger in the summer. The Earth thrives in the summer and enjoys a period of growth, which could easily explain why Uriel is more present during the hotter months (Chaignot, n.d.). However, don't be discouraged from contacting him during other seasons! Growth occurs at all times in different ways.

Chapter 2: How to Call Upon Uriel

You might be thinking that you have to be specially chosen in order to communicate with Uriel. There must be some type of message that God wants to deliver through him, some major purpose that you need to fulfill, or something of great, universal importance that you were made to do. This can't be something that any Average Joe can do, right?

If you're thinking that, you're halfway correct! Yes, there's something that only you can fulfill. Yes, there's a message God wants Uriel to tell you. And, yes, it's of a great, universal importance! However, everyone has a duty to fulfil here on Earth and everyone has equal access to the angels for assistance to achieve their goals. All of humanity is made in the Image of God, not just the Prophets and Saints! By completing a few simple steps, you'll be able to communicate freely with Uriel and recognize his energy in the world around you.

Beginning the Meditation

Although you'll eventually get better at noticing an angel's influence, the best way to connect with them as a beginner is through deep meditation. Through some focus and intentionality, you can get to know Uriel better and hear his voice clearly! If you're new to meditation, here are some tips about entering a meditative state.

- **Find a Quiet Area**. In our modern world, it's sometimes a bit hard to find complete silence. The space you choose for your meditation doesn't have to be perfectly quiet, but it's helpful to have an area with minimal interruptions so you won't be torn from your thoughts. If you're finding noise particularly distracting, try popping in some earbuds and playing white noise! There are tons of white noise videos available on YouTube for free, or you can search your app store for a white noise player.
- **Reign in Your Breath**. The breath is the rhythm of the body, and we can use that to our advantage! One popular breathing technique recommended by scientists is the 4-7-8, in which you inhale for 4 seconds, hold for 7, and exhale for 8 (Fletcher, 2019). You can always adjust the timing if that pace is difficult for you! Just try to keep your breath steady, slow, and consistent.
- **Practice Mindfulness**. Some people find it helpful to integrate an amount of mindfulness into their meditations. Mindfulness is the practice of being present in your current environment and noticing the little things around you. Try naming one thing you can touch, hear, smell, see, and taste. The act of doing so will connect you with the Earth, Uriel's domain.

- **Use Visualizations**. When my mind is particularly unfocused, I often use my imagination to help me enter a meditative state. Most effective visualizations are centered around the breath and will match your breathing cycle, such as imagining a feather flying up and down in time with your inhales and exhales. You can also imagine yourself climbing up and down a ladder, going up and down on an elevator, or any other image that calls to you. We'll just be using it to help you relax and focus, so the image itself isn't too important at this stage.

Calling Out to Uriel

After you've successfully entered a meditative state, it's time to reach out to Uriel! Don't worry, it's extremely easy. There's no right or wrong way to do it, so I'll go over a few options that are specific to Uriel that you can try. If you don't have success with one method, go ahead and try another! The only trick is to stay alert and aware as his presence approaches you. He will come; you just need to find a method that you can match your energy to.

- **Shift Your Visualization**. If you used visualization to help you relax into your meditation, it's time to change your imagery so it's more specific to Uriel. Try to imagine yourself being bathed in the red light of the Earth or the golden light of Wisdom. If your third eye is very sensitive, you might want to focus the color into your forehead (Beckler, 2017). Alternatively, you can invite Uriel to touch your arms or shoulders and imagine his hands on your skin. His touch will feel warm, stable, and strong.
- **Use a Chant or Mantra.** In 2 Esdras, Uriel responded when his name was mentioned. You could do the same by chanting his name slowly, perhaps in time with your exhales. Pronounce each syllable slowly, such as YUWR-ee-al. You could also turn it into a statement, such as "Uriel, I need your help," "Uriel, show me the truth," or "Uriel, I need you." So long as the statement you choose is genuine and comes from the heart, he will respond!
- **Use Tools**. When we're struggling to receive a direct message, we can use tools such as crystals, oils, or tarot cards to help us read energy. If you choose to use crystals, try using one that's associated with the Earth, such as obsidian. You can also use hematite or Tiger's Eye. If you choose to use a scent or oil, try to find sandalwood, ginger, or basil (Acone, 2010). Skip to Chapter 7 for more information on these tools! If you use Tarot cards, present Uriel with an open-ended question and invite him to guide your hand as you pull a card.

Hearing Uriel's Voice

In the esoteric world, we often use words like "voice" to represent a being's energy and intention, even without the use of vocal cords as we know them. It's very possible to hear direct words from an angel, as many Prophets do, but it's important to keep ourselves susceptible to the many ways that we may pick up on angelic energy.

If you do hear specific words, most people hear a masculine voice for Uriel. This is why I've been using he/him/his pronouns to refer to him. However, several others report seeing Uriel as female or receiving more feminine tones as he communicates. Others say that they've seen him as male in most cases, but female on occasion! Keep yourself open to all of these possibilities. If you're receiving feminine energy, you're probably still talking to Uriel. He's simply decided to use a female presentation for the time being (Aroche, 2018).

Other people have strong emotional reactions once they've come into contact with an angel. If you find yourself wanting to cry, that means you've succeeded! Power through it and listen closely to Uriel's message.

Lastly, we often hear Uriel's truths in the form of instincts, images, and thoughts. If you find that your instincts or emotions are pulling in a certain direction as you are connected with Uriel, he's trying to tell you that's the right way to go. Or, if an idea suddenly fills you with fear, he is warning against it. Stay open-minded and listen closely!

Chapter 3: Having the Strength to Ask

Angels are always eager and willing to help us. They're able to do endless good for us, but, like parents, they want us to learn how to ask. Through the simple act of asking, we learn how to recognize our own needs, realize our strengths and weaknesses, and stay humble (Palmy, 2020).

Now that you've learned to recognize Uriel's presence and power, it's time to allow him to influence your life more directly and with clearer intentions. As the Angel of Wisdom, think of him as a teacher or mentor in your life! In this chapter, we'll discuss a few daily exercises you can do to include Uriel in your schedule, some affirmations that will help you accept his energy, and a special technique called cord-cutting that frees you of lingering negative connections. He will be thrilled to find that you're asking for the things you need!

Daily Exercises

Being able to contact Uriel through meditation is a great way to seek his guidance, but there are many other things you can do that will allow him to influence more areas of your life! Since he specializes in the arts, sciences, and anything else that progresses humanity, many of these exercises will center around your work and career. If you feel that your life purpose lies elsewhere, such as parenthood, you can also try welcoming him into that part of your life. No obstacle is too small for Uriel; let him in and see how much more productive you become!

- **Invite Uriel Into Your Work.** Because our careers are one of the main ways we influence humanity's progress, Uriel is deeply ingrained in our work! Even before we invite him, he's present in our daily routine. By openly recognizing his influence and inviting his assistance before you begin a project or assignment, try contacting Uriel and letting him know that you're listening. Either aloud or in your head, say "Uriel, I welcome your assistance in my work" or "Uriel, I feel your hand influencing me." If it's a difficult project, ask him for help. Try "Uriel, help me to bring forth the Greater Good through my work."
- **Spend Time With the Earth**. Sunbathing is the perfect activity to connect to Uriel: You are laying on the Earth and accepting the light! You can't just sunbathe mindlessly, however; you have to intentionally listen for Uriel if you want to hear him. Try doing meditations as you sunbathe or use your sunbathing sessions as chances to brainstorm your next projects.
- **Cleanse Yourself with Red and Gold Energy**. When you're experiencing a mental blockage, such as the infamous writer's block, let Uriel clear that away for you. Allow yourself a few moments to separate from your work and focus on Uriel's energy. Let it envelop you from head-to-toe, revel in his strength and stability, and stay there for as long as you need.

When you're ready, return to the task at hand and see how much inspiration Uriel has given you!

Mantras and Affirmations

In times of stress and anxiety, we often subject ourselves to negative self-talk. We're so weighed down by thoughts such as "I'm not good enough" that we aren't able to hear Uriel's voice at all throughout our day! Using daily mantras or affirmations is a fantastic way to separate ourselves from that self-talk and open our minds to Uriel's truth. In a sense, it helps us to trick our minds into a higher vibration through the use of positive "I am" statements.

There are a number of ways to use affirmations effectively, so feel free to experiment and see what feels best for you. You may want to use them as a part of your usual meditation, or you may combine them with some of the other exercises mentioned above, such as whenever you're spending time with the Earth. To use them, just repeat the phrase in your head or out loud over and over for 30 seconds or longer. Try to sound like you mean it, even if you aren't sure the affirmation applies to you in your current state! Repeat it until you feel its intention setting in.

You can create your own affirmations if you'd like to access a particular aspect of Uriel's identity, but here are a few to get you started:

- "I am open to truth and light."
- "I am connected to the Earth and its power."
- "I feel the Earth below me and I know I am supported."
- "Through my work, I help humanity to progress."
- "I have an important mission to fulfill and I will do so perfectly."
- "I am knowledgeable and wise."
- "I am constantly growing and improving."
- "I use science as a means of helping society/I use art as a means of helping society."
- "I am humble and unafraid of asking questions."
- "I can receive new knowledge with dignity."
- "My life path is clear to me. I know precisely what needs to be done."

Cord-Cutting

Do you ever notice that your feelings of confusion and hesitation last for days, weeks, or months after the emotional trigger occurred? Perhaps you find yourself obsessing over a past decision and worrying if it was correct, overthinking the "meaning" of someone's behavior, or any other lingering thought that causes you distress. Thankfully, through Uriel's help, you can cut yourself from those negative thoughts and be free from them forever!

Cord-cutting is based around the idea that we create emotional "cords" with the people we interact with, the things we experience, and even the thoughts and ideas that we cling to. These cords can often be very positive, but sometimes they hold us back from achieving our highest good by keeping us anchored to things that no longer serve us. Since Uriel is the ultimate truth-teller, let's think about the things that keep us removed from the truth. Think about any trauma you obtained from people who have lied to you, those troubling "what if" thoughts that keep you from sleeping at night, or anything else that you think Uriel could help remove from your life.

In order to complete a successful cord-cutting, you'll want to enter a meditative state in a quiet area of your choosing. Some people like to bathe in epsom salt or Himalayan salt to weaken the charge of a toxic cord, but you can easily complete the cut without the extra help if you don't have either of those. Visualize the person, situation, or thought that you want to remove yourself from as well as a string that attaches you to it. Give yourself a few moments to ensure that the image is clear in your mind (Marcin, 2017).

Next, you'll want to call Uriel to give you some assistance. Simply call to him inside of your mind and listen for his strong, grounded presence. Let him know what's going on and ask for his strength to cut the cord. Try saying "Uriel, this cord no longer serves my highest purpose," "Uriel, this cord holds me from the truth," or whatever you feel is applicable to your unique situation (Palmy, 2020). Uriel will cut the cord using the flaming sword he used to guard Eden and you will be completely removed from the negative influence (Genesis 3:24).

Chapter 4: Calling Forth Uriel's Sword

"After he drove the man out, he placed on the east side of the Garden of Eden cherubim and a flaming sword flashing back and forth to guard the way to the tree of life" (Genesis 3:24).

Although Uriel isn't mentioned by name in this particular verse, tradition primarily dictates that the angel stationed to guard Eden was, in fact, Uriel! The apocryphal book The Life of Adam and Eve, dated all the way back in the 1st century CE, is our main source for this assumption, where he's seen stationed around the border of the Garden (Chaignot, n.d.). Alongside being a brilliant teacher, mentor, and revealer of truth, he's also a skilled swordsman and an effective guard. You can feel free to call upon his protective power at any time that you feel vulnerable, whether you're threatened physically, emotionally, or spiritually. You can also call upon his power to protect your loved ones, including your pets.

Protecting Yourself

Traditionally, prayer is the classic way to request an angel's protection. If you've been raised with faith in your household, you're probably already pretty familiar with classic prayer. It's proper to sit quietly and calmly, focus, and state your intention to the entity of your choice. You might use a scripted prayer, or you might improvise and speak from the heart.

Sounds a lot like meditation, doesn't it? That's because it is! Faiths across the world use meditation as a way of invoking protective energy, whether they refer to it as meditation or use another term, like prayer. You can ask for Uriel's protection in a Western style that involves simply asking for his help, or you can integrate some Eastern ideas such as chakra focus and aura cleaning. There is no wrong answer!

If you choose to use chakras, you can make use of your crown chakra to access the Light aspect of Uriel's being. After you've entered a meditative state, imagine your crown chakra soaring above you and swirling and white energy. Then, imagine that swirl growing bigger until it envelops the entirety of your aura, and invite Uriel's red and gold aura to take over. He'll need your permission to stand guard over you, so let him know that you desire his sword of protection by either opening your heart to him or stating it verbally. You may find it helpful to imagine his sword or shield planted in front of you, protecting you from negative energies (Taphorn, 2018).

If you'd like Uriel to focus on a particular chakra that you know you're struggling with, you can adjust the chakra you use in the exercise. Uriel will also sense your distress in that area and can help to pinpoint the issue at its core. Be open to his adept skills as a guard and allow him to step into your energy, defending your very core.

Protecting Your Pets

In the same way that we can call upon Uriel's protective sword for our own benefit, we can also use it to protect those we love. And, who do we love more than our best friends, our pets? As the elemental angel of the Earth, Uriel has a soft spot for animals and all wildlife, which makes him the perfect angel to ask for some pet protection. Whether your pet is feeling a bit sick, anxious, or could simply use some protection in their day-to-day life, you can ask Uriel to help improve the quality of your animal's time here on Earth.

One thing that's important to understand as you begin this protective, healing session is that animals have the same chakras as we do, although the placement of the chakras varies slightly. It may be worthwhile to look up the exact chakra placement of the animal of your choice, since dogs, cats, horses, and reptiles all look a little different! As a general rule, the root chakra is typically at the base of the tail, the sacral chakra is in the lower belly, the solar plexus is in the mid-back, the heart chakra is in the chest, the brachial chakra is on the sides of the neck, the third eye is on the forehead, and the crown is on the very top of the head. Again, look up your animal's specific chakras for a more tailored session (McKenzie, 2019).

Healing our pets sometimes takes a little bit more prep time than healing ourselves since we can't communicate when they should relax, how they should be feeling, and so on. Be sure that your pet had a bathroom break recently and that it's a time of day that animals typically relax, such as the peak of the afternoon. Begin by relaxing your mind and body and running your hands along your pet's chakra points. You may already be able to feel blockages just by doing so, so pay attention to any tingling, energetic pulls, and to your own instincts. Wherever you feel you need to place your hand, go ahead and stay in that spot. Since we often communicate with our animals telepathically, you may also feel connected with the crown chakra, so you can place your hand there if you feel no major blockages.

Next, you will want to channel the strength of Uriel on behalf of your pet. Let his strength flow through your hands into the animal and protect them. You may find it helpful to state your intention to Uriel through a phrase like "Uriel, please protect this animal from illness" or whatever message you would like to communicate to him (Kean, 2016). Your pet may respond to the energy since animals are often very sensitive to the movement of angels, so be sure to stay sensitive to your pet's needs. If they appear to be stressed by Uriel's presence, try again another time! Not all animals are receptive to strangers, even of the angelic sort (McKenzie, 2019).

As with any energy work, you may need to repeat the session several times in order to see a difference in the behavior or well-being of your pet. This is especially true since your animal may be reluctant to accept the protection! Remain patient and trust in both your pet and Uriel to achieve a miraculous healing.

Chapter 5: Uriel the Role Model: Aligning Your Frequency

Like all good teachers and guardians, Uriel leads by example! He is deeply connected with the Image of God that lies within all of us and leads us to desire ultimate peace on Earth. As a being deeply rooted to the progression of humanity, each step we take towards peace is a step closer to Uriel's full realization. Yet, he is not impatient with us and is willing to work with individuals to achieve his long-term goals. This consistent, detail-oriented mindset is definitely something that a lot of us strive for and may want to channel into our own personalities.

Thankfully, by aligning your frequency to Uriel's, you can begin to feel more motivated and focused! You will be able to attract more abundance to your being and manifest a more productive lifestyle that suits God's design, and you will find that it comes easily to you. This exercise may take a number of sessions to complete and will require a bit of work to be completed successfully. However, Uriel will work with you the entire way and give you guidance as you need it, so don't be intimidated!

What Is a Frequency?

The concept of aligning your frequency sounds a bit abstract at first, so let's break down the idea before we start the exercise.

Frequency is a term used in science to describe the speed at which something occurs over a particular period of time. In the same way that we might tell our friends "I go to this coffee shop frequently," scientists use frequency as a means of recording how often something happens. In the realm of science, however, the term has to be more specific in order to have meaning. Something's frequency is typically measured in Hertz, which relates to an amount of units per second. Color as we see it is created by the frequency of visible light and gives the world its vibrant shades. If the light is moving at its lowest visible frequency, 430 trillion Hertz, we see it as the color red. If the light is moving at its fastest visible frequency, 750 trillion Hertz, we see it as the color violet. Any frequency between those two shades will land somewhere else on the color spectrum (How Stuff Works Contributors, 2020).

You may be familiar with the idea of aura colors. Each person has an aura that surrounds their physical body and encompasses their energy, typically manifesting into a shape, texture, or color that is representative of their being. In order to have a color, that means that our energy is moving at a particular frequency that can be perceived by those who are sensitive to that sort of energy. If you get your aura read, the medium is picking up on your personal frequency!

Angels also have a personal aura, and it's often quite powerful. Their color typically relates to the assignments given to them by God; blue represents courage and strength, pink represents peace, white represents purity and cleansing, green represents healing, and purple represents transformation. Angels of a red aura, such as Uriel, are especially designed by God to bring us wisdom (Angel Colors Meanings and Symbolism, 2020). If you've already contacted Uriel in one of the previous exercises, you've probably felt it already! His aura feels very strong, grounded, and stable, just like the Earth itself, but maintains a lightness that he is granted through his wisdom. In order to align your frequency to his, you'll need to manifest his personal frequency into your own.

Completing the Alignment

The key to this activity is to do it slowly and often. In order to notice long-term changes in your personal energy, it's going to take a few tries! Consider doing the full meditation at least three times a week and dedicate 20 minutes to each session.

To begin, bring yourself into a meditative state with the skills you learned in Chapter 2. As before, the imagery you use to get yourself relaxed doesn't matter too much because we'll shift the image into what we need.

Uriel will need your permission to invade your personal space for this exercise. You're going to be inviting him into the very core of your being and wrap his arms around each fiber of your energy, so it's best to be okay with the idea of having him all around you. Remember that you are safe and protected in his grasp. Start by allowing his steady, red energy to fill your own aura. You'll feel his presence getting closer and closer, as though he was walking towards you, and it will get stronger as it approaches your physical shape. Spend some time focusing on the feeling of this energy and how it makes your mind feel sharper, clearer, and less cluttered. Next, let yourself relax as his mighty wings enfold over your body and his hands come to rest on your shoulders. You might envision him standing behind you as he does so.

His ruby aura will then spread into your physical self. Take this part slowly! Focus as the energy flows into your hands and permeates deep into your flesh. Through your mind's eye, watch it spread up your arms and into your torso. It will then go to your thighs, knees, calves, and feet. You'll feel it flow up into your head and tingle around your scalp, clearing your mind of all distraction and confusion. Remember that his red light has an extremely low frequency, so imagine yourself lowering into his color range and will the action into being.

Lastly, you'll feel Uriel's red energy pierce deep into your chest and touch your very core. You'll notice that it feels liberating and safe rather than frightening. You may feel his consistency, his solidity, and his pure intelligence. Let him take over every aspect of your being and affect you in a positive way. With his energy surrounding you, go ahead and slowly awaken your body. You can start by opening your eyes, wiggling your fingers and toes, or sitting up slowly. If you're doing this activity before bed, you can also let yourself fall asleep while embraced in Uriel's strength (Cooper, 2020).

Chapter 6: Meditations for Your Specific Needs

Life can throw plenty of obstacles at us. Sometimes, things seem to happen all at once and we need an overall healing of our soul. Other times, we'd rather focus on one specific problem. This chapter will walk you through three meditations that are centered around unique, human problems that you may experience throughout your life: body acceptance, and finding your life direction. If you ever find yourself struggling with these problems (or if you're experiencing them right now), reach out to Uriel and allow him to help you.

Meditation for Body Positivity

The world around us places a lot of emphasis on having the "perfect" body, and it can make us very uncomfortable in our own skin. People of all ages are becoming more and more concerned with losing weight, gaining muscle, and overall policing our bodies. While it can be helpful to adopt healthy habits, it shouldn't come with extra stress and self-hatred. Angels do not see us for our bodies, they see us for our souls and for the essence of God that lies within us, making them wonderful allies as we seek body positivity in our day-to-day life. If you're struggling with your body image, let Uriel lend you a hand.

This meditation is relatively short and can be done in any quiet moment where you can have skin-on-skin contact with yourself, such as during your shower or in your pajamas. Since we'll be focusing on your body, it will be important to bring positive attention to ourselves and the space we occupy. Do this by giving yourself a hug, slowly and gently. Place the palms of your hands on your opposite shoulder blade and experiment with the pressure, making sure that you don't hurt your shoulders or obliques. The position should feel comforting and should not strain you in any way.

With your arms around your shoulders, take a series of slow breaths. In for 4 seconds, hold for 7 seconds, and then out for 8 seconds. And then again. Notice how this position helps you to experience your breath in a new way. Where do you feel the expansion of your ribs? What do you notice? Breathe again; in for 4 seconds, hold for 7 seconds, and out for 8 seconds. One more time.

Let your breath fall into a comfortable and steady rhythm. It should be deeper than before you began, but the pace will come naturally. No need to force yourself into any pattern; you exist perfectly as you are. Take a few moments and focus on your body, noticing what you feel. If any negativity or discomfort arises, take notice of it but do not linger on the thought. Just let it go and move on to the next thought, like you're taking inventory. Where do you feel the strongest and most sturdy? Where are you experiencing pain? Where are your muscles tight and stressed? How are you feeling as you sit with your body, and what associations are coming to mind?

Now, it's time to invite Uriel into the conversation. Repeat his name to yourself for the next two breaths. In for 4 seconds, hold for 7, and out for 8. You will begin to feel his red, powerful aura surrounding you. He is here, and he is eager to help you. Tell him whatever you're struggling with during your next few breaths.

Feel as Uriel places his arms around you in a comforting embrace, alongside your own hands. You may also feel his wings around you, shielding you from negativity and outside distractions. He is solid, strong, and patient. His aura is merging with yours, filling you with his maroon light and giving you a sense of innate wisdom and knowledge. In this moment, you know that you are a divine creation, and that you are made in the image of God. You know that God made no mistakes, and that society's view of your body does not matter. You know that your body is your loving and beautiful home, regardless of its shape.

As you say these positive affirmations to yourself, Uriel will say them with you, reinforcing the statement in your heart and turning it into absolute truth. Let's begin.

My weight has nothing to do with my beauty. I don't need to be shaped a certain way to be a beautiful person. Outside perspectives of my body do not affect my worth. I am perfectly made. I respect my body and all that it does for me. I recognize my strength and flexibility. I am deserving of love and respect regardless of my shape. Society's expectations for my gender do not affect me.

Awaken yourself by slowly beginning to move your body. Wiggle your toes and stretch your feet. Wiggle your fingers and release your palms from your shoulders. Uriel's knowledge stays with you as he unravels himself and his wings from your being, giving you peace of mind and self-acceptance. Now, go ahead and open your eyes.

Meditation for Life Direction

If you're feeling lost, confused, or directionless, even small decisions can become very difficult. We know that we're created to fulfill a personal mission for God, but we don't know where to start or what to do. It's a frustrating and depressing way to live. Thankfully, God sees our struggles and created angels specifically designed to help people find their way. Uriel is one such angel! He expertly leads people to their destinies and is able to do so in a patient, loving way. If you would like his advice on how to complete your divine mission, try this meditation.

For this meditation, you will allow Uriel to guide you through a series of images designed to give you an idea of your ultimate destiny. Begin by getting comfortable; you may want to lay down, sit cross-legged, or relax in a chair. During this meditation, we will be focusing on mending the heart chakra. If you'd like, begin by holding a stone such as rose quartz, rhodochrosite, emerald, or rhodonite. These stones are known for having a strong effect on the heart chakra, so it may help make this process easier (Ancillette, 2020). If you choose to use one of these stones, you may set them before you, hold them in your hand, or place them atop your heart chakra if you're laying down. Wearing a necklace with one of these stones is another easy way to keep it close to your heart.

Reign in your breath. Breathe in for 4 seconds, hold for 7 seconds, and exhale for 8 seconds. And again. Remove yourself from any lingering thoughts about your day; you will take care of it later. For now, it is time to relax. Again, inhale for 4 seconds, hold for 7, and exhale for 8. Breathe one more time, and then allow your breath to return to a natural rhythm.

In your mind's eye, hold out your hand to Uriel and allow him to take it. You will feel his earth-like energy around your palm and fingers as he grasps you gently. Linger here for a moment as you breathe deeply one more time. Inhale for 4 seconds, hold for 7, and exhale for 8. If you have a specific question at this point, such as "Uriel, what does God want me to do?" or "Uriel, what will be the consequences of this upcoming career decision," now is the time to ask. If you don't have a question in mind, you can always stay silent and let Uriel tell you what he thinks you need to know.

Pay attention to your surroundings as Uriel draws your hand forward, moving you through the space inside of your mind's eye. Relax and breathe. Most likely, the environment will be black at first. Trust Uriel to lead you further into the darkness and know that you are not alone on this journey. Inhale for 4 seconds, hold for 7 seconds, and exhale for 8.

You will begin to feel more. You may pick up on particular imagery, emotions, energy, or sounds that relate to the question you asked. Remain open-minded, receptive, and relaxed. Pay attention to what you're feeling. What sorts of images are appearing in your mind? What emotions do they arouse? What feelings are you picking up from Uriel? Is he worried? Happy? Hopeful? Do you hear his voice in any way? What is he saying?

Stay in this space for as long as you need. When you are ready, you can return to the physical world by moving your hands, feet, and rolling your neck. If you need more time, stay in this mindset and listen, paying close attention to your body and mind. You can always perform a separate meditation later where you ask Uriel questions about what you are experiencing, but first, you must experience it.

Chapter 7: Utilizing Dreams, Crystals, and Candles

Dreamwork

Our dreams are often mysterious, abstract, and fleeting. It's often difficult to remember our most impactful dreams, even if they were frightening or emotional in the moment, and many of us find that a bit frustrating. With a little bit of extra work, however, we can begin to use our dreams as an extra means of communicating with angels such as Uriel!

Begin by keeping a notebook and pencil close to your bed. It would be a shame to receive an important dream from Uriel and then immediately forget about it when you wake, so you'll want to write it down as soon as you wake! If you plan on doing dreamwork often, you might consider keeping a dream journal to keep track of recurring imagery.

The moments before you fall asleep are your only chances to communicate with the angels. You will need to use this time wisely! Start by laying in bed and making sure you're comfortable. Try to minimize interruptions by silencing your phone and turning off all other electronics. As you begin to relax, start calling Uriel to you by calling his name, and you'll notice his red aura begin to surround you. Focus on that feeling and state your intention to him. You may simply wish to invite him into your dreams and affect them as he pleases, but you may also have a question for him that you want him to explain to you while you sleep. State whatever you need to tell him at this point.

Once you've said everything you need to say, hold onto his aura as you begin to drift off. Don't focus so hard on the feeling that you prevent yourself from sleeping, but keep it in the back of your mind. Revel in the safety Uriel grants you.

Upon waking, turn to your notebook or dream journal. Jot down any imagery, events, or emotions that occurred during your dreams. If anything stands out or seems similar to previous dreams, it may be worthwhile to research the image and its potential meaning. If anything you witnessed is confusing, you can always meditate with Uriel while you are awake and ask him for some clarification. If you didn't have any dreams or you don't remember them, it's probably that Uriel healed you during your sleep or performed some other miracle that didn't require your immediate knowledge. Write down how you felt as you woke to see if you were granted new energy, perspective, or inspiration (Beckler, 2017).

Crystals

Crystals are an age-old method for connecting with the universe and the power within ourselves! As many angel-workers have noted, they can also be a fantastic way to channel the energy of any angel. Through the use of stones, you can begin channeling an angel's frequency without even thinking about it! Here are some of the stones known to share a frequency with Uriel:

- **Hematite**: Hematite is a black stone that's very connected to both the Earth and the astral plane, making it a good representative of Uriel's power. It absorbs and destroys negativity, so it's also a favorite of healers and energy-workers. Hematite can be used in meditation to eliminate mental ailments, or it can be rubbed on the body to help relieve physical aches (Acone, 2010).
- **Obsidian**: Obsidian is a volcanic glass, meaning that it was created from lava. If the lava hit water and cooled quickly, it creates a beautiful stone with white splotches called Snowflake Obsidian! Regardless of what form of Obsidian you use, the stone is linked with the Earth and has strong, protective powers. As the guard of the Garden of Eden, Uriel is strongly linked with this stone (Acone, 2010).
- **Tiger's Eye**: Tiger's Eye is a beautiful stone known for its stripes of gold and brown. It contains very potent solar energy, giving it a connection to Uriel's nature of Light and truth. It's also known for granting a burst of energy in times of exhaustion and stress, so it can boost your productivity by a large margin (Acone, 2010).
- **Amber**: Amber is one of the most common stones associated with this Archangel. It's actually a fossilized tree resin, which ties it to plantlife, the Earth, and all things that grow. Amber can also help you to grow by fostering transformation. This stone is often used for transmuting negative energies into positive ones (Sheri, 2019).

To use a stone successfully, you will want to cleanse it frequently to make sure foreign energies do not get trapped within it. You can do this by letting the stone sit in moonlight or water, waving it through smoke, or blowing your breath onto it. After your stone is properly cleansed, hold it in your hand as you meditate or carry it in your pocket throughout your day. Doing this will allow you to channel Uriel as you complete your daily chores. After a few weeks of carrying Obsidian or Amber with you, you'll definitely notice an increase in your overall energy (Beckler, 2017).

Candles

As Uriel is the angel of Light, candles can be an especially helpful tool when communicating with him. They're also extremely easy to use and can be adjusted to suit whatever your spirit needs!

Although the flame itself is enough to invoke the energy of Uriel, the color of the candle itself is important for setting your intention. If you're aiming to use the candle as a tool for communicating with Uriel, red is the perfect color. Red is connected to the root chakra, which keeps us grounded and connected to the Earth, so a red candle symbolizes Uriel's Earthly nature as well as his Light nature. If you want to bring a specific issue to Uriel's attention, however, then you can match the color of the candle with whatever you need.

- **Yellow**: Use this color for any problem relating to your personal power and sense of self. Yellow is great for self-image issues.
- **Green**: Green is ideal for healing, whether you want to heal the mind, body, or spirit.
- **Purple**: Use a purple candle if you want Uriel's help with your spiritual journey or any type of internal change.
- **Black**: Although it looks sinister, black is a protective color and can grant you strength.
- **Orange**: If you need help sparking your creativity, use an orange candle. Uriel will work through it to give you some ideas.
- **White**: If you don't have any of the above candles, you can use white as a substitute and set a unique intention for it. You can also use it as an overall purifying candle to try to remove negativity from your aura.

Once you've chosen your candle color, you can integrate it into your meditations. Many people find that simply staring at the flame can cause images and ideas to burst in their minds, so it's worth a try if you're willing to experience some powerful energy! You can also try writing an intention on a piece of paper and burning it with your candle in order to banish or manifest an idea of your choice (Green, 2018).

Chapter 8: Seeing Uriel in the World Around You

Angels move around us all of the time without being known. They may have prevented a car crash during your morning commute, drawn your attention to a beautiful ray of sunlight, or gave you an important thought while you were making a decision. Angels have far more influence over the small happenings of our world than most people give them credit for, and archangels often lead these actions! By recognizing when an angel is present in the world around you, you will learn to appreciate the small things in life and be more mindful. You will see more beauty, light, and peace in God's Creation, and you will see your place in it more clearly.

Most people report that Uriel's influence is often subtle. When he influences the arts and sciences, he drops an idea into someone's mind and then leaves, allowing them to think that the idea came on its own. He may also influence our instincts and intuition in a gentle way. Uriel frequently nudges us in the right direction without calling any attention to himself, giving him an air of humility and introversion (How to Recognize When Archangel Uriel is Present, 2017).

Despite Uriel's quiet nature, we can still learn to recognize his presence as we go about our daily routine. By looking for signs in nature, our own minds, and some unique symbols, we can notice how Uriel helps us throughout our lives and realize that we are never truly alone!

Animal Encounters

As the archangel connected to the Earth element, Uriel often works through nature and animals as a means of communicating with us. If you live in an area where you do not experience much wildlife, pay attention when you do see animals. If you live in the country, you may want to notice when you see animals in an unusual place or at crucial times, like when you're driving to a job interview or thinking about a big decision. Here are some interpretations of common animal encounters:

- **Cat**: If you were recently approached by a stray cat, Uriel may be telling you that it's time to take a big risk. Is there something you've been holding back from because the idea of it makes you anxious? Do your research and go for it!
- **Deer**: Deer carry a distinctly gendered energy to them; a doe represents divine femininity while a stag represents divine masculinity. Therefore, seeing a doe may mean that you need to be kinder to yourself or others, while a stag may mean that empowerment and forward momentum is coming soon.
- **Rabbit**: A rabbit must make quick decisions in order to survive, making them the ultimate opportunist. If you see a rabbit in an odd spot, Uriel may be telling you that it's time to jump on an important opportunity.

- **Raven**: The raven, much like the Tarot card Death, is often associated with sadness and grief but actually represents change. Sometimes the change is desperately needed, but it doesn't necessarily bring death. Uriel is likely telling you that you need to change some part of your lifestyle very soon.
- **Hawk**: The observant hawk depends on its eyesight to navigate life, so its appearance may be a sign to back up and analyze your situation. You're missing an important detail and need to go back to the drawing board.

(Spirit Animal Meanings, Encounters & Symbolism, n.d.)

Repeating Numbers

As the patron of artists and scientists, mathematics is integral to Uriel's work. Seeing a number once or twice is probably just a coincidence, but if you're noticing a number multiple times over a few weeks or even months, it may be a sign that Uriel is pulling strings behind the scenes. Uriel is also associated with specific numbers and patterns, so keep an eye out for the following:

- **111 or 1111**: Do you always see 11:11 on the clock? Do a lot of your purchases total to $11.11? Is the number 11 relevant in your birthday or birth month? The number 111 or 1111 is seen as Uriel's number and is a strong sign that he's trying to communicate with you! Either he's particularly present in your career at this time or he's encouraging you to sit back and think. Are all of your relationships satisfactory? Do you like your job? Do you enjoy your role in your family? Examine your lifestyle and see what can be changed for the better (111 Angel Number (Uriel): Angel Numbers, n.d.).
- **2**: In the world of numerology, repeating 11s are equated with the number 2. This means that if you're experiencing 2 extremely frequently in your daily life, it carries a very similar meaning to 111 or 1111 (Bender, 2019).

Instincts and Ideas

Lastly, it's important to remember that Uriel is the Angel of Wisdom and Knowledge, especially when it's relevant to humanity's progress. When Uriel notices an opportunity for you to contribute to our overall development, he'll let you know! This influence can come in a variety of ways, so pay attention to feelings such as these:

- **Sudden Confidence**: Many believers say that having Uriel's wisdom at the ready gives them an extra boost of self-confidence, especially if they typically struggle with their self-image. If you ever feel a rush of confidence when thinking of an idea, Uriel is telling you to go for it!

- **Sparks of Inspiration**: Do you ever have ideas come to you at the strangest moments, especially if you weren't even trying to brainstorm? It's likely that Uriel is behind it! Even if the idea doesn't work out, Uriel likes to give us a push in the right direction.
- **Desire to Serve and Help**: Human progression relies on our ability to help one another, so Uriel will be eager to tell us when this is possible. If you ever feel a sudden desire to help someone, devote yourself to a cause, or you feel pulled towards a particular charity, Uriel wants you to help in whatever way you can (Hopler, 2019).

Chapter 9: Writing a Letter to Uriel

If you've ever had a pen pal, then you already know the intimacy and excitement involved in letters. In an age where texts and emails are the norm, it can be relieving to handwrite a letter and send it out. Even waiting for a reply can make our days a bit more exciting! If you've never had the chance to write to a pen pal, you're in for a treat: You can get the same feeling by writing to Uriel! Writing is an art, too, so he will definitely appreciate the effort you put in and will even give you a response. In this chapter, we'll discuss how to write your letter, look at a quick example, and discuss how to receive his answer.

How to Write the Letter

The most important thing about writing your letter is that it needs to be genuine! The content of your letter doesn't matter much so long as you put sincerity into it. You can ask any question you want, vent about things that are bothering you, or anything else you would tell a friend. Uriel is your friend, after all!

Many people recommend that you write the letter right before bed in case Uriel's response comes in a dream. If you enjoy dreamwork or often receive messages through dreams, this is a great option for you!

Format the letter the same way you normally would: by stating who the letter is for and the date that you're writing it. Include any opening that feels right for you, such as "Dear Uriel," or "My friend Uriel." Next, go ahead and write your content. It can be as long or as short as you want it to be. Uriel will read any length of text, even if you write him a novel! As you're writing, you may be able to feel his presence or at least notice that he's watching you. He will wait patiently until your letter is complete so he can read it for himself.

When you're done writing the body, close it out with your name and put it in an envelope. You may want to write "To: Uriel" on the outside of the envelope as a means of addressing it and ensuring that no other entities open it accidentally. Leave the letter on your nightstand overnight and see what happens in your dreams!

Example Letter

If you're struggling to format your letter or to think of what to write, I decided to include this example. Because it's an example it's a bit short, but remember to make the letter as long as you need it to be.

> 9/20/20
>
> Dear Uriel,
>
> The world sure is crazy lately! Thank you for taking the time to read this letter among all of your other duties.
>
> Last time we talked, I told you that I have been thinking about getting an apartment soon. You'll be glad to hear that I followed your advice and am looking for a new job first, but I've found myself in a tricky spot. There's one job that I really like and am hopeful for, but it's taking forever to hear back from them! I have to admit that I'm getting a bit impatient. I'm thinking that I should apply to some other jobs in case this one falls through, but I'm also wondering if I should just be patient and wait for the job that I really want.
>
> What do you think, Uriel? Is my impatience a sign that I should be looking elsewhere, or should I wait for a while?
>
> Much love,
>
> Angela Grace

Follow-Up

After writing your letter, you may want to keep your dream journal nearby in case you wake with new knowledge. You should also pay attention throughout your day for any signals or new emotions that Uriel is using to communicate his response to you. If you're confused about his answer, you can always meditate shortly after you completed the letter to ask for some clarification. After you hear his response, it's a good idea to give him thanks in the form of a quick prayer or another letter.

You can also choose to include some candle magic in this ritual if you would like! Many people like to burn their letters as a symbol of sending it off to the archangel, and this can be done either in the morning or at night. You may also choose to read the letter aloud before doing so. Consider matching the color of your candle to the intention of your letter in order to charge it with some extra power. If you decide to burn the letter, I would recommend keeping a journal where you track the content of the letter as well as the response you received from Uriel. This will help you to notice patterns in his communication and be more receptive to answers in the future. Otherwise, feel free to hold onto your letters for safekeeping (Guidance From Angels, 2015).

Chapter 10: Reiki With Uriel

What Is Reiki?

Reiki is a Japanese technique founded by a man named Mikao Usui in 1914, and it allows someone to channel healing energy for themselves and others. Its name consists of two words *rei* meaning "higher power," and *ki* meaning "life force energy." Combined, we see that Reiki involves using the power of the universe and God to heal the life force. It's possible to receive certification and become a Reiki master, but it isn't dependent on spiritual attunement or ability, meaning that it's available to all people of all walks of life.

It is typically completed by channeling energy through the hands, as we have done in a few other exercises already. A Reiki healer may place their hands on a relevant chakra to heal it, run their fingers through their patient's aura to cleanse it, or gather energy in their palms from the air around them. A session can often have sedative qualities as well as healing.

Although Reiki is sometimes associated with Eastern faiths or New Age practices, it isn't actually associated with a single religion! In fact, even atheists have used and enjoyed Reiki. It involves using the power of the universe, whether you see it as an energy or entity. Mikao Usui has stated that the only ideal necessary for practicing Reiki is a desire to promote peace, which people of all faiths can stand behind.

Although Reiki masters recommend using the practice in tandem with modern medicine, there have been instances of miraculous healing through the use of Reiki. It's a powerful art that should not be taken lightly (What Is Reiki?, 2019).

Don't worry, however. You can ask Uriel to guide you through the motions and ensure that you do well. Through Reiki, you can become a powerful healer for yourself and your loved ones!

Incorporating Uriel's Help

If you're new to Reiki, asking Uriel for assistance can be a fantastic way to get the hang of it. As with all angels, he is an expert at channeling God's all-powerful energy, so he can be very helpful for a beginner. However, even if you've been doing Reiki for a long time, you may notice some unique benefits to using his help in your practice.

For this practice, it may be beneficial to think of angels as a shard of God. Each angel represents an aspect of His personality and is able to perform their assigned duty with perfection thanks to His hand in the process. Archangels are particularly powerful and each have their own assignments; Raphael heals, Azrael works with the souls of those who have passed, and Uriel stands guard and teaches. By approaching Uriel in particular and channeling his energy on someone else's behalf, you can help to protect them or dispel confusion!

Light Weaving

I have found the light weaving technique particularly powerful when used in tandem with Uriel's energy. Since it's focused around light, this comes as no surprise! With this technique, we sew a cloth of divine Light intended to protect a person or area from negative energies. In Uriel's case, this cloth will defend from distraction, disorientation, and mental cluttering.

Begin by calling for Uriel by speaking his name and stating that you need his assistance with this Reiki healing. Be sure to state your intention directly! You may have a particular goal in mind, such as "I wish to protect this space from distraction while I work," but you may also keep the intention open and allow Uriel to decide what's needed in that moment. Upon feeling his presence and stating your intention, channel his frequency through your heart chakra, arms, hands, and down into your fingers. You will want to imagine Uriel's Light coming from your fingertips and creating long strings that you are able to manipulate.

Next, ask Uriel to guide your hands as you begin to weave the fabric in the air. You may notice that Uriel is encouraging large, sweeping movements, or you may notice that the situation requires a gentler, slower touch. Do whatever feels best to you, as that's what Uriel is advising. You can make the fabric directly in front of your target, a few feet away, or you may have one hand upon the person or object you are protecting while the other hand weaves. You may also use the weaving as a form of stitch to close physical wounds or mend an afflicted chakra.

The result will be a red cloth imbued with powerful, protective energy, designed specifically to defend from an energy of your choosing. Feel free to repeat this activity several times to strengthen the fabric and renew its abilities. After having the fabric around for a while, you or your loved ones will certainly feel a positive shift in their emotions and confidence (Shewmaker, 2019).

Energy Plucking

Energy plucking is a simple technique in which the Reiki practitioner literally plucks undesired energy from the aura of their client or themselves! It's often done without the help of angels, but having Uriel as a guide can improve the quality of the session, especially if the intention is to remove feelings of doubt, hesitation, or creativity blocks.

As with Light weaving, call Uriel to you and tell him what energy you intend to remove. Ask him to guide your hands as you use your fingers to pinch and pluck at the aura of your choosing. He will lead you to the right spots and ensure that you are removing the right thing! The great advantage to having Uriel's assistance with this technique is that he contains vast knowledge that we do not and knows what will assist the client in the long term. We may not understand our target's life purpose, but Uriel does!

As with all Reiki, the session may need to be repeated a few times to create the best result, but you or your loved ones will feel much freer even after the first attempt. With Uriel at your back, you can achieve great things!

Chapter 11: Spending Time With Uriel

> "Then [Ezra] asked, '…Why are our lives so short and so full of misery?' Uriel answered, 'Don't be in a greater hurry than God Most High! You are thinking only of yourself, but God has to be concerned about everybody. For God has weighed this age, measured the years, and numbered the days. Nothing will be changed until time has run its predetermined course'" (2 Esdras 4:33-37).

This excerpt of a conversation between Ezra and Uriel, although quite small in the context of the whole text, reveals a lot about the nature of angels and their Creator. Although we often imagine archangels as untouchable beings who can only be bothered with world-changing events, Uriel emphasizes that God (and therefore Uriel himself!) works carefully with individual people to ensure that everything happens at the right time. In order to achieve the greater picture of God's Creation, it's important to be detail-oriented and thorough.

This means something very special for angel-workers: We are able to call upon Uriel and his archangel brothers at any time we need them! Each of our actions has consequences and can create a butterfly effect, so it makes sense to communicate with higher beings about even the small happenings in our lives. By doing so, we can contribute to the greater good more effectively.

In this final chapter, you will learn how to foster a loving relationship with Uriel by including him in your daily life. Although there are many ways of personalizing this process, I'll share some that are common among angel-workers so you can have a better idea of where to start.

Beautiful Moments

In Jewish culture, it's traditional to say a quick blessing to God after witnessing something especially beautiful. It's a great way to show gratitude for the little things in life and learn to look for beautiful moments! One very beautiful blessing is meant to be said upon seeing a rainbow, "Blessed are You, Lord our God, Ruler of the Universe, who remembers the covenant, and is faithful to God's covenant, and keeps God's promise" (In Hebrew, "*Barukh atah Adonai Eloheinu melekh zokher hab'rit v'ne'eman bivrito v'kayam b'ma'amaro*"). However, when seeing something that is beautiful and doesn't have a specific blessing attached to it, such as a lovely cat sitting in the morning sun or children playing together, one might simply say "Blessed are you, Adonai" ("*Barukh atah Adonai*") (MJL, n.d.).

Although that formal blessing should be reserved for God Himself, we can use a similar concept to help us connect with Uriel during small moments. Think of all of the duties we know Uriel is assigned to: wisdom, knowledge, learning, light, Earth, art, science, and protection. If you see one of these items being played out in front of you, go ahead and say a quick blessing to Uriel. It doesn't have to be complicated! A simple acknowledgment of his work is enough. Here are a few examples you could use for situations you encounter:

- "Thank you, Uriel, for this burst of inspiration."
- "Thank you, Uriel, for protecting me in this moment."
- "Uriel, thank you for gifting talent and inspiration to this great artist."
- "Uriel, thank you for helping our Earth to thrive."

Venting

Do you ever send your friends vent texts? They can be very relieving. Sometimes, all we need to do is complain about our day in order to feel better. Having someone else know what we go through makes us feel appreciated and known. Never forget that you can also vent to Uriel if you need to!

I often like to use quiet moments during my commute or work day to vent to my angels. We're always in dialogue with ourselves during long drives, slow days at the office, or when we're doing errands, so why not invite Uriel into the dialogue as well? It's simple to include him in the chat. Simply address him as you begin the thought and he will start to listen in. You will likely sense his presence or at least feel that he's listening in.

When you're talking to him, be sure to pay attention to your surroundings in case he decides to send you a sign at that moment. An animal encounter, appearance of the number 111, or stumbling upon a person in need might be a major signal from the archangel. Don't be discouraged if you don't see any signs, however. Uriel will choose some other way to respond and help you, even if he's working behind the scenes.

Conclusion

Although our world can be full of deceit, misconceptions, and negativity, we don't have to face it alone! We can move forward with confidence, knowing that Uriel has our backs. With his help, we can gain a better understanding of God's intention for us and fulfill that purpose with minimal stress. Not only that, but we can also gain a valuable friend!

Now that you know how to hear Uriel's voice, look for him in the world around you, and access him through a number of different activities, you have him available at all times. Uriel doesn't care whether you've had a hard past, a troubling present, or fear for the future. He's here for you no matter what, and his advice will be very valuable as you move forward. I hope that this book gave you the self-assurance you need to contact Uriel without fear or shame, and I will be praying that he is able to communicate efficiently with you! You deserve this positive influence in your life and are hopefully willing to accept it.

As you now know, Uriel is able to grant you guidance and knowledge that allows you to be more productive and inspired in your own work. With his help, you will be able to contribute more to the overall evolution of our species, giving you a great feeling of accomplishment and satisfaction. You will feel an increase in energy, motivation, and hope!

As with other Archangels, you may want to dedicate some time to getting to know Uriel before you attempt to connect with another. Otherwise, the messages may get a little confusing and the many energies of the Archangels might be hard to tell apart. However, after you know Uriel well, I hope that you will be willing to check out the other books in my *Archangelology* series so you can continue your spiritual journey. The Archangels can all offer unique services, so you will have a more complete experience if you reach out to all of them. It would be my great honor to introduce them to you!

Good luck, and I hope you enjoy Uriel's wisdom!

References

111 Angel Number (Uriel): Angel numbers. (n.d.). https://askastrology.com/numerology/angel-numbers/111-angel-number-uriel/

Acone, S. (2010, March 1). Crystals to help connect with archangel Uriel. https://www.healingcrystals.com/Crystals_to_help_connect_with_Archangel_Uriel_Articles_1792.html

Ancillette, M. (2020, September 14). 9 powerful stones & crystals for the heart chakra. https://angelgrotto.com/crystals-stones/heart-chakra/

Angel Colors Meanings and Symbolism (Truth Revealed!). (2020, February 11). https://backpackerverse.com/angel-colors-meaning/

Aroche, C. (2018, February 7). *Archangel Raphael: Who he is and how to work with him.* [Video]. YouTube. https://www.youtube.com/watch?v=KTxlUIeZaiQ&ab_channel=CristinaAroche

Beachley, L. [Guided Meditations by Lisa Beachley]. (2015, October 20). *Archangel Raphael meditation: Heal the heartache and forgive* [Video]. YouTube. https://www.youtube.com/watch?v=MfXe6RLDs1M&ab_channel=GuidedMeditationsbyLisaBeachy

Beckler, M. [Ask Angels with Melanie Beckler]. (2017, January 15). *Archangel Raphael prayer ~ An angel prayer to invoke the help of Raphael the Archangel of Healing.* [Video]. YouTube. https://www.youtube.com/watch?v=_XrX86T8DyA&ab_channel=AskAngelswithMelanieBeckler

Beckler, M. (2020). How to invite an angel into your dreams. https://www.ask-angels.com/spiritual-guidance/angel-dreams/

Bender, F. (2019, November 29). 11/2 Life path. https://feliciabender.com/11-2-life-path/

Be Not Afraid Luke 2:1-20. (2018, December 19). https://seeyouonsunday.org/be-not-afraid-luke-21-20/

Chaignot, M. (n.d.). Angel Uriel. https://www.biblewise.com/bible_study/characters/angel-uriel.php

Cooper, D. (2020, March 29). *Day 7 - Open to health and abundance with Archangel Raphael* [Video]. YouTube. https://www.youtube.com/watch?v=yRPWkMJFFhU&ab_channel=LindaKean

Fletcher, J. (2019, February 12). How to use 4-7-8 breathing for anxiety. https://www.medicalnewstoday.com/articles/324417

Green, P. L. (2018, November 03). Uriel's candle power. https://pamsdailyangelnotes.com/2018/11/03/uriels-candle-power/

Guidance From Angels. (2015, November 26). *How to write a letter to archangels*. [Video]. YouTube. https://www.youtube.com/watch?v=yRPWkMJFFhU&ab_channel=LindaKean

Hopler, W. (2018, December 23). Rapheael, Michael, Gabriel, Uriel: Archangels of the 4 nature elements. https://www.learnreligions.com/archangels-of-four-elements-in-nature-124411

Hopler, W. (2019, January 20). How to recognize Archangel Uriel. https://www.learnreligions.com/how-to-recognize-archangel-uriel-124286

How Stuff Works Contributors. (2020, June 30). How are frequency and wavelength of light related?. Retrieved September 18, 2020 from https://science.howstuffworks.com/dictionary/physics-terms/frequency-wavelength-light.htm

How to Recognize When Archangel Uriel is Present. (2017, December 22). https://intuitivejourney.com/recognize-archangel-uriel/

Kean, L. (2016, September 28). *Archangel Raphael and Ariel healing meditation for animals | Guided meditation* [Video]. YouTube. https://www.youtube.com/watch?v=yRPWkMJFFhU&ab_channel=LindaKean

McKenzie, L. (2019, January 25). Healing and balancing your dog's chakras. https://animalwellnessmagazine.com/dogs-chakras/

MJL. (n.d.). Everyday blessings & rituals. https://www.myjewishlearning.com/article/everyday-blessings-rituals/

Marcin, A. (2017, October 19). Cutting the emotional cord - Step by step meditation. https://www.balancepsychologies.com/post/2017/10/19/cutting-the-emotional-cord-step-by-step-meditation

New International Version. (2011). BibleGateway.com. https://www.biblegateway.com/quicksearch/?quicksearch=Genesis&version=NIV

Palmy, C. (2020, May 01). How to cut cords with the angels. https://carolinepalmy.com/how-to-cut-cords-with-the-angels/

Sheri, R. (2019, June 26). Archangel Uriel. https://www.angelmessenger.net/archangel-uriel/

Shewmaker, D. (2019, July 11). Reiki and angels. https://www.reiki.org/articles/reiki-and-angels

Spirit Animal Meanings, Encounters & Symbolism. (2020). https://alltotems.com/

Taphorn, S. (2018, February 03). Angelic Protection – Using Shields. https://www.beliefnet.com/columnists/angelguidance/2018/02/angelic-protection-using-shields.html

The Legends of History. (2020, February 19). *Archangel Uriel: The Angel of Wisdom (Angels & Demons Explained)* [Video]. YouTube. https://www.youtube.com/watch?v=kw1UYJ24wCM&ab_channel=TheLegendsofHistory

Virtue, D. (n.d.). Life purpose meditation. https://www.mixcloud.com/hayhousemeditations/doreen-virtue-life-purpose-meditation/

What are the Catholic Apocrypha / Deuterocanonical books? (n.d.). https://www.compellingtruth.org/Apocrypha-Deuterocanonical.html

What is Reiki? (2019, September 10). https://www.reiki.org/faqs/what-reiki

Book 7: Spiritual Discernment

The Guide to Trusting in the Direction of God

Angela Grace

Introduction

"But the Helper, the Holy Spirit, whom the Father will send in my name, he will teach you all things and bring to your remembrance all that I have said to you" **- John 14:26, (English Standard Version)**

Here is something you probably know, but I am going to tell it to you anyway. Perhaps you don't know this or haven't thought about it. Regardless I am going to be telling you about it. Maybe the way I say it to you will help you realize and appreciate something about the world that you never have before.

Look around you. What do you see? Pictures are moving about on the screen. You hear the chirp of the birds outside. Maybe you live in the city, where all you hear is the roar of the city and the fervor of activity, not easy to pierce through with your ears or isolate. How does this book feel in your hands, is it smooth? If you are reading this on a device, how does it feel? Is the device solid and sturdy in your hands, are the buttons on the screen smooth to your touch? Is it heavy or surprisingly light for its size? How about the chair you are sitting in, is it comfortable? How about those sensations in your body, the niggle in your left knee, the way your skin stretches and contracts as you move?

This is all exciting and nice, and you might even say that it is real as opposed to something that is a dream or fictional. Here is the strange part about all of this, it is a real-time simulation being run by your brain. These feelings, perceptions, sights, and stuff you hear. This is not to say that there aren't things like tables, chairs, and bodies that exist in the world; there are objects in the world that serve these purposes and present themselves that way. The point I want you to realize is that your brain is in a black box. It gets inputs from your senses, and using a bunch of techniques, it simulates a world for you: taste, touch, sight, internal sensations, and much more. But we know, both from what we know about science and our experiences, that the way we perceive the world isn't exactly how the world is. We have technologies in our life that exploit the fact that our brains are blind to a lot that is out there. Consider the TV in your living room or any screen for that matter. When you look at it, you see people on the screen talking; when you swipe up the page, it scrolls. But you do realize this is an illusion, but like any other illusions in works by exploiting how our brain interprets visual input to build a world. It is a type of optical illusion, as you know.

The point I am making is that the world is not as it seems. We can't live a wholesome life that is tuned with nature and the world by our own wits or experience. Most of the things that happen in the universe, and I mean universe as absolutely everything that exists, including matter, are not in our direct experience or observation. They are invisible to us. And many of these things that are invisible to us have real effects on us. They have implications for our lives here on earth. Just because something is vast and far away, just because you are unable to see something doesn't mean it can't hurt you or embolden you. It doesn't make it not exist or matter less. If your goal is to live a life that is genuinely fulfilling, successful, and in harmony with the ultimate existence, it would make sense to see beyond the world that has been pulled over your eyes by the limits of your own perceptions, experience, and nature.

A person who does not see beyond their immediate reality or experience is like a person stumbling in the dark. They have no insight or perception of how their decisions reverberate beyond what they can see. Since people are more than their direct experience, they have a soul. They might also be making decisions that harm the soul in the long term.

How do you turn that around, though? How do you see beyond your immediate, small reality and make decisions that are wise beyond your direct experience? You have to learn to be spiritually aware and alert. To do that you will need some help, the best help, guidance, you get is from God. Well, you might think I am a little biased, going for God right off the bat. What if there is some other spirit, Cthulhu or Leviathan, who is more equipped to help you? Before we get into it, let's talk about what spirits are. Many people think of spirits as existing separate from or beyond physical reality. As we have seen, physical reality, or the world as we experience it, is a tiny slither of what is actually out there. Spirits are being, which are residents of this fuller reality. They see much more than the world than us. By us, I mean most of us because we have souls; at the fundamental level, we are souls. But some spirits are more conscious of others, they know more, see more and can do more than others. This is just like here in the real world. Some people are just more capable than other people.

Now, imagine if the entire world was one country. The most influential person in that country we would call the President. The word God describes something like that. It is a title. God is not the name of God. God has an actual name. Just like how your President's name isn't President. But with God, there is another element that makes them the best guy to listen to. They made everything that exists. They are the ultimate architects. So, they know everything about their existence because it is their design. That is why we say God is all-knowing; he literally is. God didn't have an algorithm to make him the universe; he designed it all. Not only does he know all, but he must also be super-intelligent. More intelligent than anything that could exist, because any intelligence that exists in the universe exists as a result of his design, meaning it is his design. So, God is your guy if you want to have the best life. He knows best because he is the best that can ever be.

There is a problem, though. This is why we have this book right here. There is an infinite number of other spirits who try to sell you the same services. Sometimes, often, it is difficult to know which one is God and which one isn't. This is because of two things. One is that we have spiritually neglected ourselves. We are spiritually malnourished, so to speak. So, we are terrible at acting in the spiritual world because of this.

The second problem is that there are forces out there that are hell-bent of destroying us or thwarting our attempts to make a connection with God. There is simply too much noise. Put simply, it takes some effort, maintained effort to hear God. Some people might be quick to ask why. My response is to ask why it should be otherwise? We like the people we are in relationships with because it is a two-way street. Relationships are built on the idea that both parties are making an effort to build something together. God is already making an effort; you are not living up to your part of the bargain. If you don't believe me that God talks to us all the time, I will give one proof that is difficult to dispute.

Think back to when you were a child and your mother baked those lovely cookies you like. She put them in a jar, told you not to have any until she gives them to you. Maybe she told you should ask first. But three or five cookies in the morning wasn't enough for you. You wanted more. It is not your fault. They were very delicious cookies. Your mouth is watering just thinking about them. Side note: Maybe you should call your mom and tell her to bake you some this instant. Be kind, though. Anyway, back to our story. You know what you did next. You went and stole some. Maybe one here and there, but soon it became ten or twenty, and you got caught. Right? But you probably remember, despite the thrill of stealing, that bad feeling in your chest or that voice in the back of your head telling you that you shouldn't do it. You knew right then that what you were doing was wrong, and there was a voice that told you it was. We call this voice a conscience; our conscience is one of the purest ways God talks to us.

But as you know, this channel can get hijacked by other influences and spirits, but when you were a kid, that probably hadn't happened yet. And God probably talked to you more often, not only when you were doing bad things, but when you were playing too. Do you remember that feeling of a presence? Of being watched over, observed, how you would sometimes talk to yourself, or to something, but you weren't quite sure what? The thing that is not your imaginary friend? Just thinking about it.

But you came to this book because, in a sense, you have lost that at a point in your life when you need more of it. One of the reasons that spirits don't spend as much effort binding kids; it is because kids make fewer decisions. They have fewer responsibilities. There the more choices you have, the more power you have, and the more useful you are as a person. This is not saying children are less important. They are, it may be part of the reason that they attack parents and adults because confused adults can confuse the children too. Since you make more decisions and your decisions echo across generations, you need God now more than ever. So, picking up this book has been one of the most clever decisions you have ever made. Perhaps God himself has guided you here.

In this book, I will talk about what it takes to hear God, how do you tell it is God. I will talk about finding your purpose and why that matters. We will explore how God talks to us day by day and how we can use that to grow in faith. The most interesting chat for most of you will be my discussion on discerning good spirits from bad spirits, good intentions, and bad intentions. We will discuss living by scripture and wisdom. This will be a lot of fun. This book is about spiritual discernment, and so far, I have said a lot about hearing God. This is because as much as discernment is having great spiritual perception, much of it grows from and is informed by two-way communication with God. So, this discussion necessitates a discussion on hearing God, listening to God, and also ways to distinguish between different voices, intentions, and spirits.

Chapter 1: Hearing God

At its most basic, God talks to us through the spirit. This is helpful because the spirit is always around us and within us. He speaks in different ways and there are many ways God uses the spirit to talk to us. God speaks to us differently, depending on who we are, where we are, and what our trajectory in life is. He talks to each individual differently, but it is all to serve one ultimate goal: achieve great intimacy and bring about his kingdom. While I can't provide a set of instructions on how you can begin to hear God in your life, I can tell you there are set ways that God does communicate. Still, the nature in which he uses these ways will differ with each person. There will be great overlaps, though.

In these chapters I will go over the readily available ways that God communicates with us, some are so used to these ways that they no longer think of it as something out of the ordinary. The most common being the conscience; this is like a built-in mechanism that connects God to each person. The only problem is this mechanism can become corrupted. We know this because there are people who disagree strongly on things that should be the same for all. These worldviews can alter our conscience.

Substitute the word 'worldview' here for 'information.' A worldview consists of a set of concepts that relate to each other in a complex manner. Imagine you are given land. The land is lush, and a lot will grow there so you decide to start growing a few crops. Before you can do that, you have to clear what's already growing there. If the information you have is that clearing the field will lead to a high crop yield, established jobs, food for others, and support for your family, clearing the field will feel like the best thing to do.

Now imagine the same situation, but you have a different set of information. For example, you know clearing the field will lead to the town flooding in the summer, causing irreparable damage and possibly loss of life. You might feel bad about clearing the field even if you know it will lead to wealth and support for your family. The information you have, the concepts, can have a great influence on your conscience and decision making. What this illustrates is how easy it is for conscience to be swayed. If your worldview is biblical, your conscience will, for the most part, be aligned with God's desires. But you can't always be sure that somehow, something has muddled your conceptions of the word to lead you astray.

Another way God communicates with us is through intuition. Intuition is most famously called a gut feeling. It can be as simple as feeling uneasy about making a particular decision. Sometimes it is confidence in knowing that you should do something, a type of unexplainable knowledge about a situation that later turns out to be true. Intuition is enigmatic in the sense that it does not appeal to the intellect; it affects and deals with something deeply spiritual about our nature.

"For the Lord gives wisdom; from his mouth comes knowledge and understanding; he stores up sound wisdom for the upright; he is a shield to those who walk in integrity, guarding the paths of justice and watching over the way of his saints. Then you will understand righteousness and justice and equity, every good path; for wisdom will come into your heart, and knowledge will be pleasant to your soul;" - Proverbs 2:6-15

Another way that God communicates is through dreams and visions. God can use them to bring something mysterious to the forefront. To make sense of problems we have been struggling with, to give us a different idea about what's next and so much more. While people may obsess about dream interpretation, often, dreams are clear cut because of language, using imagery and emotions, that we understand.

"For God speaks in one way, and in two, though man does not perceive it. In a dream, in a vision of the night, when deep sleep falls on men, while they slumber on their beds, then he opens the ears of men and terrifies them with warnings, that he may turn man aside from his deed and conceal pride from a man; he keeps back his soul from the pit, his life from perishing by the sword." **- Job 33:14-18**

God also uses other people's counsel to communicate with us. Generally, this is something you will hear from people who have a close relationship with God. For instance, if at church, people say something about you, they see something similar, like that you would make an excellent teacher. That would be a way of God showing you that you have this gift. He has paved the way for you to follow it. This is because if people see or recognize something in you, they ascribe a role for you. While you might face some challenges on a route that is acknowledged within the spiritual circle, you will receive adequate support to reach your goal. An even better sign of this is if people who don't communicate with each other say the same thing about a matter in your life.

"The way of a fool is right in his own eyes, but a wise man listens to advice."
- Proverbs 12:15

"Where there is no guidance, a people falls, but in an abundance of counselors there is safety."
- **Proverbs 11:14**

The other way that God communicates with us is through his word. Whether by reading it or through sermons and messages. You will know that God is communicating with you if a message or sermon convicts you. The word *convict* is a perfect way to describe the phenomenon. What it essentially means is that you feel like, at that moment, that the message was meant for you, made for you in mind. Of course, no preacher's message or verse was written specifically with you in mind, but you might be positioned in such a way in life that the message resonates deeply with you.

"All Scripture is breathed out by God and profitable for teaching, for reproof, for correction, and for training in righteousness, that the man of God may be competent, equipped for every good work." - **2 Timothy 3:16-17**

Another way that God communicates with us is more direct. He speaks to us through the voice in our heads, a still voice that speaks spirit to spirit. This might be the point that some people feel uneasy. Still, if you clear your head, meditate in scripture, and do some of the exercises that we will discuss in this book, you will hear ideas, thoughts and get pictures popping in her head that guide you. This thing isn't just thoughts, they are specific to your questions, and they also come with other confirmations. A confirmation is when God says something, and then something happens in the world that corroborates his will or desires for you.

The less common one, something many would love or even pay to experience, is an audible voice. This is when you hear an actual voice the same way you would hear music from your speaker or someone next to you speak. It happens in a distinctly external way. It can be scary or seem that way as you read this. This is because, in our normal experiences, we don't hear voices coming out of thin air, and when they do, it can mean mental instability. God can use this method, and when he does, you will be filled with a sense of calm, peace, and knowing.

Another way is through intense passion. This can be something like a strong, euphoric feeling that comes out of nowhere and propels you towards something. People generally have these types of experiences during worship when the spirit of the Lord comes upon them and is an overwhelming presence. At that moment, a type of supernatural knowledge comes to you; it is so clear and bright that you can't doubt or mistake it.

"So, whether you eat or drink, or whatever you do, do all to the glory of God."

- 1 Corinthians 10:31

"I can do all things through him who strengthens me." - **Philippians 4:13**

God will employ several methods to communicate with you. Just like you wouldn't only communicate with your parents or friends face-to-face. You use every tool at your disposal to transfer a message and use whatever fits best the scenario at hand. If they are far away, you might raise your voice. If you are in another city, you might call them. If you can't talk, you can text them. And if it has been a long time and you miss them, you might video chat your loved ones. God is the same way, and it will likely be the same message, the one that you need to hear right now. This is another way in which confirmations happen as well: the same messages communicated in different ways

How Can I Tell?

Now you know the ways in which God speaks, how can you tell if it is God? This is a central struggle for all believers. I call it the perpetual ambiguity syndrome. When they get a message from God, they either think the source is not clear or they can't be sure it is God as it is not very clear. I often ask these people what they would need to see to be convinced that it is God speaking to them. They never really have an answer, I guess it's because they sense it is rhetorical. I imagine they would like God to reach down from heaven and talk to them in a mass of blinding light. Perhaps that would be proof enough. But who knows for sure?

We have hinted at ways that God reveals himself and they are worth going over briefly. God confirms the things he tells you. He won't say it one time, to only you and in one way. He will say the same thing in different ways. It is like how your partner might text you not to forget the milk when you already know to get the milk. Maybe you dream about starting a 'GoFundMe' page for your neighbor. Then you hear the same voice popping in your head more as you pray, and even start to feel good about it. A friend might ask you why you don't do something similar for your friend. And then, just like that, you know it God talking to you.

You can tell it is good simply because it is good. God wouldn't tell you to do something that is ultimately destructive to you, your loved ones, or your relationship with him. If it is in line with scripture, and it is good, it advances His word and strengthens your relationship with him, then it is God.

"And Jesus said to him, 'Why do you call me good? No one is good except God alone."
- Mark 10:18

It is here that you often hear about the story of God and Abraham. This story often makes people think that God doesn't always tell us to do things that are good or at least look morally acceptable. If you don't know the story, God tells Abraham to sacrifice his son. Abraham comes close to it, right as he is about to strike his head, God tells him to stop and that Abraham has proven his faith. It seems like a cruel joke. Why would God do something like that? How can God be so cruel? Surely then, God doesn't always ask us to do what is good. He is more than capable of telling us to do things and change his mind at the last minute. This seems to be the picture that many people draw from this specific story in the bible. They hear that story, and they see a God who is capricious and capable of instructing people to do morally reprehensible acts for no reason. And with that description, you might feel better calling this entity a devil instead of God.

The people who think this is are often quick to ask questions like, "If God tells you to kill your neighbor, would you do it?" I am afraid I am going to be a bit morbid for the next few sentences. But this only for the sake of argument. Not saying God would do this, but I think the question is worth examining. If you were in this scenario and a voice came to you and said: "I am the Lord your God and savior, and I command you to kill your neighbor." The first thing to go through your head is probably not "Wow, God is speaking to me," it is somewhere between "I am going insane" and "This must be an evil spirit." This is exactly where your thoughts should be. Why? God is not counter-productive. He works to make things better, not to make them worse. The question to ask yourself is: if I were to go to my neighbor and kill him, how would it make me feel? How would those feelings impact my relationship with God and the community? If the answer to that, from what you know about the world, is overwhelmingly negative, then it isn't God. If it means breaking ties with family, disgracing your church, making it hard for you to trust God's message, and leading to potentially irreversible psychological and emotional damage, this isn't God. He would never ask you to do something that might jeopardize your relationship with him.

Now one can imagine a clever terrorist saying, "Well, God would never do anything to harm you. So, he knows that if you kill this person, it will be very good for you."

But remember what I said. If, from what you know now, at this moment, according to the intelligence you have earned, doing such an action looks like it would damage your relationship with God, the church, your family, and bring about hurt and pain, it is not God. The moment you allow yourself to act on ridiculous, wild impulses or invocations because "the spirit knows better," you are opening yourself up to outside influences. A sign that God is speaking to you is that he will make what he says to you intelligible to your current situation. It won't be a complete mystery. I advise you to apply this criterion in the very serious of circumstances. If God tells you to go have pizza, there would be no need for such a review.

"The Lord is good to all, and his mercy is over all that he has made." - **Psalm 145:9**

When you spend time studying and praying on scripture, you get used to the voice of God. God's spirit works with you during those times to illuminate the word and bring insight into your life. When you read the word, and you feel convicted by it, you will know it is God speaking to you. And when you are in doubt, you can rest assured that that message can be confirmed outside of scripture. One of the other benefits that come from reading scripture and immersing yourself in the word is that you spend so much time with God's spirit that you can easily recognize God the next time he communicates with you. Your mind will be filled with his word, and when you look out into the world, it will be shaped in such a way it becomes easy to perceive his ways and actions in the world and to recognize him. This may sound weird, but you have had a similar experience before. The spirit opens up our minds or our spiritual eye in the same way knowledge can change how we see things around us.

For example, as any student of varying subjects will tell you, before learning something new they have to know the world around them is full of unseen features. Not because these invisible things aren't there but because the student's mind has yet to be trained on how to recognize them. Before psychology students begin to study their subject, they start off seeing other people's behavior in two-dimensional ways as either good or bad. They make poor judgments about the motivations of others, the way they act, and might see mental health challenges as personality quirks or even bad behavior.

It's when the student begins to see a world that is even more multifaceted, where things are way more complex and intriguing than they appear at first. They are more ready to look at a situation and behavior and then come up with better judgments about the reason for the behavior and if it is normal. Immersing yourself in the word of God gives you the ability to see more than the world that is in front of you, to recognize patterns, hidden influences, and the significance of events around you.

"Your word is a lamp to my feet and a light to my path." **- Psalm 119:105**

That is why the best way to hear God or prime yourself to easily recognize his ways in your life is by acquainting yourself with his word. This will help you easily discern evil spirits.

To reiterate, God is not destructive. God uses more than one way, and he will confirm what he says and if you immersive yourself in scripture, you readily perceive him in other areas in your life.

Now What?

Now you have a good idea of some of the things you should pay attention to or do if you want to discern God's ways in your life. You know why it's important to read and analyze scripture. That is true, but so far, we have talked about how God talks, and how you can know it is him, but we haven't talked about the ways you can actively listen to him. Most of the time, it is not that God is not talking to us; we just never listen. So, I will talk about ways we can listen to God.

Be Bored

Yes, you heard me right, allow yourself to be bored. People nowadays are so afraid of non-activity that they always preoccupy themselves with some form of digital stimulation. In this age and economy, there is no shortage of things to keep us busy if we don't want to be bored. And boredom is uncomfortable, so we avoid it a lot. When we keep ourselves busy, preoccupied, and entertained, we shut out a lot that God might be saying to us because we are too focused on something else. It's like talking to someone who is texting someone else, they aren't paying attention, and sometimes don't hear you at all. Being busy all the time is what texting someone else while in a conversation is to spirituality.

"But when you pray, go into your room and shut the door and pray to your Father who is in secret. And your Father who sees in secret will reward you." **- Matthew 6:6**

So, I am assuming you go to a place of worship, you read scripture, and you are keen to hear God speak to you. Try this exercise if you want to hear God. Disclaimer: This is my way of doing it, but there are other ways. Find a room where you can be alone, where no one can interrupt you. For me, this is the bathroom. Clear out this room of any reading material, or anything that might attract attention or something you might be tempted to use if you get bored. Take out the toys, interesting figurines, or stuff like that. Finally, turn off notifications on your phone and other devices. Make sure these devices are not in your room. Then stay or lock yourself in this room shutting out the world for about fifteen minutes. If you must, ask a trusted friend to stand near the door to hold you accountable until time is up. You can do this if you don't trust yourself to follow through. So far, so good.

A few things you should not do once you are in this protected room, don't partake in any strenuous physical activity such as stationary jogging or push-ups. Do not pray; do not speak much at all. Just let yourself do nothing. You are likely to feel very anxious at first if you aren't used to not having something to do. You might even think you hear a phantom notification from your phone or computer. Let yourself feel this slight anxiety. Just let it happen, do nothing. Now just listen and sit there. You will notice your mind starts to become more active, there are new thoughts rushing in, things you have never thought about before, or buried memories. You might begin by thinking about things that bother you, and strangely see some of these things more clearly when making the connection in this moment. You might even have completely new ideas come to you.

This might be followed by feelings of joy, passion, and motivation to act. This is a sign that God is speaking to you. You have allowed yourself to be porous and receive from him, so you hear him. These thoughts might feel intrusive, sharp, and sometimes loud, don't falter just listen. Congratulations, you have learned how to listen to God. Other ideas that can serve the same purpose is taking a walk in the more silent hours. This may be at night or very early in the morning. Do this alone, with no conversation, and no electronic companions.

Listen for the Right Thing

Sometimes people allow themselves to be bored and go through the process only to claim they didn't hear anything. Sometimes it might indeed take more than one occasion before you get anything from God. I find that most times, when people don't hear anything is because they are ignoring what they are already being told. In their minds, they have very specific expectations about what they look forward to hearing. There is nothing wrong with that because sometimes God speaks to that. Sometimes, it might not be the perfect time for the thing that you are most concerned about. God might have other ideas for you. Ideas that are judged to be more important. So, God speaks to you about other things, but you refuse to listen to that because you are focused on something else. This doesn't only apply to moments when you allow yourself to be bored. It applies to any moment. Allow yourself to be open to anything God might be saying even if that thing isn't quite the most important thing to you at that point.

Scanning

What you can do is pray about a particular question, let that sit in your mind, and go about your day. Usually, God will reach out to you about that particular issue in one of the ways we have talked about. Just scan your surroundings and your mind. My favorite way of using this technique is by allowing the question to percolate in my head and then read scripture. It won't be long until I get an "ah-ha!" moment or scripture speaks to my question, or helps shed some light on it.

Consult Other Believers

If you have questions, listen to what the believers around you are saying about the matter. Remember that God can use them to communicate with you. And if what they say is the right thing you will know it in your heart, your soul will resonate. Not only will this be the case, but it will also line up with what you have learned about in scripture.

Pray for Answers

You can pray for answers before bed and hope that God will speak to it in your dreams, sometimes he won't, sometimes he will. Sometimes God has already answered you, and you have to look closely around you, consult his word, spend intimate time with him and open yourself up to hear him.

What you can also do is do what I call a listening prayer. You ask God a question, like "What should I study?" And then you wait, waiting for thoughts in your head to appear, to be filled with ideas and information regarding the topic. God will put ideas and thoughts in your head to answer those questions. It is usually the most random ones, the ones that are more difficult to shake, ignore, or forget. The more commanding they are, the more confident you can be that you are hearing God.

"Call to me and I will answer you, and will tell you great and hidden things that you have not known." **- Jeremiah 33:3**

Make Observations

Words matter, they matter a lot, that is why we watch what we say. But we all know that actions speak louder than words. Sometimes what is real is a far stronger message than what you are hearing. Circumstances, situations, and reality are far more powerful and affecting than flowery, dressed up language. One of the best ways to hear what he is saying is by looking at where you are, what he is doing, and what your options are. Sometimes words won't do; God knows this, and your situation will reveal to you what God's will is, or what he is trying to tell you. This can range from something small to something big. If you have reservations about living in a particular city. Then suddenly, a once in a lifetime opportunity appears there, maybe a position opens up in another company that suits you better. This might be how God is speaking to you, especially if you find you can carry on your faith there. There are measures in place to safeguard it. God might be telling you it is time to move on and cultivate new experiences. Sometimes he speaks to us by taking away options. Things don't quite turn out the way we want so that we may start down a path more suited for us, a path of greater growth and happiness.

Nobody knows why God does this, but he does it. I believe that sometimes God knows the things we are not ready to think about or understand. And we just have to do them. When this happens, your response should be to trust. Trust that whatever is happening is for the best. Because in the end, it always is, even if it takes a while before you realize this.

You should always trust that God is communicating and working hard to help you.

Chapter 2: Purpose

My nephew has a strange question that he likes to ask about specific wildlife. I never ask him why he does this because I never give him a satisfying answer, but he keeps asking anyway. The question is: "What is this for?" Now it would make some sense if he was asking this about tools or toys or something like that. But in each situation, he only wants to know about the animals. As such an odd question, it stays in my mind and I think about it anytime I see a strange creature on TV or online. But I think the question my nephew asks comes intuitively to adults. We are used to things fitting into a category or playing a role. And when I think that way, asking what things are for is no different from asking what they do. The reason why this question stuck with me is that it hints at the deeper question of purpose. Our purpose is the role we play in the grand scheme of things. It is the thing we should be doing with our life. It is the grandest of goals. All your goals or actions in some way, big or small, are in service to this larger mission.

Think of someone making a hammer. What are they making it for? They make it for a purpose. One purpose is to put nails in place, but this tool is multifunctional with many different versions. Not all hammers are made equal, for the same purpose, or used for one thing. Sledgehammers bring down walls and you wouldn't use it to pin a nail. Some hammers are used for smaller tasks like making birdhouses, some are heavier and would come in handy when building a treehouse. Other hammers are just right to use as a paperweight, or their owners use as doorstops. Some hammers come with extra features that allow them to take out nails; some are round enough you can use them to grind grain.

The person making a hammer may have a generic reason behind making it. But hammers are bought with a specific task or several tasks in mind. Their owners give them purpose within this larger set of activities. A hammer is a hammer because of what it does and its features. Not surprisingly, so are people. It may seem strange to talk about humanity in this way because surely, we weren't made for something. People, as a whole, not individuals, were made for the sake of it because it is good. But God has a use for us in his kingdom. He shapes each one of us in a way that serves some purpose because he creates us; he gives us mission, meaning, a point because he has called us to him.

Why Does It Matter?

Humor me for a moment. You are sitting in your living room minding your own business, you have your feet out, nestled in the soft furry carpet or propped up. You like how the carpet feels between your toes and under your feet, it is an enjoyable moment. Now, imagine I come in stomping while wearing shoes with hard soles or heels, and step on your toe. You look at me in pain, a bit confused. But I don't move my foot. I press hard, glaring at you. You could yank your foot back, but you are afraid that you might hurt yourself even more by tearing your skin. The sole of the shoe doesn't feel that smooth. I keep pressing. You could kick me off or push back, but there is something about that glare that makes you think you shouldn't. Now, why does it matter if I am inflicting such pain on you? If I ask you why I should take my foot off, what would your response be?

Think carefully before you answer this question. Don't say something obvious. Clearly, from your groaning and moaning and your disfigured face, you must be in a great deal of pain. So, don't tell me that. Think. Oh, did you just say because it is a nice thing to do? How about how nice it feels to hurt you? That can be nice too. Why does it matter if it's nice or the right thing to do?

If I were to do that and ask for real answers, you wouldn't be able to come up with one satisfying enough. This is because some things just are. I should take my foot off because it hurts; there is no other reason necessary. Also, because it is nice, being nice is good and there is no reason except that it is just the way it is.

Purpose matters because it is nice, and it hurts feeling like you have no purpose. That is just the way it is. People who demand a better answer than that are never successful. But still, people appreciate the exercise, fleshing it out and twirling big concepts in their minds. There is nothing wrong with that. But in the end, it will all circle back to one answer, it hurts not to, and it is good to have a purpose. You don't believe me? Let's toss around the concept of purpose for a while and see where we end up after a few lines.

When we don't have a purpose, we lose our sense of direction. We do not know why we do what we are doing, why it matters, or why we should care a lot about it. You can see just from that set of problems that it is bad. Oops! We're back there again, aren't we? We go back to talk about how feeling like you have direction, meaning and that you matter is nice. See? I can try to come up with other explanations, but they all come back here. Should we give it another try? Okay. A life without purpose is empty, and – no, I can't do it. Sorry, not sorry.

Finding your purpose matters on a cosmic scale because it fulfills a role in the larger divine realm that far supersedes anything we know about the world. Maybe that is why where this strong feeling comes from, from the fact that they are about the best thing that anyone can do in the entire universe, a reason and significance that transcends everything we know and understand. We can speculate about this forever, So I won't spend any time here. In the next section, we talk about how we can find your purpose, God's desire for your life, or his will.

The bottom line is this. We want to know what our purpose is in the world because purpose gives our life meaning and makes us feel fulfilled. The formula is simple, purpose equates to happiness, both earthly happiness and divine happiness. It is the thing that completes us.

Here's How You Know

One way you can find out what is God's purpose for you is to look at your design. Earlier, we talked about hammers and how particular types of hammers are made with a specific purpose in mind. With people, it is like that. We have a collection of traits, abilities, and talents, and these are an indication of what roles we are meant to play. They tell us what our mission is or should be. I can imagine some of you reading this, someone with a misstep between what they are good at and what they are passionate about. I can relate to that. In school, I was very good at science and I was asked by one teacher to join an extracurricular activity involving a science team competing in expos. While I enjoyed traveling and being part of a team, I didn't enjoy these activities very much. With science, I always felt insecure, inadequate, and anxious. But when I was with my fellow nerds, I felt fine. I liked the social side of these events, not the actual science, and I knew it.

Continuing with this logic, it may appear that I was meant to do science, at least something science-related or STEM. I can see that if I had gone down that road and stayed the course long enough maybe I would have found success, but I would have been miserable, as I was most of the time in school. If this was my purpose in life, it sure wasn't pleasant and didn't make me feel passion. I didn't feel I was contributing to something bigger than me, and if I had, I wouldn't have thought it was because I deeply care about it.

Consider another possibility. Sometimes you are passionate about something that you are not good at. Sometimes, although it might be something you were meant to do, you are so horrible at it, and you never seem to advance. Just because you are passionate about one thing, or good at something else, it doesn't automatically mean it is your purpose. But a lot of the time, our purpose is aligned with our passions, with what we are reasonably good at and experience as a defining moment.

Your first clue to what God is saying about your life is both the things you can do and the things you are passionate about. It is this intersection where your purpose lies. Opportunities where these two things come together, are a sign of God calling to you. So, you look at yourself and your personality, and look around you for things that are molded in your shape, these things are what you should be doing. It is in the design.

"The Lord has made everything for its purpose, even the wicked for the day of trouble." - **Proverbs 16:4**

"For we are his workmanship, created in Christ Jesus for good works, which God prepared beforehand, that we should walk in them" - **Ephesians 2:10**

Another way to find out what God wants to do with your life is to listen to what other people around you are saying or what they have said or suggested in the past. Going back to my years as a student, I was told to look towards science as a career and encouraged to do so. If everyone was saying this, this might have meant this is something I should look at closely, something I should work hard to find my passion in because clearly, God wants it for me. But only my science teachers were the ones who thought this. Everyone else saw something different. They talked about my sharp intellect, clear thinking, my beautiful speaking ability, and how I was able to form interesting concepts. They didn't know what I could do with it, but when I found God and started talking about God, this felt right to me and to them too. This group of people was much broader and diverse, not coming from the same teachers, social circle, or school.

This way of looking at things can work for you too. Listen to what different people have always said about you. These people should know you well enough to have valid points about the matter at hand. They shouldn't be people who know little about the subject at hand, or about you or people whose interests are aligned in such a way that they might not be honest with you.

Sometimes God talks to you directly. You begin to hear his voice telling you what you need to do. This way won't be the most common, but it happens if you listen closely and immerse yourself in the word of the Lord. Doing so makes you sensitive to his voice. And when you are that sensitive, God communicates easily about what the next goal in your life should be, or what you should dedicate your life to.

What You Should Do Before Listening

We have talked about yearning for purpose and direction about your life and how it can be communicated to you and how to find it. But you also need to know about the steps you should take so that this revelation comes to you.

The first step you should take should be to clear out the way. Sometimes we can't hear what God desires or is saying about the direction our life should go because we are just too busy building a life we want. We are so hard set on the things we want. We don't stop to listen to what God might want from us. This is the equivalent to pressing mute on God because although we might yearn for him to guide us and point us in a direction, we are only willing to hear it if it lines up in some way with what we want. The noise of our lives, our desires, crowds out God. So, the first step, which is a very difficult one, is to put our desires and wants aside. It is to be willing to reassess and head over in a different direction altogether.

I want you to take a moment to look at your plans for the future, the things you hope to see happen. Now, are you willing to change all of that if God asked you to, or are you so attached to these desires that you might find it difficult to give them up? How about the life you are living now, your job and your lifestyle? Are you willing to change these things? If the answer is no, it might be harder for you to hear what God wants for your life because you have already decided what you want for your life, and you are clearly committed to it. Now that you are committed, find a way to be happy with it. God is not in the business of pushing people to act the way he wants. He likes it if you have a choice in the matter and values autonomy.

"For I know the plans I have for you, declares the Lord, plans for welfare and not for evil, to give you a future and a hope." **- Jeremiah 29:11**

"Many are the plans in the mind of a man, but it is the purpose of the Lord that will

stand." **- Proverbs 19:21**

The way to put your heart in the right place is by realizing that all these plans, desires, the life you lead now are not where purpose and meaning reside. Purpose and meaning reside with God; whatever sense of satisfaction you get from all these other things is nothing compared to what God desires for you. Secondly, all things in life are transient, but it is God's will that is eternal, there is nothing better, more wholesome or complete than putting your life in the hands of God. It is the grandest of endeavors you will ever experience. Who would want anything less? Thirdly, God does not want you to be miserable, so you should be open to his idea, even the very idea that you might need to change your life considerably. He does not promise the process won't be difficult or hard at times, but he guarantees that you will be fulfilled doing it, and you will have a purpose in your life.

Now, it is time to accept God's help in your life. Be willing to lay down your life for him, if you can't do so simply, work at it. One way of doing so is by starting small. That is what the next chapter will explore.

Chapter 3: Day to Day

Here is something you probably already know, but it's worth saying anyway. Big things are made up of smaller things. Life is also made of sets of little decisions and events that add up to something bigger than the sum of its parts. Involving God in your day-to-day activities, even on the smallest scale, works to infuse the very fabric of your life with his presence. We need to feel God's presence in our lives, get accustomed to it and who he is to us; this will make it easier for us to trust him with the rest of our lives. Maybe all we need to do is just trust him with the small things, and those small things make a life.

The Small Things Matter

When looking at your day, it is composed of small transient decisions that you don't spend a lot of time thinking about. You wake up and decide to shower or skip it; if you should make breakfast or grab a pastry on the way; if you should wear one particular outfit instead of another. Then when you leave your house, if you should take one street or go the back way depending on known traffic delays so you can get to work on time. Or if you should have a second cup of coffee or drink more water. Our days are filled with these little insignificant decisions. You might think of these as little detours in an otherwise busy day filled with activity, but I have news for you: They make up a good portion of your day, time-wise. And way more than you think.

If you had to split your hours for a day, they would account for more than a third of that time. I realized this when I downloaded an activity tracking app on my phone that also linked to my laptop. It would note any and all movement throughout the day, and it also kept track of which apps I was using and how much 'screen time' I was using. At the end of the day, I would have a comprehensive grouping of information on how I spent my time. There would always be a huge chunk of time that went unallocated. From this report you would say I spend more time playing than putting in actual work hours. This was a surprise because in my mind I thought I spent a lot of time being productive with my work or work-related tasks and I do, but not as much as I originally thought.

The missing time was made up of those little unavoidable things. Little things that have nothing to do with being productive or having fun, they are what happens in between work and play. The bad part is you don't really notice how much time they take up in your day and add up to make up for a good portion of your life. Like when you see statistics online for how much of your life you spend in traffic on your daily commute or how much your life consists of sleeping. But you rarely see any numbers on decision making, or small menial tasks that are neither work nor play.

Let's talk about play. Play is made up of these little decisions that take up a lot of time. I choose these areas because they are the ones that most people are themselves when they do, offering a great deal of freedom. If you invite God into these areas of your life, you give God a large share of your life. The good part is that you don't have to do anything drastic, you just have to let him choose which movie or show you should watch, or to read instead, if you should have sugar with your coffee, or take a walk in the neighborhood. In this way, you are getting acquainted with the spirit of God. You normalize his presence and his ways and soon learn to trust him. And when you trust him, it will be easy for you to start listening when he tells you something about your life. God will also entrust you with bigger things if you have shown your faith in the small stuff.

Here are just a few examples of the small stuff, yours will look different than mine and make it your own by adding more to the list because it is meant to be extensive.

- What you should watch.
- What you should eat.
- What you should drink.
- What you should do with your leisure time.
- What books you should read.
- Where you should spend your time on social media and how long.
- Should you get a pet or a plant?
- What should you do for physical activity?
- Should you take a nap?
- Should you be drinking more water?
- Should you engage in small talk with that woman from work every day?
- Should you say hi to your neighbor?

How to Listen

I apologize if I make it sound like you should always pray, close your eyes, wait for God to answer every time and want an extra slice of toast. Well, no, that is not a very practical way to live, and in fact, it might cause you more problems than ever bringing you closer to God. Living a life where you are always waiting for an answer from God, for him to weigh in every little decision will not work out the way you want. But God does have input on many of the small things we do every day. So, what is he saying to you, and how do you hear him?

Nagging

The truth is most people don't hear what God is saying about their everyday decisions because they don't like what he is saying, or they are too busy avoiding or assuming he never speaks or never speaks to them specifically. God has already spoken about something in your life. You're probably waiting for him to say something else, or something new, but he won't say any more than he already has said if you are not listening.

You know that voice in your head that tells you maybe you shouldn't have another donut, or another glass of wine, or you should watch how much sugar you take each day and start answering your mom's phone call? That might actually be God talking to you. Because of how often this voice is with us, telling us what we should and shouldn't do and making us feel bad when we do something we know we aren't supposed to, I call it the 'nagging'. It's as if someone is standing behind you, nagging you to do something. Sometimes people are so set on an objective that hearing this voice has little to no effect at all on their decision. They have given up on feelings of remorse if it doesn't affect them.

Sometimes this voice is just our subconscious, compiling the past, present, and dreams of the future putting together appropriate thoughts and ways we can behave, guiding our behavior to reach assorted goals. It is our self-policing voice. When it is God using this voice, there are a few signs. What the voice has told you is often in the back of your head; it lingers there no matter what you are doing. It convicts you, and it bothers you. It is the same feeling you get when a picture on your wall is hanging crooked, and you can't resist the urge to set it straight. Except in this situation, it is this feeling and this voice about something you are doing or should do, but unlike the crooked picture in your hallway, it is usually something you find daunting to do. So, you put it off, the longer you put it off, the more desensitized you become to this sensation.

If you want God in your life, you should start by listening to what he says about the little things in your present day situation. Start with something simple; do the bare minimum if you have to. But whatever that thing is, do it now, and you will notice God speaking to other areas of your life, and it will be easier to trust him. You will find that you become a lot lighter and happy with yourself. It's like putting on glasses for the first time. You never quite know how bad your vision is before putting on prescription lenses. You don't know how tense, miserable, or out of balance you are until you start listening to that voice.

I have made it sound like this voice will only talk to you about do's and don'ts. Sometimes this voice brings about ideas, too, it brings passion and inspiration. You know it is from God when it lines up with scripture, is constructive instead of destructive, and it adds a sense of direction to your life. When you show your faith in this area of your life, God will start opening doors for you and speaking to you about things that are life-defining; because small things make up big things.

"Do not be anxious about anything, but in everything by prayer and supplication with thanksgiving let your requests be made known to God. And the peace of God, which surpasses all understanding, will guard your hearts and your minds in Christ Jesus."
- Philippians 4:6-7

Reading Scripture

Make it a habit to start each day by reading scripture, even if it is a few lines or a paragraph, meditate on it and think about its application to your life and relevance. If in some way it connects or speaks to your situation you will spot little things you can start doing differently on that day. Sometimes ideas will come, and other times there will be nothing. The best part is that no line can go to waste; one day in some other situation, these words will come to the forefront of your mind and guide you.

"My sheep hear my voice, and I know them, and they follow me. I give them eternal life, and they will never perish, and no one will snatch them out of my hand."
 - John 10:27-28

Chapter 4: Light of Darkness

In the introduction, I mentioned the spirit world being abundant, and how some of them may want to influence you in some ways. I gave you a reason to prefer God, above all else. But you might have wondered how you will know if these are bad spirits trying to speak and make a connection with you. How can you have eyes that look out in the world and easily pick out the good from the bad? I will answer this question at the end of this chapter. First, I feel I have to explain terms like the spiritual world/realm and the spirits themselves. I am not going into demonology here, think of it as metaphysics.

Nature of Spirits

First let's get one thing out of the way: The thought that the spiritual world is a place inhabited by all things spiritual is misleading because it gives the idea that the physical world and the spiritual world are separate. Like I said, spirits and spiritual things mingle with and live within the same universe created by God. They are phenomena that we don't observe directly with our mind or tools, but since it exists within this universe, it interacts with and can influence our observable experience. It is a bit like we have spiritual blindness, spiritual things exist and interact with us every day, but we have a hard time perceiving them.

Spirits are consciousness that exist away from our direct observation. Because they have desires, they like and dislike just the same. Think about humanity and imagine that we were largely invisible to creatures who we share the world with. Imagine they couldn't see us, but could sometimes sense us, that we could influence their events and themselves to achieve a state of affairs that is most desirable to our desires. That is what spirits are. There is something else too, like how other species interact with others, there is a bit of speciesism going on. They act on self-interest, often at the detriment of humans, our wellbeing and success. This is because it is much better for them this way. Some people like to think of spirits as unreasonably bad to humans. It may very well be that they are. But think of how humans are bad to other species for our own good. Spirits don't need us; unlike us, we need our environment, but spirits treat us the way they do because of their interests, ruthless because they think of themselves as superior, deserving of more. Sounds familiar?

"Be sober-minded; be watchful. Your adversary the devil prowls around like a roaring lion, seeking someone to devour." **- 1 Peter 5:8**

God and his pals, the angels, are the ones saying we are special, and they want to protect us and all that. The other guys are maddened by this, perhaps filled with jealousy because of it. So, they want to sabotage us for this reason and others unbeknown to us, the reason that has to do with their wants and interests separate from envy and anger. When you are not with God, you open yourself up to a lot of other spirits, whose interest doesn't necessarily align with yours, they have little to no reason to care about your well-being. But God does.

"For I am sure that neither death nor life, nor angels nor rulers, nor things present nor things to come, nor powers, nor height nor depth, nor anything else in all creation, will be able to separate us from the love of God in Christ Jesus our Lord." **- Romans 8:38-39**

Here's How You Know

I have given away how you can tell if a bad spirit is trying to connect with you. The ways I will discuss here relate to that element of self-interest in the expanse of people.

Spirits speak to us a lot through negative talk. They attack us at the very core. This is often seen in how they make people think that they are selfish, undeserving, or just bad. They breed and maintain a state of mind and perception that sell the story that human beings are terrible, or you as an individual are bad, unclean, unlovable or incapable. They breed low self-esteem, doubt, anxiety, and distorted self-images. If we can't find love for ourselves in our minds, the natural thing is to neglect ourselves and even harm ourselves, and we do so through acts that are detrimental to our wellbeing. We may abuse alcohol. We may act in ways that destroy our relationships, refrain from taking on opportunities because we are too afraid. We may even put off doing work because we feel ill-equipped. All these acts stem from a deep-seated sense of inadequacy. If you have persistent thoughts in your head that contribute to these feelings, you have a bad spirit in your hands. It's even worse if the spirit has you convinced that it is God.

Here are some examples of ways this spirit will speak to you:

1. "You are a nobody."
2. "Nobody cares about you."
3. "You are worthless."

4. "You can't do anything right."
5. "You are a sinner, and a hypocrite. That is why you keep having these dirty thoughts."
6. "Things will never work out. Everything always falls apart."
7. "You really thought you could do that? Have you looked at yourself?"
8. "You are a loser and a failure."
9. "Everything you touch fails, stay away!"

These types of thoughts will hijack your normal sense of guilt if you do something wrong. They exaggerate and embolden your guilt to such an extent that is overwhelming and morphs into feelings of inadequacy and highlights your imperfections. God would never torture you about your mistakes. He wouldn't spend every minute of the day telling you are unworthy just because of a passing sultry thought about a colleague. He expects you to acknowledge what you did was wrong, but to also move on from it, and he will work quickly on making sure this happens. If it means that you should forgive yourself, give yourself a slight slap on the wrist and laugh about it, good! Being miserable about it is a sure way to get yourself dragged into more sin. So, if you are driven to a point where you can't forgive yourself, you might have a spirit on your hands, tormenting you. God works to heal you, and self- forgiveness is an important step in that process.

"There is therefore now no condemnation for those who are in Christ Jesus."
- Romans 8:1

"If we confess our sins, he is faithful and just to forgive us our sins and to cleanse us from all unrighteousness." **- 1 John 1:9**

But wait, what if you actually are a bad guitar player, or learning a new language? Then this can't just be some spirit trying to hurt you, right? In other words, what if you are making a good personal judgment about your abilities or traits and this observation is somewhat uncomfortable to admit or painful to think about. For me, it was when I had to come to terms with the fact that perhaps I wasn't the best singer, even after all the while thinking I was. And that I am really bad at cooking. These are what I call objective judgments, and they are different from negative talk in many ways.

If you are convinced of a truth about yourself that is not actually true, you might already be suffering from that inability to appreciate your reality. Objective judgments work well for us because they are freeing. They free us from problems of self-delusion. Objective judgments feel more like a weight being lifted off your shoulders, although at first, they might create some pain and discomfort. This is normal because you are adjusting to a new reality while letting go of something you invested a lot into. Negative self-talk does the opposite. It brings more misery, confusion, and it actually makes us more blind and disconnected from our reality.

How do you see it in other people, how do you know they are under the influence of bad spirits or if they harbor bad intentions against you? The way to discern this is by paying attention to your underlying emotions or gut feelings. The spirit speaks to us about others this way. The spirit of God can perceive what we cannot, and if something is off, it will communicate this, and it is up to us to listen and act accordingly. How many times have you heard someone say, "I knew there was something with that guy" or "I totally saw it coming, I don't know why I didn't say something"? Probably a lot. In these cases, it might have been the spirit telling you about something it can see, and you cannot. So, listen closely to that feeling whenever you interact with others.

So, what if you are often very gullible believing whatever you are told? Seek the counsel of others who are acquainted with God and the spirit in the way that you are, they might be more attuned to what God is saying then you are. Here is a safe place where your suspicions can be confirmed or corrected.

Positive Talk

So, when is positive talk good? We are constantly told to be positive and allow only positive things in, but we just now established that this is not always a good idea. We should be vigilant of the influences we let in even when they are nice sounding. Positive talk is good when it is not binding to the things in your situations that need you to work at. God has probably been talking to you about those things in your life and how you should work on them, you do the difficult thing of being honest and hearing that deeper voice in you that is telling you about the flawed thing in your life. Good positive talk does not feel dirty. There is a sense in the back of your head or elsewhere that makes you feel bad, anxious, or confused.

We all have bad, positive talk voices in our heads. Mine tells me I am the right weight for my height. But when I calculated my BMI, it shows I am in the overweight range for my age and height. I looked at myself in the mirror and said, "What now?" The voice in my head says, "You still aren't as fat as your friend Mary or cousin Katie. So, it's not that bad," even though it is. Other people's challenges don't make mine any less meaningful; this voice in place is a distraction. So instead of agreeing with this voice, I took steps to fix my problem. I started watching my diet, and how many hours I was active a day.

Think about the gambler who loses his life savings and still thinks if he bets on this horse or draws one more time, he could make the money back? That may seem like a positive outlook on life, but it is not helpful, it is harmful. Chances are the gambler who will lose all his money will put him in debt, miserable, and maybe even without a home. It comes in other forms too, like denying that you are addicted to a substance. You have heard this before, "I can quit anytime. I don't need it." This can be reassuring to the person who says that it just makes them feel good, invincible, or superior, but this is a trap to lure them into complacency and a state of ignorance until it is too late and the substance has caused them a great amount of pain or loss. Think about the student who looks at her mid-term grades and says, "It's not that bad. I can make it up." We love when people stay positive and are motivated to achieve their goals and overcome great odds. But ideally, we don't want to live in a world where people have to overcome the odds to achieve something that doesn't need to cost that much to achieve. This is why we want to avoid it because we know that most of the time, attempting the unlikely leads to failure.

One of the blatant ways that spirits attack us is through negative talk. It is so very easy to recognize that for some of you, you wonder why I even mentioned it at all. Well, I've got to cover my bases. By the most insidious one I find is positive talk, which sometimes takes the veil of denial or lying. We have quickly mentioned how self-delusions can cause a lot of pain; this is like that but not always like that.

Separate Bad Things from Evil

Evil spirits work in your life by making bad things happen. A lot of bad things can happen to you, but there are broadly two types, those that are a result of nature and those that happen because of evil spirits. The trick is being able to distinguish between the two.

Terrible things, as a result of nature, can be harmful and traumatic—like death and natural disaster. Another type is accidents that happen because of human failings or human error. People are not perfect; they make mistakes, and sometimes these mistakes lead to very sad outcomes. These are car accidents, an explosion at a chemical plant, or a partnership ending in divorce. The way we know these events are as a result of how the world is or of how we are, they aren't intent on destroying our faith, distancing us from God. Yes, they may be depressing, but they won't taunt us to abandon God or our faith. They also won't make us feel extraordinarily stuck. Our efforts to overcome a bad situation will feel successful, even when it happens in a very slow way. Don't feel stuck. These situations might demand a great deal of patience to overcome, and we will see this because our efforts count towards something. You may give up, but you will know it is not because things are fundamentally broken or not working.

Bad things that happen as a result of bad spirits will challenge your faith. They attack, taunting you to give it up, just like the story of Job. You will notice in this story that the more faithful Job becomes, the worse the situation becomes, and he is constantly being challenged to give up his faith in God. When you face a challenge that hacks at the core of faith, and when you try to be faithful and read the bible or go to church, these activities feel very difficult. It might be an evil spirit attacking you. You shouldn't feel like the thing is getting worse the more you turn to God; you should be filled with hope and a sense of working towards a desirable end. Now, things might turn out badly, your spouse might die from a terminal illness, but it is the desirable end in the grand scheme of things. You shouldn't feel stuck, trapped, or completely out of control. You shouldn't feel alone or abandoned by God. If you feel this way, you might have a spirit on your hands.

People Under the Influence of Spirits

If you can be that kind to yourself, you should be that way with other people. Bad spirits form entire world views, ways of thinking that can make people act against their interest. Spirits are more clever than we are, they see more, they need to possess people to be effective. They just need to nudge things the right way.

You will meet people in your life that are not good for you. Some of them are just flawed humans, and others are under the influence of a bad spirit. Now, I don't mean possession. I am not going to tell you that your annoying neighbor is trying your faith because they are possessed. Talking about possession or using it as an excuse for foul behavior dehumanizes people, and demonizes them. And once you demonize people, it becomes very difficult to find love or understand them in your heart. And when you find it difficult to find love or understanding in your heart for others, you are not listening to the spirit of God. People that are influenced by spirits to do certain things are the same as you. You are just as vulnerable to bad influence if you don't examine yourself carefully. You can't say to me, honestly, that there isn't an area in your life where you feel challenged, or you struggle because of your weaknesses, and there aren't spiritual entities trying to exploit that and often succeed. Sometimes spirits don't need to say anything. They just need to crowd your environment and create a situation that challenges your faith and make you falter. And if/when you do, don't be hard on yourself, the goal is to grow intimacy with God not to chastise yourself for every mistake you make.

People in your life under the influence of spirits will work to undermine your faith and relationship with God in the things they do directly and indirectly. I want to emphasize that people who do this are not evil, it might be comforting for you to think that they are this way, but it is simply not true. It is the kind of thinking that takes away your love for others and makes enemies of people who are victims. These people don't really hate you; they might have hate in them, but it comes from a largely ill-advised place. So, your response should be that of compassion and try to help them or get yourself out of the web spun around you.

When you begin to tease out the light from the darkness, be careful of the following emotions and thoughts. I want to list them here and make it easy to remember.

- Judging other people.
- Thinking people are evil or possessed.
- Despising others or feeling a strong sense of dislike or hatred.
- Thinking the world might be better off without certain people instead of others.
- Harboring anger for those who protect harmful ideas and ways of living.
- Being tempted to take drastic measures bordering on immoral or illegal acts to protect yourself.
- Closing yourself off to other people when they explain to you their experience or reality.
- Trying to enforce your way of seeing things on others.

You should watch out for these things because they drive you back to the swamp that you are trying to clear. Instead of fixing things and advancing God, you are recruiting yourself into the auxiliary forces of the enemy. And these spirits like this type of soldier, the one who thinks they are on the right side because they do the work for them without even realizing it and they also demonize fellow believers sowing discord.

Chapter 5: Wisdom

In the introduction, I briefly touched on wisdom without openly mentioning it. People often conflate wisdom with knowledge and intelligence. Wisdom is about the optimum application of tools like knowledge, intelligence, and talent. The big question is, how do you obtain wisdom? Wisdom is such an ill-understood but a widely desired attribute among believers. They think it has a lot of benefits, and it is true it is. God wouldn't want it for us if it were for nothing.

What It Is

Wisdom is a much broader meaning of what discernment is. Discernment concerns itself with the spiritual world over the readily experienced world. It is about being spiritually perceptive while going about your life and in the world and develops after establishing an intimate relationship with God. This relationship will serve to sharpen your spiritual instincts that you may walk out into the word with little that passes by you. This is why the emphasis of this book has been on communication with God. It is the fertile ground form in which discernment grows.

Wisdom is about how the knowledge you have, both the things life teaches you and formal education, come into action in your life, especially in matters that have little to do with spirituality. This is a fine distinction, one that doesn't hold to powerful scrutiny. It is essentially the story of how the experience makes us more adept in our dealings, both spiritual and not.

God's Wisdom in Action

When you are filled with God's wisdom, you grow in confidence, peace, and conform to the decisions you make. Your decisions and how you go about in the world promote love, peace, they shun all prejudice, and advance God's kingdom. Your undertakings in the world are done through patience, from a position of empathy, sympathy, and humility.

It is difficult to explain wisdom, but there is an analogy. Before you start your relationship with God, you have had world experiences, and they make up your worldly wisdom. You are like a crudely shaped hunk of marble, sharp edges, rough surfaces, and ungainly curves. You are something, but not quite it. When you get to God, he whips out his hammer and chisel, and he knocks off some of the unwanted stone, he might remove entire curves altogether. You might look misshapen at first, but he soon gets to work creating new shapes and curves. He gives you a striking form and a new shape. He smoothens out the edges, surfaces, and the curves bringing out a god/goddess.

Through his relationship, you become endowed with traits and features whose application is wisdom.

- Knowing when to quit or work harder.
- Knowing when making a deal is best.
- Having foresight.
- Having sensibility for appropriateness.
- Going through difficulties and still retaining a spirit of calm.
- When you have an acute awareness of your abilities and know how to apply them.
- You are about the outcomes of your whole life, not just yourself.
- Your instincts are to seek cooperation not competition.
- You value knowledge for its sake, not what it can do for you.
- You realize there are no such things as time lost.
- You know how to listen and hear exactly what others are saying.
- You come to appreciate the power of observation.
- You don't get into debates to win; you seek to learn something new and correct your mistakes.
- You aren't ashamed of your mistakes and flaws to the point of inaction. You recognize that everyone has them too, the wise thing is to move forward.
- You value consistency over sudden flashes of genius.
- You are not scared of your mortality.
- You realize judging others is fruitless.

There are many other traits out there that are the mark of wisdom. You will know them when you see them.

"But the fruit of the Spirit is love, joy, peace, patience, kindness, goodness, faithfulness, gentleness, self-control; against such things there is no law." - Galatians 5:22-23

Conclusion

"And when he had said these things, he knelt down and prayed with them all. And there was much weeping on the part of all; they embraced Paul and kissed him, being sorrowful most of all because of the word he had spoken, that they would not see his face again. And they accompanied him to the ship." **- Acts 20:36-38**

With this text we have done a lot for ourselves. I started off by talking about the typical ways that God speaks. Then I showed you how you could know it is God speaking. I also shared some tips about how to listen to him when he speaks. Realizing that this information could be limited. I created two chapters that deal with purpose and everyday living. These chapters are related because small things make big things. We talked about giving god charge of the little things, he may trust you with the bigger things. We also acknowledged this would make you more comfortable with God taking over, for those who were a bit reluctant to relinquish control over. I hope this can be spread to those you care about, and with active practice, it will.

Even if you stopped reading there, it was a good start, but something was missing. You also needed to understand that there are various influences out there that don't have your best interest at heart. We had to talk about them, learn how to recognize them and how you should treat them when all is said and done. This information helps you see your enemies, externally and within. It also taught you about lapses in thought that make it easy for these influences to upend your life. This was far from the longest of all parts, but it was nice.

The last thing we did was talk about wisdom. More like I showed that if you practice everything we have talked about in this book consistently, you will have it and God will shape you. This is great because we finally understood that wisdom is a process; it isn't a set of instructions.

I am on the porch sipping on tea looking out in the yard, watching the children play about the street and all is calm once more. And I say to you, dear friend, it has been a journey. Thank you for joining me on it.

BONUS FREE 10 Minute Guided Meditation Mp3

Wouldn't it be nice to have even more motivation, inspiration, and courage on your spiritual path? As a sincere "Thank you" from the bottom of my heart, i've given you access to a free audio Mp3 violet Flame guided meditation below.

If you're ready to drop all the negative energy that no longer serves you then get your Violet Flame meditation below.

- Easily use the violet flame to free blocked energy within you
- Cleanse your Karma to skyrocket your joy
- Start growing spiritually again & get back on your path to your destiny.

Go To: *bit.ly/zadkielmeditation* To Get Your FREE Violet Flame Guided Meditation Mp3!

Please Leave a Review on Amazon

From the bottom of my heart, thank you for reading my book. I truly hope that it helps you on your spiritual journey and to live a more empowered and happy life. If it does help you, then I'd like to ask you for a favor. Would you be kind enough to leave an honest review for this book on Amazon? It'd be greatly appreciated and will likely impact the lives of other spiritual seekers across the globe, giving them hope and power.

Thank you and good luck!

Angela Grace

Why not join our Facebook community and discuss your spiritual path with like-minded seekers?

We would love to hear from you!

Go here to join the 'Ascending Vibrations' community:

bit.ly/ascendingvibrations

Want Your Next Book/Audiobook FOR FREE?

You can request copies of any of my books or audiobooks **FOR FREE!** Find out how by emailing me at contact@stonebankpublishing.com !
(By emailing, you agree to sign up to my spiritual help e-newsletter & receive exclusive offers & promotions!)

I would love to hear from you!

Love and light powerful warrior

Claim the life YOU DESERVE

Angela

www.ingramcontent.com/pod-product-compliance
Lightning Source LLC
Chambersburg PA
CBHW081353070526
44583CB00020B/2545